T0319707

Institutionalist Theory and Applications

For Dale

Institutionalist Theory and Applications

Essays in Honour of Paul Dale Bush

Volume 2

Edited by

Sasan Fayazmanesh
California State University, Fresno, USA

and

Marc R. Tool
California State University, Sacramento, USA

Edward Elgar
Cheltenham, UK • Northampton, MA, USA

Published by
Edward Elgar Publishing Limited
8 Lansdown Place
Cheltenham
Glos GL50 2HU
UK

Edward Elgar Publishing, Inc.
6 Market Street
Northampton
Massachusetts 01060
USA

A catalogue record for this book
is available from the British Library

Library of Congress Cataloguing in Publication Data

Institutionalist theory and applications: essays in honour of Paul Dale Bush
    / edited by Sasan Fayazmanesh, Marc R. Tool.
      ISBN 1 85898 561 7 (v. 1) — ISBN 1 85898 562 5 (v. 2)
      1. Institutional economics.   I. Bush, Paul Dale.
    II. Fayazmanesh, Sasan, 1950– . III. Tool, Marc R.
    H899.5.I583 1998
    330—DC21   97–46640
                                        CIP

Printed and bound in Great Britain by
Biddles Ltd, Guildford and King's Lynn

ISBN 1 85898 562 5

Contents

Figures

Tables

List of Contributors

Clark, Charles M.A., *Department of Economics, St. John's University, Jamaica, NY 11439, USA*

Cypher, James M., *Department of Economics, California State University, Fresno, CA 93740, USA*

Groenewegen, John, *Department of Economics, Erasmus University Rotterdam, 3000 DR, Rotterdam, The Netherlands*

Hayden, F. Gregory, *Department of Economics, University of Nebraska, Lincoln, NE 68588, USA*

Kavanagh, Catherine, *Department of Economics, University College Cork, Cork, Ireland*

Klein, Philip A., *Department of Economics, Pennsylvania State University, University Park, PA 16802, USA*

Miller, Edythe S., *Professor Emeritus of Economics, 580 Front Range Road, Littleton, CO 80120, USA*

Peterson, Janice, *Department of Economics, SUNY College at Fredonia, Fredonia, NY 14063, USA*

Söderbaum, Peter, *Ekologisk Ekonomi, Malardalens Hogskola, Institutionen for Energiteknik, 721-23 Vasteras, Sweden*

Tool, Marc R., *Professor Emeritus of Economics, 5708 McAdoo Avenue, Sacramento, CA 95819, USA*

Preface

In the spring of 1995, Professor Paul Dale Bush informed the Department of Economics at California State University, Fresno, that he would retire from active teaching in June 1996. The news did not come as a surprise; after all, Dale Bush had been teaching in the department for over thirty years. There was, however, a general sense of disappointment. Bush's contributions to the department and to the university at large were multifaceted and irreplaceable. He was an outstanding scholar who had published many articles, notes and book reviews. His work, especially in the field of institutional economics, was widely cited in the United States and around the world. He participated in numerous professional conferences, and served on the editorial board of the *Journal of Economic Issues*. He also served as the President of the Association for Institutionalist Thought (AFIT) and the Association for Evolutionary Economics (AFEE). Such scholarship did not go without notice in our department. Even those of us who did not consider ourselves institutional economists, and therefore did not fully comprehend Bush's theoretical work, could not but admire his active scholarship.

When it came to teaching, Bush was exemplary. Over the years, he taught just about every course listed in the university catalogue under 'Economics'. His encyclopaedic knowledge of economic theory and policy, history of economic thought, methodology, philosophy of science, general history, and even such subjects as the history of art and music, would impress even the most unimpressionable minds in his classrooms. Bush's intellect was the magnet that attracted some of the finest students on our campus to the Department of Economics. Many of these students, in turn, have become scholars in their own rights.

Our general sense of loss following Bush's decision to retire, however, was not due solely to foregoing the company of an active scholar and an exemplary teacher. Many of us were also concerned about losing our everyday contact with a colleague who possessed those characteristics that create and sustain a collegial and supportive environment. He is an individual who, in addition to his fine scholarly contributions, was always available as an adviser offering reasoned counsel in times of need. He is a selfless individual willing to devote much time and effort to helping others. Above all, he is a person who sets and observes high ethical standards for himself and his institution. He urges colleagues and students to share and defend that sense of scholarly commitment and integrity that is the *sine qua non* of meaningful collegial life for both faculty and students.

In appreciation of Bush's contributions as a scholar, a teacher, and a selfless colleague and friend, the Department of Economics decided to honour him with a festschrift volume. For this, we asked the assistance of Professor Emeritus Marc R. Tool, California State University, Sacramento, a noted institutional economist and one of Bush's close friends and colleagues. Tool generously agreed to participate in the project; he accepted the role of co-editor for this two volume work.

In the fall of 1995, a letter of invitation was sent to many of Bush's colleagues, friends and former students, requesting contributions of essays toward a festschrift volume. The response was immediate and overwhelming. We received far more proposals than we expected; indeed, far more than we had space to accommodate in a single volume. The problem of selecting from so many fine proposals was in part resolved when Edward Elgar kindly proposed publishing the festschrift in two volumes. The result is the present work.

We would like to acknowledge and thank a number of individuals who made this work possible. First, we are grateful to all individuals who submitted abstracts and essays; we extend our sincere regrets to those whose work could not be included.

We also thank Provost and Vice President for Academic Affairs Alexander Gonzalez and Dr Peter Klassen, the former Dean of the School of Social Sciences at California State University, Fresno, for their generous support of this project.

As the co-editor of this project, I would personally like to acknowledge the support and the encouragement of the members of the Department of Economics, particularly Professors James Cypher, Donald Leet and Linda Shaffer, and Ms Shirley Pennell. Above all, however, I am indebted to my co-editor, Marc R. Tool. Without his help, his relentless devotion to the project, his keen insight and expertise, his efficiency, his calmness and flexibility, none of this would have been possible.

Sasan Fayazmanesh
Fresno, California, USA

June 1997

1. Instrumental Inquiry and Democratic Governance

Marc R. Tool

Freedom is to be found in the widest possible area of significant, genuine alternatives . . . Knowledge and freedom are inseparable.

Francis M. Myers, 1956

The decisive step toward a good society is to make democracy genuine, inclusive.

John Kenneth Galbraith, 1996

INTRODUCTION

Throughout his long career as a professional scholar, Paul D. Bush has been a cogent theorist, a model practitioner and an ardent defender of academic freedom and of democratic practices (for example, Bush 1976; Seib 1979, p. 60). This essay is intended as an analytical recognition of that exemplary contribution and as an extension and refinement of the inquiry focus of which that contribution is a part.[1]

To choose freedom requires a concurrent understanding of the philosophical character of, the analytical commonalities between, and the necessary interdependencies of free, especially academic, inquiry and democratic theory and policy making. Accordingly, in pursuit of that understanding, the nature of a free inquiry process must be elaborated at some length. Similarly the conceptual character of genuinely democratic processes of governance must be developed well beyond the cliché level.

The general character and perspective of this essay, in exploration of these processes, reflects and encompasses the following: The locus of inquiry is the social process and the institutional configurations that organize behaviour in that context. The methodological attributes are those of pragmatic instrumentalism. The communal reservoir of scholarship in political economy drawn upon is mainly American neoinstitutional economics. The normative tenets are derived from instrumental social value theory. The purpose here is analytically to contribute to the maintenance and expansion of unfettered scientific social inquiry and to democratic creation and modification of

1

institutional structures.

A brief clarification of the referential content of 'free inquiry' is required at the outset: Free inquiry encompasses both causal and non-causal intellectual explorations. The purpose of causal inquiry is to explain in means–consequence terms. Its theories are explicative in fashioning if-then propositions that rest on empirical grounds; they are fact-dependent. It poses questions of: Why? In what way? With what outcomes? Its creativity is reflected in part in the formulation of hypotheses that purport to explain causal phenomena. Causal inquiry generates tests of causal congruity, consistency and evidential plausibility. It is intended to account in causal terms for observable phenomena, to explain choice and consequence, action and reaction. Its outcomes are evidentially warranted assertions subject to subsequent confirmation, revision or refutation. Its truths are demonstrable.

The purposes of the non-causal inquiry are more discursive. This universe of discourse is addressed to ontological certitudes and perceptual puzzles of a speculative character. Its advocates generate tests of elegance, conformity, historical congruity and cultural ethos. It is not necessarily or designedly fact-dependent. It may embody and defend received pre- or non-causal doctrines – Cartesian dichotomies, maximizing rationalities, eternal verities or cultural givens. Those committed may seek to impede divergent or contrary modes of inquiry. Non-causal accounts often reflect ideological characterizations and certitudes. The inquirer's responsibility is not explanation but affirmation. Its truths are conjectural.

Even so, free inquiry must be permissive of both causal and non-causal explorations. Inquirers have the right to be 'wrong' as well as 'right'; and the distinction and substance remain arguable. It is the process of inquiry that permits this distinction to be drawn and the consequences to be assessed. Moreover, there is continuing and productive intellectual stimulation generated by the juxtaposition of these conflictual perspectives in reference to each other. Each, in its challenges, is an inquiry prod for the other. If the process of inquiry is kept open, coercion free and is culturally supported, inquirers can continue to generate provocative insights and explanations as they compare, expand, contrast or dismiss these differing approaches to inquiry. In this paper, free causal inquiry is the universe of consideration pursued; non-causal inquiry-generated perspectives and formulations are not addressed. However, as Bush has observed, 'it is the very nature of ideology to be restrictive of freedom of inquiry . . . while ideology can thrive in the absence of freedom of inquiry, causal explanation cannot'.[2] The focus here is on unimpeded causal inquiry.

This inquiry is prompted, in part, by the character of continuing scholarly and journalistic discourse on the state of the current social order and, by implication, on the nature and credibility of professional political, economic and social inquiry. While the matter cannot be pursued here, it is my view that in the realm of social, and especially economic inquiry, it is the continuing deference to neoclassicism as the defining discipline of economics (and its recourse to critical non-causal constructs of rationality, equilibrium and the like) that is eroding the analytical credibility and policy relevance of economic inquiry generally (Leontief 1983, p. xi). And while democracy has indeed come to be the criterion of 'good' governance, locally and globally (Foster 1981b, pp. 975–80; Galbraith 1996, p. 139) its manipulation through mass media, and its suppression by *de facto* political elites, reduce it, in many places, to a distorted, verbal promise rather than an actual, viable realization. Accordingly, the central task here is to reconfigure and reconfirm the nature of social and economic inquiry as causal inquiry, and the character of democratic governance as enhanced by causal inquiry, in an effort to help provide contemporary theorists and activists with fresh, credible and warranted analyses to facilitate their formulation and advocacy of public policy.

An additional task here will be to demonstrate that instrumental causal inquiry and continuing self-governance are necessarily interdependent. As constructs, they share common modes of reflection and conduct. The comparative absence of either, imperils the other. Only with the continuing presence and interdependence of free causal inquiry and democratic governance, it is argued, can the continuity and developmental efficiency of a modern community be assured.

The first section addresses the social context, knowledge-generating purposes, analytical categories, and distinguishing characteristics and facets of free causal inquiry in political economy. The second section, in comparable fashion, addresses the discretionary context, public purposes, warranted assumptions and characterizing attributes of democratic governance in politico-economic communities. The third section briefly explores the interdependencies of free inquiry and democratic governance and summarizes the argument.

FREE INQUIRY

Social Context of Free Inquiry

Social inquiry is a continuing, deliberative and exploratory component of an inclusive social process. Two major and interrelated functions in this inclusive social process are the production and distribution of real income and the determination and administration of public policy. Economic inquiry examines the former; political inquiry examines the latter. Social inquiry (including economics and politics) is necessarily an undertaking mainly of those seeking to comprehend, explain and appraise what their sensory and reflective capabilities disclose about this social process as the current evidential reality.

Those who undertake social inquiry are necessarily themselves products of a cultural order. They have been schooled in particular, sometimes prevailing, modes of exploration, explanation and evaluation. Such inquirers draw on, and are dependent upon, the enormous magnitude of outcomes of prior inquiry. They are participants in a community of scholars in which questions, issues, interests, ideas, tools, techniques and goals of inquiry are debated and shared. They acquire skills of ordered reasoning, of analytical dissection, of verbal communication, of calculation and computation, of factual characterization, of synthetic distillation, of theoretical discrimination and of judgmental assessment, all in communal and intellectual interaction.

The nature of social conditioning reflected in economic inquiry of scholars remains a focus of contemporary debate (Mäki 1992). Some see the content of theory as being causally generated by social factors. Others contend that the goals of scientific inquiry are socially determined. Still others see the justification for scientific claims as a function of 'social negotiation and rhetorical persuasion' (Mäki 1992, p. 66). While we cannot here pursue these respective sociologies of science, the following assessment by Uskali Mäki is instructive:

> It may be granted that at least some variation of beliefs and standards is socially conditioned. This poses no threat to the notion that beliefs may be true or may be false. On the contrary, the idea of social conditioning opens up an important dimension in regard to the role of truth in our conception of science. . . . What are the favourable social conditions, both internal and external to a particular science such as economics, that help direct a discipline to approach the truth. . . . Not all social conditions are . . . equal in this respect. (Mäki 1992, p. 97)

The exploration and pursuit, in context, of 'favourable social conditions' that support free inquiry in search of warranted knowledge set a significant agenda for professional scholars and for the community generally. For social inquiry to be free, inquiry topics must be chosen by thinkers/researchers as doubts emerge in their perceptions of social conditions and as they tentatively identify the pertinence of questions posed. Inquiry approaches must be adapted to the particularities of the problem to which inquiry is directed. Instrumentally pertinent criteria must guide choices in all stages of inquiry. Procedures and methodologies employed must remain openly accessible and demonstrably relevant. Outcomes as consequences must be continuously assessed for warrantability and significance.

Knowledge-Generating Purposes of Free Inquiry

For neoinstitutionalists social inquiry is demonstrably purposive only when and to the extent that, directly or indirectly, it is addressed particularly or in general to problem solving in the inclusive social process. Problems are identified, for example, as impairments in, or impediments to, the production and distribution of real income, or the popular determination of public policy. Institutions, as prescribed patterns of correlated behaviour and attitudes, organize and coordinate the economic and political facets of the social process. Problems consist of breakdowns (non- or malperformance) in the institutional fabric that correlates behaviour in these functional areas. Problem solutions consist of institutional adjustments revamping behavioural conduct and attitudinal habits of mind. Routines are revised; beliefs are reconsidered; rules are rewritten; assessments are recast; new laws are passed; loci of discretion are changed; behaviours are modified; institutions are adjusted.

The resolution of problems is made possible only through an emerging and enhanced comprehension of the actual causal determinants of problems, for example, as archaic beliefs, invidious behaviours, power impositions. Problems have causal antecedents! Those antecedents are disclosed only through free warranted inquiry. Deliberative inquiry, then, is addressed to the identification of particular causal determinants that generate problematic conditions (Dewey 1938, pp. 460–61).

Purposive inquiry is a quest for comprehension of if-then propositions, an understanding of the elements of causal interconnectedness. Acts of judgment produce behavioural and material consequences. Inquiry discloses the character, impact and import of such consequences. But 'means' and 'consequences' have no anterior or external meaning; their identity is established by their placement in the continuum of which they are determined to be a part. The causal sequence addressed is a processual phenomenon. What is 'cause' in one setting may well be 'consequence' in another. Causal comprehension is an evidential determination. The basic purpose of social inquiry is, then, to explain observations of evidential connections in causal terms.

Accordingly, any inquiry the purpose or consequence of which is to provide an apologia for sustaining existing problematic institutional structure, and/or power centres, can neither be explanatory nor scientific. In this case, the purpose of inquiry is not to comprehend causal determinants of structural problems but to provide a diversionary gloss over such impairments.

Purposes of credible social inquiry are aborted as well to the extent that anterior methodological techniques, sometimes technical, delimit or foreclose questions of institutional non- or malperformance. For example, neoclassical inquiry is an event-predictive not an explanatory approach (Lawson 1994, p. 185). Its basic model assumes rational maximizing behaviour in agents, a given enterprise market structure, inherent market movements tending to equilibriums, and a determinate outcome if price setting is unfettered. Causal comprehension may be suggested but must be otherwise established. Moreover, inquirers' mathematical prowess risks esoteric irrelevance unless its formalistic methodological use discloses causal connections bearing on institutional performance (Dennis 1994, pp. 251–5). Formal rigour, in itself, is not a sufficient goal for inquiry.

In sum, the goal of social inquiry is to contribute to the community's comprehension of the causal determinants of the problematic conditions to which it is exposed. Free and causal inquiry is purposive in the enhancement-of-understanding sense. Its purposes are not to sustain established power systems, preserve antiquated and ungrounded beliefs, affirm systems of invidious discrimination or reinforce the status quo.

Analytical Categories of Free Inquiry

For present purposes, categories of inquiry include ontology, methodology, analysis and evaluation.

Ontology

A branch of metaphysics that addresses the nature or essence of being is ontology. It generally involves a priori affirmations concerning the nature of reality. The instrumentalist approach to free inquiry does not rest on or incorporate non-existential ontological presumptions or content. As Dewey put it, instrumental inquiry is 'logical rather than ontological' (Dewey 1938, p. 462). 'Beingness' is not at issue. But 'institutionalist methodology is based on realist foundations' (Bush 1993, p. 73). Reality exists independently of the observer (Bush 1993, p. 72) and is perceived and identified through sensory and reflective capabilities of inquirers. Instrumental inquiry is addressed to existential and demonstrable facts and realities in real-time and real-life problematic situations (Bush 1996, pp. 13–17). Hypothetical guidance, empirical characterizations, causal demonstrations and evidential grounding are manipulative aspects of the inquiry process. In the following, Paul D. Bush ably summarizes the realist foundations of neoinstitutional thought:

> It incorporates an ontological *hypothesis* that *logically* entails . . . the view that society as a system of institutions is real and not merely a figment of the intellectual imagination; that continuity in human experience is not only a convenient theoretical construct but is a real process, the disruption of which has consequences independent of our ability to conceptualize them . . . that social and individual value formation are real processes and, as such, must be subject to investigation rather than postulation; that the process of institutional change is not merely a matter of shifting ideologies . . . but changes in real habits of behaviour that have real consequences . . . that physical and cultural processes are part of a contingent universe that guarantees nothing, thereby imposing the necessity of choice on the human agent; and, finally, that human choices have real consequences for the physical and cultural processes of which they are a part. (1993, p. 73, emphasis added)

Methodology

That which encompasses the constructs, modes and procedures of conducting inquiry is methodology (Bush and Tool, forthcoming). Neoinstitutionalist methodologies of inquiry may be sharply distinguished from other approaches:

First, they are not foundationalist or essentialist. There is no injection of or recourse to eternal verities, non-experiential essences, first causes, or substantive structural or behavioural givens. There is, for example, no deference shown to antecedent natural laws, to inherently given, agent-maximizing rationality, or historical determinism. There is no anterior non-evidential foundation premise that undergirds instrumental inquiry.

Second, instrumental methodologies are contextualist in the recognition that inquiry is induced by doubt in context, by the stimulus to turn an indeterminate situation into a unified one that involves an 'existential transformation and reconstruction of the materials with which it deals' (Dewey, quoted by Bush 1993, p. 66). Such inquiry is not a mere subjectivistic exercise; the transformation occurs in an identifiable context of existential and temporal modification. The situation (context) has become problematic because it is understood to be indeterminate. Knowing how to think, to proceed, to accommodate, to reject is 'up in the air'; one is unclear, uncertain, unconfident. Inquiry is addressed to the transformation of objective materials from indeterminate and unknown status and context to determinant and causally comprehended status and context.

Third, instrumental methodologies embody no versions of Cartesian dualisms. The knowing–doing (mind–body) dualism generates the inadmissible 'spectator theory of knowledge' (Bush 1993, p. 63) that places the inquirer outside the context of the problematic situation. 'What is known is [presumed to be] antecedent to the mental act of observation and inquiry' (Dewey quoted in Bush 1993, p. 63). Objective knowing, then, is mistakenly thought to be uncontaminated by subjective doing.

Neoinstitutionalists (following Dewey) argue against all such Cartesian divorcements of objective and subjective material. Scientific social inquiry is an activity conducted by self-conscious and self-aware participant observers who, as inquirers, are inescapably involved in the generation and verification of knowledge. They make no a priori affirmation of realities, premises and assumptions, that are anterior to or otherwise outside of the inquiry process.

Fourth, instrumental methodologies employ holistic approaches to inquiry in which the initiation, integration and assessment of factual accounts and causal explanations generate encompassing patterns of inquiry (Wilber and Harrison 1978, pp. 71–85). Such patterns are emergent, not a priori, and consist of interconnections and interdependencies linking data and account. The inclusiveness of patterns is demonstrable. What can be shown, with appropriate placement, to have a substantive bearing on explanations and consequences becomes a part of the then-current holistic pattern. Tests of evidential 'correspondence as a conjugate correlation of ideas and facts' and of coherent ordering as 'a necessary characteristic of warranted assertions' (Bush 1993, p. 69), are routinely made and redetermine the configuration of causal connections and evidential support. Accordingly, all such inquiry is evolutionary, holistic and provisional; it is, then, problem-pertinent and non-dogmatic, as well.

Analysis

Activities that identify, trace and determine the import of disaggregatable causal connections are commonly characterized as analysis. Their role is to pump causal substance into if-then propositions at various levels of inclusiveness. Free inquiry as social analysis provides for creative model building to facilitate demonstrations of causal connections. Analytical models are patterned constructs (tools of inquiry) that disclose, connect and order the causal patterns discerned. Distinctive and analytically potent neoinstitutionalist models of recent vintage, for example, include Hayden's 'social fabric matrix' (1982, pp. 1013–36), Munkirs's 'central planning tableau' (1985), Hayden's 'institutionalist metapolicymaking' (1993, pp. 283–331) and Bush's 'axiomatic system' of institutionalist constructs (1983, pp. 35–66). They are prominent and applicable models of warranted economic inquiry that, atypically, take cognizance, for example, of the locus and use of economic power in directing the economic process. As an analytical exercise, model building involves the fashioning of patterns and interconnections that help identify, select and isolate for inquiry purposes, aspects of phenomena that are thought to be causally operative and therefore significant.

Model building, utilization and adaptation require a critical and continuing flow of choices involving grounding in evidence, relevance to problems, coherence of reasoning processes, magnitude and extent of suitability, credibility of inferences drawn, confirmations of connections perceived, and the like. The design of the model must be such as to open and sustain inquiry, not to channel or close inquiry in favour of anterior constructs not themselves amenable to inquiry and tests of pertinence. Causal sequences ordered by pattern models are generally multiple, complex and discursive. The causal data may well reflect cumulative causation in which causal connections are increasing in magnitude and complexity; their import is shifting from prior patterns. The causal data may, as well, disclose circular causation, in which feedback loops appear and multiply, requiring new analytical constructs, and changes in models, to encompass their impact on causal understandings and conduct.

Evaluation

Judgments are omnipresent in all social inquiry. Free inquiry is impossible in their absence. Evaluation necessarily connotes unexceptional use of criteria of appraisal. The succession of choices in warranted inquiry compels in every case the application of one or another criterion of choice. There is no way of breathing meaning into terms like 'pertinence', 'relevance' or 'problem', except as some criterion of judgment, some evaluative tenet, is employed in terms of which the choices are made. Evaluation, then, is an incessant and critical responsibility for any researcher! The logic of social inquiry compels use of social value theory; the purposiveness of inquiry is defined by the character of value judgments employed.

Neoinstitutionalists often employ instrumental social value theory. As I have argued elsewhere:

> Choices that function to advance and facilitate the inquiry process to reach its provisional conclusion reflect use of instrumental judgments. In choosing and judging the grounding and relevance of assumptions, the directive hypotheses created and employed, the pertinence of evidential material, the assessment of the appropriateness of tools used, of theories employed, of evidential tests conducted, of coherence achieved, of inferences drawn . . . the researcher must choose what is instrumentally required, what will demonstrably function, for the continuum of inquiry to proceed and for tentative and warrantable conclusions to be derived . . . [Thus] in every facet of inquiry – from the framing of an initial question, to the culminating and provisional choice of the hypothetical account that most adequately explains the causal phenomena under review – choices are made continuously. Every choice requires use of [a criterion or] criteria of judgment . . . [T]he process of instrumental valuation provides the primary judgmental standards for modern causal inquiry. (Tool 1993, p. 129)

Neoinstitutionalists sometimes identify social value as that which provides for 'the continuity of human life and the non-invidious recreation of community through the instrumental use of knowledge' (Tool 1979, p. 293). This criterion is at once realistic, experiential, processual, normativist, logical, functional and applicable. It addresses real-world and real-time disjunctions in experience. Its referential content is grounded in empirical evidence of how people think and what people do as social beings. It is drawn as an evolutionary, adaptive and processual construct. It is openly a normativist premise without any deference to the fictive normative–positive dichotomy. It derives from the instrumental logic of pragmatic instrumentalism of Dewey. It does function as a major criterion of choice in determining which direction is forward. It is the criterion actually applied in credible and scientific social inquiry.

This instrumental value principle presumes no eternal verities. It is consonant with warranted conceptions of the nature of human nature and the construct of culture. When the institutional fabric has actually been modified to restore the continuity and efficiency of the social process, instrumental value theory has provided the operative criterion. Instrumental value-driven social inquiry is necessarily devoid of absolutist, utopian, status quo-preserving, power retention, or other invidious criteria of judgment in defining purpose, substance and significance of inquiry. Each and all subvert the purpose – the instrumental purpose – of inquiry to explain in causal terms the actual determinants of real problems addressed or confronted and to guide consequential problem-solving efforts. Indeed, instrumental inquiry, as characterized, appears to be the closest approximation of free social inquiry available! Other social inquiry modes, in different ways, delimit and suppress both normative and positive instrumental inquiry.

Distinguishing Characteristics and Facets of Free Inquiry

The inquiry approach of neoinstitutionalists is here characterized as creative, combinatorial, cumulative and processual. Its continuing instrumental relevance to problem analysis and resolution is dependent upon the presence of these particular attributes and facets. Its transformation over time is accounted for in these terms.

Creativity

Instrumental inquiry is, and must be, creative. To be fertile and productive, inquiry must be exploratory, inventive and insightful. Can doubts be articulated as questions? Posing questions as hypothetical queries are expressions of imaginative inquiry: Given doubt, is there interest in its removal? Given opportunity, can its character be explored? Given an assumption, can its credibility be established? Given an assertion, could the contrary be true? Given a particular, can its representativeness of the general case be established? Given an event, can its origins be traced? Given a universe of inquiry, in which there can be no sacred cows or forbidden turf, can received doctrine be challenged with alternative accounts?

Exploratory inquiry is reflected in the opening of new avenues of consideration of both empirical and analytical approaches. Inventive inquiry generates new sources of data to be tapped and fresh ways of securing and assessing data. It creates a need for new or revised models to be employed in ordering data. Theories formulated in one area may generate fresh insights if applied to new areas: What was the initial warrant for an earlier inquiry approach? What circumstances forced a revision or abandonment? What, if anything, can be salvaged, reconfigured and used for instrumental inquiry?

Combinatorial

Instrumental inquiry is and must be combinatorial. New knowledge, as Clarence E. Ayres made very clear half a century ago (1944, pp. 105–24), is always a recasting of old knowledge often joined in combination with new knowledge. Present scholars do and must stand on the shoulders of their predecessors, albeit at times uncomfortably. In all the sciences – physical and social – progression is a combinatorial process of adding new empirical data and new theoretical accounts concerning the new data. It may, as well, compel modification or abandonment of prior beliefs and mind sets. The theory–evidence connections are always tentative and provisional. They may last a day or a lifetime depending upon a continuing demonstration of conjugate correspondence between theory and fact. Theories tell us which facts to gather and how to arrange them for analysis. Facts tie us to the reality of the present and theory explains their significance.

Cumulative

Instrumental inquiry is and must be cumulative. That warranted knowledge has been expanding at exponential rates is now widely acknowledged. The magnitude of what is warrantably known in the physical and social sciences is multiplying dramatically decade by decade. More inquirers in more cultures are creating and accessing information more discursively and more electronically and making it more available globally. Predictably, where social conditions permit, the accumulation of warranted knowledge will extend well beyond what has been previously known. Although evolutionary changes are typical, breakthrough innovations sometimes accelerate the opening of wholly new fields of inquiry, as occurred with Keynesian economics and DNA biology. What is involved in part is a winnowing process, in which prior constructs, tools, techniques and models all must continuously pass muster in current use as contemporaneously pertinent. Keynes spoke exemplificatively of his 'long struggle of escape . . . from habitual modes of thought and expression' (1936, p. viii). Some theories no longer explain; some data are no longer credible; some methods become archaic. Under tests of relevancy, they may be abandoned. What must be retained is that which can be shown to have continuing explanatory and evidential pertinence. What is added are creative explorations of new theories explaining new data.

Processual

Instrumental inquiry is and must be processual. As implied above, inquiry is an adaptive procedure because the reality to which it is addressed is itself a processual phenomenon. Change is the constant; doctrines, dicta, data are inconstant. Constructs of analysis, then, must themselves be drawn in evolutionary and developmental terms. Institutions are created; they become settled conventions; they are adjusted and/or abandoned. Habits of mind are learned, tested, revised and/or cast aside. The functional realities of the social process – production of real income, communal governance, education of the young – remain as continuing categories of inquiry and areas of conduct, but the manner of implementing these functions institutionally is constantly and necessarily changing. Inquiry is and must be evolutionary. Doctrines which purport to apply ancient dicta and data to contemporary problems are static, not processual. For example, economic ideological isms do not solve problems: free enterprise capitalism was not a sufficiently pertinent doctrine for guidance of change in European transition economies (Tool 1995, pp. 181–212); socialist state planning systems in the USSR and elsewhere were far from exemplary in their adaptability to changing   factual circumstances. The social reality is processual; to be relevant, the inquiry model for that reality must also be processual.

Facets of inquiry

It remains here to consider the differing aspects of instrumental inquiry or modes of drawing warrantable assertions of causal determination. Neoinstitutionalist conceptions of free inquiry encompass specific modes of generating inferences that are largely at variance with traditional (especially neoclassical) patterns and models of inquiry. Neoinstitutionalists reject singular or primary dependence on the logics of either empiricism or rationalism and argue that warranted inquiry must necessarily involve not only inductive and deductive aspects but abductive facets as well.

There is a long tradition of distinguishing between empiristic and rationalist theories of knowing and therewith a distinction between the relative roles of induction and deduction in the search for warrantable propositions (Dewey 1938, pp. 513–35). Empiricist logicians perceive truth as a product of amassing factual materials; rationalist logicians perceive truth as correspondence with some antecedently given dictum or absolute. The corollary views that induction involves reasoning from the particular to the general and that deduction involves the contrary, reasoning from the general to the particular, are, from an instrumentalist perspective, archaic and misleading.

In distinguishing these logics from neoinstitutionalist logic, Dewey's critique of empiristic and rationalistic logics is, in the main, accepted and incorporated. His summary follows:

> The fundamental defect of traditional empiristic logic is its failure to recognize the necessity of abstract hypotheses, involving deductive relations of propositions, for control of the operations by which the singulars are instituted that sustain the evidential-testing burden. The inherent defects of the traditional (formally rationalistic) theory are (1) its failure to recognize that the procedures of experimental science transform the singulars from which inductive generalization proceeds; and (2) its failure to recognize the strictly instrumental relation borne by hypothesis [sic] to experimental determination of singulars. (Dewey 1938, p. 440)

For neoinstitutionalists, then, both inductive and deductive procedures are incorporated in warranted inquiry. Indeed, they are but different facets of the ongoing process of inquiry; neither is sufficient by itself to establish warranted assertions. Induction is not a matter of inferring from some cases to all cases (Dewey 1938, p. 479); it is a matter of demonstrating that a particular case, a singular or a sample, *is* representative. Deduction, in turn, is not a matter of deducing or predicting a consequence from an a priori generality (for example, maximizing rationality), it is a matter of creating contingent, exploratory and plausible hypotheses to shape and guide inquiry and to transform and arrange existential materials in a manner to facilitate an empirical check.

Dewey and neoinstitutionalists are particularly emphatic and instructive about the character and significance of the formulation of hypotheses. This exercise is perceived to be the most creative and important facet of inquiry. What C.S. Peirce referred to as 'abduction' – an addendum to induction and deduction – calls for the most imaginative and astute reasoning processes in the exploration of indeterminate situations (real institutional impediments or impairments). Inquiry concerning causal determinants is prompted by doubts and engendered by the recognition of a difference between what is and what ought to be. Given the availability of pertinent evidence of the problem, insightful but warranted conjectures as hypotheses are fashioned in the search for causal explanations of the determinants of the problem. Dewey speaks of the crucial role of hypotheses in inquiry as follows:

> [All] general conceptions (ideas, theories, thought) are hypothetical. Ability to frame hypotheses is the means by which man is liberated from submergence in the existences that surround him . . . It is the positive phase of abstraction. But hypotheses are conditional; they have to be tested by the consequences of the operations they define and direct. The discovery of the value of hypothetical ideas when employed to suggest and direct concrete processes . . . marks a great emancipation and correspondent increase of intellectual control . . . Scientific conceptions are not a revelation of prior and independent reality. They are a system of hypotheses, worked out under conditions of definite text, by means of which our intellectual and practical traffic with nature is rendered freer, more secure and more significant. (1929, p. 165)

In sum, it is the argument here that the pragmatic instrumentalist approach to inquiry, as characterized above, provides extensive and continuing discretion over the inquiry process. It generates warranted assertions as the causally accounted outcomes of inquiry. And because of its evidential grounding, logical coherence and normative guidance, it contributes a most pertinent and relevant approach to social inquiry in general and to economic and political inquiry in particular.

DEMOCRATIC GOVERNANCE

Context of Democratic Governance

All human communities – and there is no continuity of human life outside of communities – have created and implemented, formally or informally, a political process. Such communities, through one mode or another, continuously determine and administer public policies. These are patterns of conduct that causally impact on, indeed determine the character of, the community as a community. Discretion is exercised over the public life of the community by creating and recreating the institutional structures that politically determine and administer public policy, that economically produce and distribute real income, and that socially provide for the procreation, education and well-being of the members of the community. However awkwardly and conflictually, or sensibly and effectually, those with discretion define and redefine the character of the public interest. The political process exists to guide and facilitate the development and implementation of the institutional adjustments that keep its own and other functional categories of community life operative and effectual. How, by whom and with what rationale these determinations of conduct and structure are accomplished constitutes the primary universe of political inquiry and discourse.

The political process necessarily involves the acquisition and use of power, the exercise by some of discretion over others. If there is to be determination of policy, some persons must actually exercise discretion, make choices and implement those choices. But political inquiry is not just or mainly about the machinations of individual quests for, and struggles over, the exercise of power. It is more broadly about the institutions constituting the fabric through which political choices are made and the undergirding normative and analytical premises that confer legitimacy upon the political decision-making process.

Questions for instrumental inquiry include: What ought to be the character of these correlative structures of the political process? Where should the locus of power be placed? What warrant for such placement is offered? How and why ought wielders of power to be held accountable? What criteria of judgment should guide their policy making? What kinds of consequences should be sought? Why should citizens obey laws passed by decision makers? When are political judgments perceived as being legitimate? What obligations should citizens accept and observe in a democratic order? How can communities modify or reverse political decisions if they are deemed to be adverse?

Responses to all of the above questions require the introduction of normative tenets and power considerations: Value judgments are everywhere embedded in, and endemic to, the political process. They are not obstructive and subjective 'contaminants' of inquiry; they are primary and defining components of all purposive inquiry. Responses require, as well, consideration of the locus, use of and constraints on power. The presence and accountability of power are everywhere pervasive in the political process. That process is any community's vehicle for reordering its structural fabric of habits, rules, laws and customs.

Democracy is defined here as continuing self-rule; rulers are accountable to the ruled. The power premise directs that those who receive the incidence of policy must have the opportunity effectively to participate in the formation of policy. Discretionary powers reside basically in the community-at-large, not in a self-defined fragment. Possession of discretionary responsibilities by elected or appointed leaders is time-contingent, provisional and revocable. Modifications of institutional forms as prescriptive and proscriptive rules and routines are, in effect, self-imposed (Tool 1985, pp. 204–6).

The normative premise, in democracy theory, stipulates that political fragments, segments, parties, factions, groups and individuals are not to be defined or treated odiously. Participants are 'ungraded' with reference to inherent worth, social status, work options and, most importantly, participatory access to economic and political processes. The formulation of democratic norms depends upon pragmatic instrumentalism to provide causal, hence warranted, knowledge for the identification of problems, the preparation of institutional revisions, and for fashioning and facilitating their political adoption as public policies. Earlier, I wrote:

> In communities which carry out the political function via participatory democracy ... actor–agent men and women create and recreate the government and its agendas as their cognitive and reflective scrutiny of existential fact and their concern for the retention of procedural guarantees for continuing control over their own lives suggest. Such involvement and participation provides discretionary dignity. (1979, p. 204)

The normative (value) and discretionary (power) aspects of political inquiry are joined in the construct of legitimacy. Implicit in the political context defined by the queries above is a continuing and underlying concern with the 'oughtness', 'rightness', 'acceptability' and 'credibility' of existing institutions and practices of governance. As John Livingston puts it,

> The question of legitimacy . . . is the question of whether a political system is regarded by its citizens as entitled to make a moral claim on their loyalty and obedience . . . The fundamental political problem is always that of seeking to support the structure of political power with the voluntary support of those who are governed . . . Before any political regime can be considered stable, the exercise of power in that regime must be judged to be legitimate by the majority of those over whom it is exercised, so that their participation in its processes and their acquiescence in the execution of its laws are a matter of willing obligation, not of brute force or the threat of force. (Livingston and Thompson 1971, pp. 19–20)

Democratic processes actually provide the only credible and available route to the realization of political legitimacy in the governance of communities.[3]

Purposes of Democratic Governance

What do neoinstitutionalists mean by the public interest and how is it served by the pursuit of public purposes? How does one distinguish between the public interest and private interests? Is the former merely or mainly a vehicle for the achievement of the latter? Is the latter mainly a matter of ownership, of power and/or of pecuniary wealth? We are now aware that power as discretion over others, and norms as criteria of social value, are necessarily embedded in any such distinction between public and private interests.

Private interests are activities, judgments and institutions that serve the pecuniary and power interests of a self-defined fragment of the community-at-large, at the expense of that community. The acquisition and sequestration of discretionary control by this fragment over matters of public significance is used to shape structural change so as to establish, sustain and extend such fragmentary control. Galbraith contends in a recent observation that '[m]oney, voice and political activism are now extensively controlled by the affluent, the very affluent and the business interests' (1996, p. 140). Amassed financial resources, conservative print and vocal media, a plethora of right-wing 'think tanks' (Stefancic and Delgado 1997), and private funding and direction of electoral processes are now indicative of the extent to which private interests have influence on, if not control over, the public agenda in the United States. Such private interests are characterized by neoinstitutionalists as invidious or ceremonial; they differentially serve and sustain fragmentary segments of the larger community. Each power centre seeks to retain and extend its financial identity and political influence.

Recent instances of the pursuit of private economic interests at the expense of public purposes (well-being) include: administered pricing of sources of energy without adequate public review or accountability; erosion of environmental protection laws permitting increased pollution and ceremonial waste; diversionary manipulation of financial accounts and institutions to enhance private fortunes in the debacle of massive closures of savings and loans institutions, and insider-trading scandals; and downsizing of major corporations separating thousands of workers in deference in some measure to CEO salary increases and stockholders' interest in quarterly profit distributions. The private status and interests of the power fragment override concerns with the welfare of the larger community.

There is a stark inversion of power foci and normative outcomes where the public interest is paramount and public purposes define the agenda for political action. The initial and overriding public purpose for any democratic community of any size is to find credible, imaginative, efficient, acceptable and continuing ways to resolve problems that impair or threaten the continuity and instrumental efficiency of the social process. Problems consist of institutional mal- or nonperformance of the warranted tasks and functions with which they are identified. 'What is' is not 'what ought to be'. Over time, lower rates of generation of new warranted knowledge, its increased 'encapsulation' (Bush 1986), erosion of worker competencies and sabotage of the 'instinct of workmanship' (Veblen 1914), for example, permit the curtailing or abandonment of instrumental functions or forestall their expansion. The continuing primary public purpose is to transform institutional forms and fabric from what our causal understanding indicates are ineffectual, inefficient or discriminatory patterns and structures into institutions that demonstrably accomplish instrumentally warranted political, economic and social purposes the community's continuity requires.

An additional purpose served by democratic rule is the stimulus, encouragement and resources it provides for individuals to become 'tribunal-worthy' (Tussman 1960, pp. 105–6); that is, to develop analytical capabilities for rational reflection, normative skills for appraising issues and proposals, and collegial incentives for accepting participatory responsibility in making their political presence both socially significant and personally rewarding.

To be tribunal-worthy requires the maturation of habits of reasoned judgments in order to participate effectually in the collective endeavour of problem identification and policy making in pursuit of public purposes. By reasoned judgments is meant those that reflect identification of and concentration on means–consequence connections, on credible distinctions between fiction and fact, on assessments of constructive vs. destructive outcomes. Tribunal-worthy democrats seek evidence of causal initiations of problems. They are prepared to distill and assign demonstrable significance to perceived acts, events and outcomes. They seek validation for judgment or conduct by proffered causal explanations of events experienced and of consequences induced and appraised. Warranted knowledge is intended to guide social action.

Tribunal-worthy democrats perceive recourse to violence, except in self-defence of democratic tenets, as an irrational and unreasoned act because it represents the cessation of deliberative discourse and conduct. Reflection and judgment no longer bear on the outcomes; muscle supplants reason. Fascists (generic) revere violence as an inescapable vehicle to serve invidious purposes; coercive dominion is their fundamental goal in politics. People are inherently at your throat or at your feet. Democracy is at once impossible, given contrived and natural hierarchies, and undesirable, given a weak and incompetent populace. Contemporary neo-Nazis and some private militias exhibit this tribunal-trashing posture.

Tribunal-worthy democrats normatively recognize their own interdependence with the community; they seek to provide for their own and the community's continuity. They acknowledge the fact of their dependency and of their responsibility to contribute as acquired skills permit. They expect that change will at times be dislocative, that habits and routines will be appraised for pertinence, that some mores and folkways will need to be revised. But self-directing engagement and contributions help guide the character of change and ease the transitions.

For democrats, then, to be tribunal-worthy implies participatory involvement as options and resources permit. Access to democratic participation prompts inventive institutional adjustments and timely social action. It involves the communication of intent, coalescing of purpose, deliberation over strategy and tactics, assumption of responsibilities and acquisition of skills of advocacy.

Such involvement enhances self-identification, self-acceptance, self-confidence and self-reliance in citizens. Political skills are acquired in the context of their development and use; democratic processes are learned by doing democratic processes. Dewey, early on, well understood the critical interdependency between education and democratic governance (Dewey 1916). Democratic participants learn how and why to think critically, coherently, cogently and continuously in pursuit of public purposes. Where, however, people perceive that the existential political system is largely unresponsive to their demonstrable needs, is governed by a self-serving fragment or fosters dismissive treatment and denigration, participation will be stillborn.

Warranted Assumptions of Democratic Governance

The foregoing characterizations of democratic modes of conduct and reflection rest on several underlying and warranted assumptions. Those addressed here include rational human nature, social conditioning and institutional generation.

Developmental rationality

An undergirding and demonstrable assumption is that actor–agent participants in governance are rationally able to develop the capacities to comprehend means–consequence connections; they are educable. Herewith is the credible meaning of 'rationality'. They can learn how to use reason and emotion to drive and direct their interactive involvements in self-governance. They can acquire the capacity to think in causal terms and behave pragmatically to secure and extend their access to the means of life and experience. Such actor–agents have genetically acquired the physiological capability to reason in if-then consequential form. Humans are not the only tool-using organisms; simians use sticks as reaching tools, and so on. But humans are the only theory-building organisms. Men and women perceive and mentally anticipate and/or rehearse causal outcomes, and with the development of meaningful language, communicate those understandings to others in a level of complexity unique to the species. Causal understanding (warranted theory) permits actions and responses to be appraised in advance of actual occurrences experienced. Some outcomes can accordingly be avoided; some can be sought. But it is this developed capacity to think, and to adjust behaviour in consequence of such thinking, that is distinctively human nature. Accordingly, democratic self-rule can be rational rule.

Sociality

That people are both products and producers of culture is assumed and is well understood. The nature–nurture debate has long been largely sterile. Humans are socially dependent. Lingual, attitudinal, behavioural and reflective capabilities are only acquired in an interactive social context. (Feral children are inescapably and massively deprived.) Human interdependencies are defining and determining. Accordingly, all tastes and preferences are culturally and continuously acquired and reconstituted in an interactive process with instituted markets, social cohorts and cultural exemplars. To take such wants and tastes as given, as do the neoclassicists, is to misdirect the inquiry process at the outset. They have no interest in discerning the origins of tastes and belief, to explain their impact on the social order or to assess the consequences resulting therefrom. Preferences are given. In a democratic polity, the political debate will necessarily include considerations of the character of wants and tastes and the consequences for the social order of their being fulfilled.

Institutional creation

Democrats assume and recognize that all societies are necessarily habit-ridden; they are replete with routines, conventions, customs, traditions, ideologies and patterns as institutional prescriptions and proscriptions. But democratic orders provide responsive mechanisms through which disjunctions, malfunctions and inefficiencies in habitual practices and attitudes can be identified, explained and restorative adjustments introduced. Democracies are political systems whose main function, as noted, is to resolve problems – institutional breakdowns – by marshalling intellects and agents in the pursuit of corrective and developmental institutional adjustments. Inquiry identifies problems within the existing structure.

Institutional creation in a democratic order, then, is primarily path-determinant, not designedly path-dependent or *aprioristically* path-independent. The structure of the social and economic order is created, institutional piece by institutional piece, by conscious will and, in a democracy, by popular choice. Although there may be some spontaneity in initiation, the structural adjustment option itself must be consciously formed. Habitual patterns and practices are acknowledged, but discretionary agents do not routinely or necessarily defer to their continuity. Assured employment, universal health care, use of the central government as growth stimulant are, for example, contemporary options for institutional adjustments of a path-determining character.

A democratic order is, in one sense, path-dependent because it must draw in large part on knowledge and experience previously accumulated. Habits of thinking as with behaviour are acquired and revised only as their credibility and relevance are questioned. A democratic order is not path-dependent, however, where habit defines option, where retention of the status quo is the dominant choice, and where proposed change is niggardly minimal and resisted. Path-dependency permits past judgments to delimit or deny contemporary adjustments.

A democratic order, finally, is not path-independent. No institutional recipe for a utopian order (socialist, capitalist, communist, et al.) is relevant to democratic problem solving. Institutional change must be tailored to revamp the correlated patterns of behaviour in a particular area problem by problem. It must be limited to adjustments in structure that are minimally dislocative, warranted by reliable knowledge, and acceptable to those who must bear the incidence of the shift (Foster 1981a, pp. 923–35; Bush 1988, pp. 125–66).

Attributes of a Democratic Order

Five central attributes distinguish a genuinely democratic order from a non-democratic system: the majority rules but minority rights are assured; accountability of leaders to those led is continuous; noninvidious standing provides open access; democratic leadership roles are uniquely required; and processual problem solving is accomplished.

Majority rule – minority rights

Jefferson's dictum bears repeating: 'The will of the majority is in all cases to prevail' but that will 'to be rightful must be reasonable' (quoted in Livingston and Thompson 1971, p. 88). Continuing our concerns with power aspects and normative issues of governance, clearly Jefferson acknowledges that majorities will possess the power to act, but the exercise of that power is to be judged by a normative appeal to reasoned perception, not to criteria grounded in discriminatory prejudices, ideological certitudes or natural law absolutes. The power configurations and governance rules must be such as continuously to provide for dialogue and organization by minority segments so that they may have genuine and continuing opportunities to become or join *de facto* majorities. The normative implications must be such as to facilitate the re-identification and recasting of what is in the public's interest. Contenders need to explain the character of, and demonstrate the warrantability for, the envisioned outcomes of policies they advance as alternatives. A blending of the power and normative aspects is provided in the following observation by Livingston:

> The minority is obligated to obey the laws passed by a majority, but not to believe that the majority or its laws are correct. The final political loyalty of both majority and minority is to the *process* through which majority opinion is formed and continuously tested . . . The process of majority rule puts limits on the power of temporary majorities and guarantees rights for temporary minorities. (Livingston and Thompson 1971, p. 90, emphasis in original)

That deliberative process is buttressed by the procedural guarantees of public law, especially governing informational and participatory access. That process encompasses the diverse yet substantive agendas of public policy offered by both majorities and minorities. In the current period, where negative political attack advertisements and simplistic legislative agendas are commonplace, the call for reasonableness in deliberation seems often unheard.

Accountability of leaders

The democratic attribute of political accountability is at the heart of the democratic ethos. Basically it specifies that those who exercise discretion over social, economic and political policy, and therewith produce altered circumstances, must themselves accept responsibility for the character and extent of the consequences induced by those enactments. There must be no anonymity, no 'hiding place', that conceals the identity of, or withholds information about, the author(s) of, and the rationale for, public policy. Indeed, one of the continuing, if frustrating, characteristics of bureaucracies, public and private, is that they endure in some measure, precisely to provide concealment for such authors and the sources of their rationales. In the public sector, hierarchical layers of pyramided individuals sometimes permit, indeed encourage, denials and concealments. A common bureaucratic query is 'Am I covered?'. In the private sector, similar conditions obtain. The existence of the corporate form, as a legal entity, permits judgments to be made in the name of the corporation but the actual designers and authors of policies are unknown and unknowable outside the upper levels of the bureaucracy. The corporation typically stands as a shield between the decision makers and those who experience the incidence of decisions made. Corporate responsibility can sometimes be pressed; executive accountability is more difficult to establish.

Noninvidiousness

An absence of discriminatory standing is central to democratic theory and conduct. The term 'invidious', as used herein, has the referential content supplied by Veblen. The term describes 'a comparison of persons with a view to rating and grading them in respect of relative worth or value' (1899, p. 34). The distinctive feature of a genuine democracy is that 'worthness' is not at issue. In the sense of participatory access to deliberations designing and implementing public policies, all are recipients of consequences; all are entitled as members of the political community to contribute as they are willing and able; all are politically worthy. That, in the history of the United States, some segments were/are invidiously defined and excluded is common knowledge. Property ownership, skin colour, gender, age, ancestry, ethnicity and nationality (among others) have at times officially or unofficially been used to deny persons access to the political process. Historically, the removal of discriminatory standing and treatment has, of course, been sought through the Emancipation Proclamation, post-Civil War constitutional amendments, Voting Rights Act, Affirmative Action measures, Fair Housing laws, and so on.

In addition to continuing invidious discrimination based on race, gender and ancestry, for example, differential income levels have also become a major and pervasive invidiously construed distinction impeding a fuller realization of the democratic process. With the top 5 per cent of families in the US getting a larger share of income (before and after income taxes) than the bottom 40 per cent (US Department of Commerce 1995, p. 475), those in the lower income category perceive that their economic conditions and political interests are not of central concern. It can hardly be surprising, then, that the bottom third of family income recipients are also mostly nonparticipants in the political process. Voting in national elections is comparatively low for young, black, Hispanic, less educated and unemployed people; voting is significantly higher for the aged, white, educated and employed members of the community (US Department of Commerce 1995, p. 289).

Participation by the low income group seems to them not to make a large difference in their income levels or life options generally. Their concerns – jobs, health care, safety nets, better education, rising living standards – seem not well enough recognized and responded to. Indeed welfare status itself has become an invidious distinction and the object of heavy political assault. A democracy cannot realize its potential if nearly half its members at lower incomes are denied real and adequate opportunities, through public policy making, significantly to support and shape their own lives.

Democratic leaders

The attribute of democratic leadership is *sine qua non* for the development and maintenance of any democratic order. In a representative democracy, as noted, those elected to office do and must wield power; that is their charge and responsibility. They have a contingent grant of authority to propose and act. The instrumental roles of democratic leaders are both extensive and determinative. Their primary instrumental function 'is to help frame public-policy options, to explore and communicate probable consequences and, where authorized, to enact and implement structural change under the continuing aegis of popular control' (Tool 1979, p. 213). A democratic leader is a thinker and proposer who generates reasoned and reasonable solutions to problems; he/she is not a shallow opportunist who pushes the cliché fad of the day (for example, annually balanced budgets). A democratic leader is an instructor and educator who explains to those affected the probable consequences, positive and negative, of structural change; he/she is not a power broker who intimidatingly serves private interests of social and financial elites. A democratic leader is a creative communicator who enhances awareness of real problems and articulates the need for their remedial treatment; he/she is not a propagandist who offers simplistic slogans seeking to manipulate consent. A democratic leader is a person who is an exemplar of integrity and commitment to public purposes; he/she is not a purveyor of factual misrepresentations, or one who generates or caters to endemic fears and frustrations in service of private purposes.

A cautionary observation is that a political community, in generating its own leadership and accountability, must recognize that holding an elected leadership position is, with rare exceptions, a major conditioning and transforming experience. Holding and exercising power is, for most, a heady and exhilarating experience. Those elected come rapidly to define themselves with reference to the position held with whatever perquisites and hierarchical recognition it offers. Their self-images incorporate a sense of status and purpose associated with the position held and are reinforced by political activity. Their predictably aggressive desires to retain office, then, are a concern to sustain an acquired and potent sense and image of their own self-defined worth and significance. They have achieved a position to which they would very much like to become accustomed.

A corollary observation is that folklore notions of leadership still retain a hierarchical content. Bureau heads and shop foremen alike are prone to describe the significance of their positions with reference to 'the number of people under me'. The more of the latter, the higher the rank and status. Unless one can place one's self in the hierarchical ordering of power holders, one cannot define one's own significance. The extent of one's power over others, then, is invidiously indicative of one's own sense of self-worth. Accordingly, sustaining communal accountability of political leaders is a difficult but continuing obligation.

Problem solving

A democratic system is distinguishable from an undemocratic system in part by its focus on constructive institutional adjustments. The continuing factors in the existential reality of the social process, that characterize this problem-solving dimension of democracy, include most prominently the evolutionary and emergent growth of warranted, reliable knowledge, its applications in the growth of technology, and its contribution to the maturation of causal comprehension of problems experienced. The non-continuing factors in the social process are the prior institutional forms created to organize the instrumental functions that no longer serve this purpose. Necessarily continuing institutional adjustments require 'creative destruction' of some institutional forms, modifications of others and creation of new forms.

This growth of knowledge, technology and understanding both causes and illuminates the emergence of problems perceived as differences between what is and what ought to be. A social, political and/or economic problem is a normative identification of institutional disjunction, disrapport or disharmony among or between existing institutional arrangements. The elegance and persuasiveness of democratic processes are a consequence of contributions such processes make to the efficient and nonviolent recreation of institutional forms that enhance warranted knowledge. Alterations in habits, routines, rules, laws, and prescriptive arrangements generally, are guided in a genuine democracy by normative commitments to instrumental efficiency, noninvidious participation and popular governance.

In this context, then, continuing alterations in structure are needed   on occasion to diminish or remove, for example, involuntary unemployment, absence of educational access, uncontrolled inflation, deprivation of medical care, destitution of the aged, poverty of children, environmental destruction, invidious discrimination, non-accountable use of political power, and the like. All are problems reflecting a perceived difference between what is and what ought to be. Democratic processes of election of officials, deliberations in legislative assemblies, resolution of conflicts by judicial bodies, and the like, are continuously to be appraised for their contributions to the continuity and efficiency of the social process.

Efforts, as noted, to miscast the nature of problems, to conceal pertinent facts and *de facto* power, to disclaim responsibility and accountability, do indeed occur. Mistakes in judgment are made; manipulation of sentiments is attempted; contrived malfunctioning is concealed; 'damage-control' stories for the press are released. But democratic processes, where viable, expose and correct for these corruptions of the problem-solving process.

In lieu of cliché-like policy options, that represent conclusions regarding which little further inquiry is needed, a viable democratic system reflects a problem-solving approach of successive approximations. Given the complexity of any significant social or economic problem, proposed solutions must be understood as time and inquiry bound, and therefore as tentative recastings of habitual institutional structure. Inquiry can initiate, feed and foster a trial, a testing out of consequences expected and sought. Implementation is always an approximation, a provisional reordering, that is itself to be appraised and revised again as experience discloses outcomes and as further inquiry suggests modifications and adjustments.

An initial attempt is an approximation; subsequent revisions as successive approximations are to be expected. A trial-and-error characterization is too simplistic, but the process of inquiry, checking hypothetical analyses and expected outcomes against emerging data of consequences actually experienced, permits the redesign as needed of the policy shift. Given community concurrence, it may be done as often as is required to restore congruity and efficiency in pursuit of instrumental functions given effect in institutional structure.

Successive approximations implies continued inquiry into processual phenomena until expectation and outcome are congruent and acceptable. But successive approximations must, at some reasoned point, reach closure, not because further inquiry is not allowed, but because subsequent adjustments must wait upon assessments of experiential history of adjustments already made. Institutional adjustment is problematic for those affected. The fashioning of new habits, new routines, new expectations is unsettling. There is insecurity about the expected outcomes. Change must not be allowed to become functionally disabling; accommodation and absorption take time. Provisional closures accommodate the 'getting used to' phases. People must go on with their lives. The problem and its impact can be revisited for inquiry and policy whenever conditions warrant or require.

INTERDEPENDENCIES AND COMMONALITIES

Free Inquiry and Democratic Governance

Free inquiry and democratic governance are but the flip sides of a folio page of a pragmatic–instrumentalist guide to inclusive social theory. Each is, in principle and in fact, an integral part of the other. The following commentary is intended to identify and summarize some of these commonalities of concept and construct.

Reason

Free inquiry and democratic governance each encompasses an appeal for, and a dependence upon, reasoned judgments. Rationality as causal comprehension is the shared root tenet of deliberate reflection on social concerns. The capacity to discern means–consequence connections and to draw inferences therefrom is a common human capability. For example, no analytical credibility is accorded the neoclassical tradition of rationality as utility maximization (cardinal utility), ranked preferences (ordinal utility) or revealed preferences. Each such mistakenly requires the a priori postulate of preferences as an anterior given that is a non-causal, even pre-causal, tenet of inquiry.

Reality

Neither free inquiry nor democratic governance admit or depend on preternatural, a priori or unexamined constructs of reality. Existential awareness of the inquirer and of the democrat are presumed. Inquiry discloses the nature of empirical reality. In inquiry and in governance, all are participant observers. There is no place to stand intellectually or behaviourally except in the factual world of causal circumstances and perceptive comprehension of that reality. There is no body of beliefs or 'knowledge' that is anterior to or outside the continuum of warranted inquiry. For the democrat there is, for example, no deference to a mythic, given, absolutist state to which loyalty and service must be pledged. The human experience continuum is neither damned nor doomed; it is and will continue to be a product of human choices and their implementation.

Experience

Free inquiry and democratic governance share a dependence on the continuum of human experience that is cumulative, developmental and evolutionary. Each is emergent as a selected composition of, and extension beyond, prior experience and prior learning. Free knowledge is a combination of ideas, tools, techniques, explanations, theorems and distillations generated by inquiring minds. Free governance derives from and represents an assessment of extensive and varied prior experience, consequences experienced and inferences drawn therefrom.

Purposiveness
The mission of free inquiry is to extend human understanding of causal phenomena and to utilize that understanding in enhancing the human condition. The mission of democratic governance is to provide mechanisms through which a reasoning community can govern itself and resolve the institutional problems of discontinuity, disruption, malperformance in its political economy through adjustments of non- or malperforming structures. The former directs and guides the latter and is indispensable in that contribution. There is no search in free inquiry for elegance, mathematical rigour or deductivistic certitude. There is no search in free governance for the 'perfect' policy option, for conformity to politico-economic ism models. Purposiveness in each case is a discretionary drive to revamp institutions where dysfunction exists, restore understanding where doubt obtains, and provide continuity where disruption threatens.

Creativity
Each inquiry and governance is dramatically a stimulus for, and highly dependent upon human creativity. Free inquiry is utterly stillborn in the absence of creations of imaginative and pertinent hypotheses, skill and insightfulness in securing and ordering data, and originality in fashioning fresh alternative accounts. Tentative explanations of causal determinacy must be checked against marshalled evidences for pertinence, congruity and explanatory capabilities. Creativity is probably the most demanding and provocative aspect of such inquiry; it is also the most crucial. Democratic governance generates, in parallel fashion, policy options and assessments of their probable significance and outcomes. Problem solving means, for example, using self-governing institutions to create new, more efficient, more humane arrangements through which to generate and distribute the flow of real income.

Value-laden
In both inquiry and governance, normative facets or dimensions are central, pervasive and continuing. In each there is rejection of all forms of the normative–positive dichotomy. Any such divorcement of means and ends reflects self-deception. Inquiry and governance inescapably involve a succession of choices. Logically no choice can be made except as a criterion of judgment is employed. Normative judgments in inquiry are those instrumental to the continuity and maturation of understanding pursued therein. Normative judgments in governance are made, though not necessarily admitted, in every

selection of one policy option over another. Indeed a policy option cannot be conceived except as value theory guides the character of its formulation. Those promoting free inquiry and democratic governance employ the instrumental theory of social value as developed by neoinstitutionalists, although it is not necessarily recognized as such.

Evolutionary
The pursuit of inquiry and of governance never arrives at any final or terminal stage in the sense of there being no post-conclusion process envisioned. Free inquiry and governance are processual, developmental, evolutionary and always open-ended. Generating support for, and confidence in, the credibility of a hypothesis leads always to the posing of subsequent questions for inquiry; many new questions are generated in the process of answering initial queries. All terminations are temporary and provisional. Concluding one inquiry is a time for regrouping, reconceiving and redirecting inquiry for generating new understandings of gaps, inconsistencies, anomalies and limitations in existing knowledge. Similarly, democratic governance is never concluded; it is always on the way. The solution to one problem may even aggravate or create other problems requiring institutional adjustment.

In sum, the choice of freedom encompasses the development and use of instrumental inquiry to guide the identification and resolution of social and economic problems and the maturation and employment of democratic governance effectively to direct and implement the political process of making needed institutional adjustments. Pragmatic instrumentalism provides a liberating, demanding and profoundly optimistic perspective in a time when liberal cynicism, conservative manipulation and pervasive indifference drain individual commitments and corrupt public discourse. Choose freedom; it is a direction that is forward!

NOTES

1. The author wishes to thank Sasan Fayazmanesh and Paul D. Bush for comments on an earlier draft. The customary caveat applies.
2. Personal communication from Paul D. Bush, 8 October 1996.
3. For an incisive comparison of pluralist democracy (broker rule politics) with participatory democracy, see Livingston and Thompson (1971), pp. 117–51. For a more contemporary comparison with neoclassicists' public choice theory of democracy, see Brennen and Lomasky (1989), passim.

REFERENCES

Ayres, Clarence E. (1944), *The Theory of Economic Progress,* 3rd edn, Kalamazoo: New Issues Press, Western Michigan University, 1978.

Brennen, Geoffrey and Loren E. Lomasky (1989), *Politics and Process: New Essays in Democratic Thought*, Cambridge: Cambridge University Press.

Bush, Paul D. (1976), 'Academic Values and the CSU Fresno Governing Experience', in *Supplemental Statements for Senate Education Committee Hearing* on Preprint S.B. 18 concerning The Collegial Model of Academic Governance in the California State University and College System (November 18, 1976, Los Angeles), Typescript, pp. 29–32.

_____(1983), 'The Structural Characteristics of a Veblen–Ayres–Foster Defined Institutional Domain', *Journal of Economic Issues,* **17** (March), 35–66.

_____(1986), 'On the Concept of Ceremonial Encapsulation', *Review of Institutional Thought,* **3** (December), 25–45.

_____(1988), 'The Theory of Institutional Change', in Marc R. Tool (ed.), *Evolutionary Economics I: Foundations of Institutional Thought,* Armonk, NY: M.E. Sharpe, pp. 125–66.

_____(1993), 'The Methodology of Institutional Economics', in Marc R. Tool (ed.), *Institutional Economics: Theory, Method, Policy,* Boston: Kluwer Academic Publishers, pp. 59–107.

_____(1996), 'First and Second Order Complexity in American Institutional Economics: An Elaboration on Delorme's Thesis', Paper presented at meetings of the European Association for Evolutionary Political Economy, Antwerp, November.

_____ and Marc R. Tool (forthcoming), 'The Evolutionary Principles of American Neoinstitutional Economics', in Kurt Dopfer (ed.), *The Evolutionary Principles of Economics*, Dordrecht: Kluwer Academic Publishers.

Dennis, Ken (1994), 'Formalism in Economics', in G.M. Hodgson, W.J. Samuels and M.R. Tool (eds), *The Elgar Companion to Institutional and Evolutionary Economics, A–K*, Aldershot: Edward Elgar, pp. 251–6.

Dewey, John (1929), *The Quest for Certainty,* New York: Minton, Balch.

_____ (1938), *Logic: The Theory of Inquiry,* New York: Holt, Rinehart and Winston.

_____ [1916] (1964), *Democracy and Education*, New York: Macmillan.

Foster, J. Fagg (1981a), 'The Theory of Institutional Adjustment', *Journal of Economic Issues,* **14** (December), 923–8.

_____(1981b), 'The United States, Russia, and Democracy', *Journal of Economic Issues,* **14** (December), 975–80.

Galbraith, John Kenneth (1996), *The Good Society: The Humane Agenda*, Boston: Houghton Mifflin.

Hayden, F. Gregory (1982), 'Organizing Policy Research Through the Social Fabric Matrix', *Journal of Economic Issues ,* **16** (December), 113–26.

_____(1993), 'Institutionalist Policymaking', in Marc R. Tool (ed.), *Institutional Economics: Theory, Method, Policy,* Boston: Kluwer Academic Publishers, pp. 283–331.

Keynes, John Maynard (1936), *The General Theory of Employment, Interest and Money,* New York: Harcourt Brace.

Lawson, Tony (1994), 'The Limits of Econometrics', in G.M. Hodgson, W.J. Samuels and M.R. Tool (eds), *The Elgar Companion to Institutional and Evolutionary*

Economics, A–K, Aldershot: Edward Elgar, pp. 179–86.

Leontief, Wassily (1983), 'Forward', in Alfred S. Eichner (ed.), *Why Economics is Not Yet a Science*, Armonk, NY: M.E. Sharpe.

Livingston, John C. (1976), 'Authority and Responsibility in a Collegial Model of Academic Self-governance', Testimony before the [California] Senate Education Committee on Preprint S.B. 8 (November 18, 1976, Los Angeles), Typescript, pp. 1–5.

_____ and Robert G. Thompson (1971), *The Consent of the Governed*, 3rd edn, New York: Macmillan.

Mäki, Uskali (1992), 'Social Conditioning of Economics', in Niel de Marchi (ed.), *Post-Popperian Methodology of Economics*, Boston: Kluwer Academic Publishers, pp. 65–104.

Munkirs, John R. (1985), *The Transformation of American Capitalism: From Competitive Market Structures to Centralized Private Sector Planning*, Armonk, NY: M.E. Sharpe.

Myers, Francis M. (1956), *The Warfare of Democratic Ideals*, Yellow Springs, Ohio: The Antioch Press.

Seib, Kenneth A. (1979), *The Slow Death of Fresno State*, Palo Alto: Ramparts Press.

Stefancic, Jean and Richard Delgado (1997), *No Mercy: Conservative Think Tanks*, Philadelphia: Temple University Press.

Tool, Marc R. (1979), *The Discretionary Economy: A Normative Theory of Political Economy*, Boulder: Westview Press, 1985.

_____(1993), 'The Theory of Instrumental Value: Extensions, Clarifications', in Marc R. Tool (ed.), *Institutional Economics: Theory, Method, Policy*, Boston: Kluwer Academic Publishers.

_____(1995), *Pricing, Valuation and Systems*, Aldershot: Edward Elgar.

Tussman, Joseph (1960), *Obligation and the Body Politic*, New York: Oxford University Press.

US Department of Commerce, Bureau of the Census (1995), *Statistical Abstract of the United States*, Washington, DC: USGPO.

Veblen, Thorstein B. (1899), *The Theory of the Leisure Class*, New York: Modern Library, 1934.

_____(1914), *The Instinct of Workmanship*, New York: Viking Press, 1946.

Wilber, Charles K. and Robert S. Harrison (1978), 'The Methodological Basis of Institutional Economics', *Journal of Economic Issues*, **12** (March), 61–90.

2. The Interdependence of Theory and Practice

Edythe S. Miller[1]

A strand of methodological agnosticism has been manifest in economic thought over the years, taking form as the belief that no policy has greater claim than any other to authenticity or legitimacy, that prescription is strictly a matter of taste and perception. It follows that professional judgment must be suspended when it comes to economic practice. *Chacun à son goût.*

Within institutional economics, this is one basis for rejection of the Veblenian dichotomy. The Veblenian dichotomy, as is well recognized, distinguishes ceremonial and instrumental patterns of thought and behaviour, and finds the former harmful and the latter serviceable for humankind. In contrast, economic agnosticism maintains that because we are creatures of our culture, and see the world through culturally tinted prisms, such assessments are flawed. Policy decisions are, and can only be, matters of rhetoric and persuasion. One purpose of this paper is to contest this view, and to demonstrate that it is inconsistent with institutional economics. In my view the belief that the overriding objective of economics is the general well-being, and that economics is a problem-solving discipline, is at the very core of institutionalism.

I will proceed by examining some foundational precepts of institutionalism that distinguish economics as social, evolutionary, indeterminate and interdisciplinary. These precepts will be contrasted to their counterparts in mainstream economics. The relationship of policy to principle and of these to the general well-being will then be explored, by examining within this context three of the policy goals of the current (for the most part a 'wannabe' neo-classical) economic order: deregulation, employment policy standards and globalization.

Before proceeding, however, a word on the question of the nature and purpose of economic theory. Theory, in the accepted definition of the past 25 years or so, has come to have only one meaning, and that an exceedingly restrictive one. When most mainstream, and even some heterodox, economists refer to economic theory they have in mind abstract hypothetico-deductive mathematical models based upon sophisticated quantitative statistical techniques, and yielding value-free, objective results (Beed and Beed 1996, p. 1082). In equating theory with mathematical modelling, normal economic science seems to be trying to adapt the methods of the natural to the social sciences in order, as often has been noted, both to achieve comparable success and to secure for itself a similar status.

The implication is that while other approaches to economics are not entirely beyond the pale – they may be characterized as methodology, philosophy or (horrors!) ethics – economic theory they are not. An important underlying premise is that the future is predictable, itself predicated upon a belief both in regularities in nature (Lawson 1994, p. 516) and in the subject matter as non-contextual, ahistorical and acultural (Beed and Beed 1996, pp. 1082–3) – unchanging aspects of human existence.

An alternative view follows from a different vision of the nature and purpose of economics. In this framework theory is defined as causal explanation. The approach substitutes a quest for understanding for the certainty and predictability that mathematical modelling provides. From this perspective, that of institutional and some of the other heterodox schools, mathematical modelling is not theory. It explains little, if anything, and provides few, if any, guides to action based on comprehension of actual forces at work. In this alternative view, the purpose of theory is seen not as predictability, nor precision, nor certainty, but as social control in the service of humankind. Social control requires, first of all, causal explanation that is the basis of understanding.

These alternative interpretations are in conformance with underlying precepts of these schools and influence their conclusions. It should go without saying, although often ignored, that all economic schools, irrespective of self-perception, adopt a prescriptive role, and that a directive to 'do nothing' is as much a charge as one to 'do something'.

DO PRECONCEPTIONS MATTER?

Milton Friedman, responsible for shaping so much of both current economic thought and its agenda, is well known to have remarked that it is not reality of assumptions but accuracy of predictions that is the measure of economic science. Putting aside the question of mainstream predictive accuracy, except to note that monetarist predictions have been widely off the mark in recent years, the perspective cannot be appraised without comprehension of the influence of the (frequently unspecified) assumptions on policy and, in turn, of policy on economic condition. I contend that conflicting assumptions of the schools are largely responsible for opposing policy prescriptions.

Two cases of unrealistic assumptions in economics are delineated in a recent article. The first is partial description, unrealistic because it omits certain factors, and therefore does not give an exhaustive description. In this event, the omissions have no, or negligible, impact if they have no, or negligible, import for real world cases. The second is false description, in which omitted factors have an effect, in some cases a non-trivial effect, on real world cases (Rappaport 1996, pp. 220–24).

I propose to add to these a third case of unrealistic assumptions: that in which assumptions constitute ideal types to which policymaking should aspire. Economic thought historically has been and continues to be centred on such exemplars. Ideals of individualism, equilibrium and certainty take shape as free private enterprise, competition, free contract and free trade, and are posited both as a natural order toward which forces incline the economy, in the absence of artificial restraints, and as conditions toward which policy should aspire. The natural order perceived has the force not only of inevitability (if we would but recognize it and respond accordingly), but of superiority. The sections that follow expand on these themes.

A SOCIAL ECONOMICS

Institutional economics is social. It recognizes a two-way flow between individuals and society, with humans viewed as both creatures and creators of their environments. Individuals are born into ongoing social systems. From the start, custom and convention shape preferences. Moreover, persons are as often driven by such incentives as emulation, affection, insecurity, status seeking and the desire for dominance as by the rational stimuli depicted in mainstream thought. Indeed, individualism, and the one-way flow from individual to social depicted in normal science, is seen as itself a social ideal.

Individuals are members of structured groups (the family, corporation, union, church). As such, they partake of the loyalties and hierarchical ordering that characterize these groups. Neither individuals nor firms are rational, passive, atomistic 'homogeneous globule[s] of desire of happiness' (Veblen 1961, p. 73). Firms are at least as often price makers as price takers. Individuals are as often, or more often, subject to direction and manipulation as they are autonomous decision makers.

Exchanges are not necessarily, doubtless not often, between equals. Even the bargaining transactions of John R. Commons, the one type of transaction that he envisions as occurring between relative equals, and therefore as allowing for negotiation, he specifies as occurring between legal and not economic equals, and as taking place within existing working rules. There is no doubt that Commons recognized that working rules include hierarchical gradations and proprieties. Institutional economics takes account of the part played by power and inequality (for example, between employer and employee, between producer and consumer) in economic life. The realistic foundation of institutionalism demands that power and inequality be taken into account in analysis.

AN EVOLUTIONARY ECONOMICS

Institutional economics is evolutionary. An evolutionary view is processual, accepting neither a beginning nor an end point to the social process. The constants of mainstream economics – preferences, customs, technology, social and economic structure – are posited as variables. The method of abstraction employed by mainstream economics, and necessary for the construction of its sophisticated models, is faulted not for application of Occam's razor, but because of the determinative factors left out of account and those adopted as guiding precepts. It is recognized that in the real world, *ceteris* will not stay *paribus*, that the method constrains and distorts both inquiry and conclusion.

An equilibrium view of the economy explicitly or implicitly posits the existence of regularities in nature. It posits also the existence of a 'grand design' benignly controlling events and of a 'natural order' to which all things appropriately tend. An equilibrium view is necessarily static; disturbances jar the system from its natural path, removal of impediments generates correctives that return it to a prior, and suitable, course. The normal order is one of private property, free contract, free trade and free private enterprise. The private market is the proper arena for all 'economic' endeavour. Any existing power disparities are 'in the nature of things'. Institutionalism is informed by no such sense of the normal.

AN INDETERMINATE ECONOMICS

Institutional economics is indeterminate. Its evolutionary viewpoint precludes determinate outcomes. The existence of guiding tendencies is denied. Lacking a 'purpose' in nature, the path of human history is unspecified, distinguished by unpredictability and uncertainty, with the uncertainty itself influencing events.

No tendencies are perceived in nature, but humans are viewed as bundles of (often contradictory) proclivities and propensities (as in the Keynesian 'propensity to consume'). Although the term has lost favour, Thorstein Veblen's 'instincts' (for example, of workmanship, for predation), carry much the same sense. Regularities in nature yield exact predictions and certainty. Conflicting and reinforcing individual propensities produce only approximate results – inexact probabilities and possibilities. Possibilities are different from necessities. They may be negated by unforeseen turns of events. There is leeway for misperception. There is latitude for human choice.

Institutionalism apprehends human choice as real. Ends are not 'given', but selected. Possible paths of development are varied. There is a role for chance, for happenstance, for luck, for Keynesian animal spirits. Veblen's 'imbecile institutions' may or may not prevail. Predictability requires rationality on the part both of observer and participant, and regularity on the part of the observed. Individuals are not 'rational', they are neither prescient, nor unbiased, nor motivated solely by self-interest. Changing comprehension sways evaluation. Unacknowledged precepts influence interpretation. Passions overcome logic. Choices are not foreordained. The social and economic world is not characterized by regularity.

Moreover, that which is accepted as fixed in standard theory is notably inconstant. For example, and as institutional economists repeatedly have pointed out, the historical process of development (as opposed to mere growth) is distinguished by structural and qualitative change in legal and social frameworks perceived as undeviating by orthodoxy, and in human and physical means of production, that is, the qualitatively fixed and homogeneous stocks of land, labour and capital of normal science. The contemporary 'representative firm' does not resemble its counterpart of a century ago. Revisions in law, technological advance, changes in fashion have indeterminable impacts. Analysis in the social sciences is time and fact dependent. Time passes, circumstances evolve, facts change. J.M. Keynes is reputed to have stated, when chided for revising a policy recommendation, 'When the facts change, I change my mind. What do you do, Sir?'.

Uncertainty plays a role in both institutional and Keynesian economics. Each recognizes that persons do not act strictly as self-seeking automatons, cognizant of future result of present activity, but attempt, sometimes blindly, to protect against an unknown future. The recognition of uncertainty itself has important economic consequences. Joan Robinson, in her Richard T. Ely address to the American Economic Association in 1971, observes that a major point of original Keynesian thought (as opposed to the later 'bastard' variety) is that economics need recognize that there is a yesterday, today and tomorrow, and that 'the past is irrevocable and the future . . . unknown' (Robinson 1972, p. 3). Undoubtedly, until Keynesianism was clothed in neoclassical garb, the uncertainty evidenced in such key concepts as the marginal efficiency of capital appeared to lay to rest much of the certitude of traditional economics. In institutionalism, the certainty of equilibrium conclusions consistently is denied.

Although institutional economics rejects the certainty of timeless equilibrium solutions and natural regularities, this does not detract from its affirmation of time- and fact-based knowledge and truth, characterized by John Dewey as the 'warrantably assertable'. The rejection by institutionalism of the dualisms of standard theory, dualisms which wall off from each other such elements as principle and policy, theory and practice, knowing and doing, means and ends, is based in its perception of the components of these pairings as reinforcing and informing each other. Its rejection of dualistic thought includes recognition that facts and values infuse each other. That knowledge is not representational makes it no less real, however. Knowledge is interpretive, subject to dispute but also to confirmation by the test of its consequences. Knowledge and truth are not absolute and universal, but tentative, experimental, fallible and corrigible when facts change or results prove them in error.

AN INTERDISCIPLINARY ECONOMICS

Institutional economics is interdisciplinary. Economics is not a 'pure' science. Defining it in the conventional sense as 'the study of the allocation of scarce resources to given ends' widely misses the mark. Economics is defined more properly in terms of provisioning. As such, it is broadly cultural, affected by and affecting all of the social and physical sciences.

Economics is historical. Means of provisioning change over time and build upon those of the past. Economic knowledge is time and place dependent. Economics is sociological. Group dynamics affect the economic order. The received wisdom influences public and private opinion. The state of the industrial arts is a common possession, both production and consumption are group activities. Law and economics are inseverable. Legislation permeates economic process. Economics is linked to the physical sciences. The level of technology determines productive potential.

Economics is perceived to be a science of scarcity only because of the closed, static, full employment, limited resources models it adopts and permits to define its reality. Indeed, to allow models to define reality, rather than having reality shape the models, is one of the more foolish errors of mainstream economics. The view of scarcity as an economic organizing principle is a misperception. Over time, unemployed and underemployed human resources have been more rule than exception. Human understanding of physical processes increases, resulting in technological advance. With the development of new tools, techniques and knowledge, previously useless physical resources (coal, oil, uranium) become useful. Indeed, so potentially productive are we that it is deemed necessary to suppress production (Veblen's 'conscientious withdrawal of efficiency') to enhance exchange value. Institutional economics has described for a long time the ability to withhold as an element in private alienation (Veblen's and Commons's intangible property) and consistently has contrasted workmanship and ownership, the industrial and pecuniary, use and exchange value. It is maldistribution, rather than inherent problems of production, that lends credence to the view of scarcity as a defining feature of the economy. And distribution, as has been known even by mainstream economists at least since the time of J.S. Mill, is a matter of power and discretion.

Moreover, economics is interdisciplinary because it is affected by almost all aspects of government policy. Economies are governed by what governments do and what they leave undone. Government policy may be off course, but to deny its use sacrifices one of the major tools available to mitigate the jungle-like 'nasty, brutish, short' aspects of economic life.

I have so far been discussing contemporary neoclassical schools as if they were one. I have done so because I believe that their differences pale before their similarities (Miller 1990, pp. 239–44). Whether classified as monetarist, rational expectations, new institutionalist, new classical or new Keynesian, common precepts and policies turn minor discrepancies – basically, subtle shadings about weightings and trivial disagreements about points of emphasis – into differences without distinctions. That 'new institutionalists' soften the rationality of the unadulterated model with 'bounded rationality', and build upon neoclassical self-seeking by adding guile and re-labelling it opportunism (Miller 1993, p. 1045), and that 'new Keynesians' relax automatic market-clearing doctrines in face of market imperfections, constitutes little more than trimming around the edges. Irrespective of designation, the new orthodoxies are founded in concepts of the old: individualism, rationality, maximization, consumer sovereignty and timeless equilibrium. Moreover, fundamental assumptions determine prescribed practice. Without exception, as is evident in the policy examples discussed below, these legatees of neoclassicism accept principles of limited government, balanced budgets and laissez-faire, defend the proposition that 'what is' is 'what should be', and serve as guardians of the status quo.

REGULATORY POLICY

As is well known, deregulation and privatization currently receive broad support in the US. They are advocated as extensively applicable – appropriate for banking, health and education as for traditional public utilities – and endorsed as a means of achieving a competitive ideal. Nor is the view confined to the US. Convictions, like consumption patterns – Coca Cola, McDonald hamburgers, blue jeans – spill across national borders, extending a pattern of US imperialism.

Public utilities long have been recognized as inhospitable to competition and beyond the reach of private market control because of inherent structural impediments.[2] It is the presence of particular operating characteristics, and not regulation, that compels a monopoly form of organization and fosters the potential for exploitation of consumers. Needless to say, social control does not occur automatically. It often is adopted only after periods of sustained public outcry.

Partly because of the hold of the economic myth in the US, the tool adopted for control of monopoly power was that of regulation – private ownership restrained by social control. In most of the rest of the world, public ownership was the instrument adopted. When it comes to public utilities, the current trend in the US is thus one of deregulation, elsewhere it takes shape as privatization.

Despite the presence of acknowledged market imperfections, the mainstream economic literature, over at least the past half century, has included a virtual *cri de coeur* for deregulation, based upon numerous perceived regulatory flaws.[3] Even highly imperfect competitive markets are depicted as preferable to regulation. The criticism of regulation worked its way down from academy to popular press, halls of government and public consciousness. Deregulation was pursued as the remedy.

For example, the 1982 settlement of the anti-trust suit against AT&T by the US Department of Justice was widely viewed as the initiation of deregulation of the telephone industry. Although it was less deregulatory than decentralizing, decentralization was either equated with or viewed as a first step toward deregulation and, in any event, approved as similarly pro-market. As is well known, the settlement decree mandated, among other things, the divestiture of the Bell operating companies from AT&T in regional holding companies (RHCs) that retained much of the market power of the former parent, prominently including control over bottleneck access to end-use consumers. The decree also terminated many previously imposed restrictions. Traditional service, product and geographic barriers fell. Diversification became a common pattern. Telephone companies added nontraditional to traditional offerings, and established bases all over the world.

All of this was accompanied by a drive toward combination. The telecommunications industry at every level has been actively engaged in mergers, acquisitions, takeovers and joint ventures. The recently completed Pacific Telesis/SBC (Southwestern Bell) and the pending Nynex/Bell Atlantic mergers are but the latest in a long string of intra-industry and inter-industry, vertical and horizontal, national and international combinations.

Remarkably, the integration is undertaken in the name of competition. Consolidation is necessary, it is asserted, to compete both at home and abroad. That is, if one is to swim with the sharks one must bulk up. Raymond Smith, chairman of Bell Atlantic, in commenting upon the motive behind the planned merger with Nynex, is quoted as saying: 'We needed more scale to *compete* with AT&T' (quoted in Naik 1996, p. R12, emphasis added).[4] Economies of scale, once viewed as the enemy of competition, now is proposed as a means of its achievement.

The trend toward consolidation traverses industry and national borders. Anti-trust seems almost a nostalgic revery. Overall merger activity in the US has more than doubled in the last five years with most applications receiving regulatory approval, reflecting relaxed controls. The prospect for future mergers is even more favourable. Recently slackened Federal Trade Commission/Justice Department rules permit efficiencies such as cost-cutting to offset anti-competitive effects in merger applications (Wilke 1997, p. A3). Among utilities, there has been a strong move toward consolidation in transportation, and significant combination within both the electric and gas industries. There is also a renewal of a drive toward electric and gas amalgamation (Holden 1997, p. B4; Lipin 1997, p. C2).

Deregulation in public utility markets has resulted in high levels of concentration and consolidation of power, conditions inconsistent with competition. It also has been accompanied by high profits, price discrimination, cross-subsidization, and cost and risk shifting, familiar patterns of behaviour in monopoly enterprises producing multiple products in segmented markets. An additional fallout of deregulation is the ability of oligopsonistic customers to achieve rate and service advantage. Moreover, there is a strong probability that diversification and mergers are occurring at the cost of network reinvestment and deterioration of service in local markets (Trebing 1994, pp. 384–6).

The trend toward combination has been accompanied by rigorous cost-cutting. This often takes the form of 'downsizing', 'outsourcing', early retirement and other euphemisms for layoffs of employees. It has added to the simultaneous reduction in other sectors of the economy in secure, unionized, reasonably remunerated employment. Moreover, there is the strong possibility that many of the eliminated jobs are important to core performance. An additional effect of the consolidation is a further erosion of regulatory control. When consolidation occurs across state lines, and even more so when cross-national, regulated activities are positioned ever further beyond the reach of administrative, and any national, control.

In the name of ideals of competition and efficiency, then, a policy of deregulation was adopted for highly imperfect markets. Deregulation is not tantamount to competition, however. Market power, rather than being diminished, was enhanced.

EMPLOYMENT POLICY STANDARDS

It is unquestionable that the concept of the non-accelerating inflation rate of unemployment (NAIRU) has been decisively important for US employment policy during the past few decades. The NAIRU is the successor concept and synonym for the natural rate of unemployment, a hypothesis first formally introduced by Milton Friedman in his 1968 Presidential Address to the American Economic Association, but with roots far back in normal science. At unemployment rates below the NAIRU, accelerating inflation is foreseen; at rates above, deflationary pressures. Only at rates approximately equal to the NAIRU will there be relative price stability. Current estimates of NAIRU are in the 6.0–6.2 per cent range. Recently, there has been pressure to revise the NAIRU in face of price stability at unemployment levels below the accepted level (for example, Stiglitz 1997, pp. 6–7; Gordon 1997, p. 30).

The NAIRU clearly is an equilibrium concept,[5] founded in a natural order prototype. A tendency in economic affairs is perceived. The unemployment rate may at any time be above or below the natural level; if so, correctives will (or should) be set in motion. The NAIRU hypothesis also conforms to the mainstream full employment model and, in fact, defines that measure. Whatever the NAIRU, it is posited as including only voluntary and frictional unemployment.

The NAIRU hypothesis also is tautological. The failure of specified results to occur at the designated NAIRU does not result in a challenge to the thesis. If prices are stable, full employment is said to exist, irrespective of the level of unemployment. If prices are stable at levels of unemployment below the accepted NAIRU, it is taken as an indication that the NAIRU has changed. The specification of a norm is not challenged. Price stability is thus the only factor it is necessary to consider when assessing economic health. No need to inquire into actual labour market conditions. The current inflation rate tells us all we need to know.

As with proponents of deregulation, supporters of NAIRU advance a conservative cause. The concept rests on the proposition that unemployment is a function of a free-floating supply and demand for labour, rather than of the aggregate demand for output. The thesis thus undercuts the use of demand-stimulating policies, even when wages are stagnant (Galbraith 1997, pp. 95, 102) and favours the view that tight limits be imposed on growth.[6] Acceptance of the NAIRU hypothesis has virtually eliminated the use of fiscal policy to correct for unemployment, irrespective of its level. Monetary policy is all that is required, with many a preemptive strike on inflation at the slightest hint of economic vitality. Inflation perennially is perceived to be just over the horizon. James Galbraith points out that there seems a greater willingness on the part of 'NAIRUvians' to raise than to lower NAIRU estimates, a sign that 'the NAIRU, like the wage rate, is downwardly sticky' (Galbraith 1997, p. 102). When it comes to employment, the policy adopted has been a case of the proverbial 'pushing on a string'.

The acceptance by the economics profession of the NAIRU hypothesis, as with its endorsement of deregulation, is in line with mainstream assumptions, in the one case of the existence of natural forces inclining the economy toward equilibrium and, in the other, of private market autonomy and legitimacy. These are important facets of the ideal world of economics. In each case, a normal or natural state which, as it happens, is also a meritorious state, is posited.

GLOBALIZATION

Along with its emphasis on gains from deregulation and price stability, public policy has focused upon the benefits of increased international trade, with no apparent recognition of any costs. The illusion is that of a 'global village'. It has been enacted in such programmes as the North American Free Trade Agreement, and the General Agreement on Tariffs and Trade, and further advanced by outspoken opposition to policies of border protection when it comes to transfers of goods (although not of people). The removal of constraints on trade is viewed as an overall gain, or at least as a condition in which total benefits outweigh total costs. A Paretian, or in any event, a Kaldor–Hicks optimum thus is achieved.

The concept is based upon neoclassical notions of free trade, comparative advantage and equilibrium. Free trade, it is maintained, ensures the concentration of each country on what it does best, yielding a more efficient allocation of resources in each, and an overall increase in world productivity and output (Milberg 1994, p. 588). It is assumed that markets will clear; the usual market-clearing conditions apply. No increase in unemployment is contemplated; the traditional full employment model is employed. No decline in standards is anticipated; rather, it is assumed that wage levels and practices of lesser developed countries will be pulled up by those of their more developed trading partners.

The reality is different. Lower environmental, working conditions and wage standards of lesser developed countries have served as magnets for businesses solely focused on cost cutting. Companies have shifted operations, either through the use of outsourcing or by establishing a multinational presence, to avail themselves of lower cost opportunities. Of at least equal importance has been the impact on wage earners of more developed countries of the potential for the transfer to lower cost countries of industrial processes. Actual moves have cost jobs, the threat of moves has intimidated workers, resulting in moderation of demands, depression of wages and throttling of labour activism.

Multinational corporations know their rights; acceptance of responsibilities is more limited. The nation state is a tool that has been used historically to specify responsibilities, enforce fulfilment and provide a shield against the 'slings and arrows of outrageous fortune'. But multinational corporations are not subject to national control. In surrendering national standards, we relinquish an important instrument for social protection and betterment. Reversal of this pattern will require that a choice be made among reassertion of national modes, design of controls within an international context or abandonment of hard won protections. In my view, the first course seems improbable at this point, and the last is unacceptable.

CONCLUSION

Theory and practice are not separate realms, but interrelated and interdependent aspects of the economics discipline. Theory flows directly from assumption, and prescribes practice. The term 'positive economics' is an oxymoron.

I have attempted to illustrate the effects of application to the real world of an ideal model, using as examples policies of deregulation, adherence to NAIRU and globalization. Needless to say, other cherished policies that express the ideal could have been used, for example, that of a balanced budget. The point is that assumptions and policies are inextricably bound, and that assessment of validity of assumptions is crucial to any evaluation of the serviceability of practice.

Adherence to the assumptions and prescriptions of mainstream theory has, over the past 25 years or so, resulted in the unshackling of private market power, threatening the integrity of the public infrastructure and the supply of necessities to certain groups. It has caused a slowdown in economic growth, a retardation in productivity, the loss of secure, middle-class jobs and the replacement of a permanent with a 'contingent' labour force. It also has induced instability of employment (on a world-wide basis), stagnant real income, an increase in inequality along with a hollowing out of income distribution, and growing polarization (Peterson 1994, pp. 35–42, et passim; Levy and Murnane 1992, pp. 1333–6).

The loss of secure, middle-class jobs frequently is attributed to technological advance that renders worker skills obsolete, and to foreign competition. The resulting labour insecurity also sometimes is cited approvingly as contributing to the decrease in the NAIRU in recent years (Stiglitz 1997, pp. 6–7; Gordon 1997, p. 12). But technological advance has always been with us. When labour markets are tight, employers provide training sufficient to upgrade skills. Foreign competition is a threat only because costs of production in lesser developed countries are low as a result of unacceptable standards and practices. It is not technological advance and foreign competition to which these conditions are attributable, but an imbalance in the distribution of power caused by a national and international abandonment both of tools of social control and of pro-growth, full employment policies.

The policies of deregulation, acceptance of the NAIRU and globalization were intended to establish ideals of competition, stability and efficiency. But a funny thing happened on the way to utopia. The result instead has been the reinforcement of established power, economic instability and an increase in income inequality. It is not too difficult to discern that current conditions result directly from attempts to mandate the establishment of the mainstream myth. A more difficult task will be that of putting Humpty Dumpty back together again.

NOTES

1. Presidential Address to the Association for Institutional Thought, April 1997, Albuquerque, New Mexico.
2. As is well known, these conditions include the existence of economies of scale and scope, a high minimum threshold level of investment, the need to build plant in advance of demand implying chronic excess capacity, the requirement for widespread interconnection, the control of access, an inelasticity of demand engendered by the presence of a high element of necessity in demand in some of the markets served, and the presence of externalities. They also include the existence of asymmetric information, risks and burdens. That these enterprises produce multiple products under conditions of a high and increasing proportion of joint and common costs in total costs, in an environment of pervasive market segmentation containing customer groups that themselves possess oligopsonistic power, facilitates price discrimination, cross-subsidization, and cost and risk shifting among markets.
3. Familiar criticisms of regulation include its stifling of both innovation and technological change, its encouragement of rate base padding including the gold plating of investment, its incentive to expenditure inflation because of cost-plus biases, its distortion of investment and consumption decisions, and its undue focus on equity as opposed to efficiency goals as exemplified in the use of embedded historic cost and value-of-service costing and pricing techniques, producing cross-subsidization. Various behavioural flaws of regulation also are specified, such as in capture theory in which regulators are posited as either pawns of industry or in thrall to powerful consumer interest groups, that is, as acting from a political, rather than an economic, interest.
4. Raymond Smith's remark has reference to the passage of the 1996 Telecommunications Act, the alleged purpose of which is to ease entry into long distance and local markets, an entry that long distance companies and RHCs are by turns vigorously pursuing (when it comes to the turf of others) and resisting (when it comes to their own).
5. Joseph Stiglitz states: 'I think of the theory behind the NAIRU essentially as a description about how the economy behaves out of equilibrium' (Stiglitz 1997, p. 3).
6. Thus, for example, Robert J. Gordon rejects the proposal to use even monetary policy to stimulate an increase in the growth rate from 2 per cent to 3 per cent, on the grounds that the recent decrease in the NAIRU is insufficient to prevent such a rate of growth from creating unacceptable rates of inflation (Gordon 1997, p. 30).

REFERENCES

Beed, Clive and Cara Beed (1996), 'Polarities Between Naturalism and Non-naturalism in Contemporary Economics: An Overview', *Journal of Economic Issues*, **30** (4), December, pp. 1077–104.

Galbraith, James K. (1997), 'Time to Ditch the Nairu', *Journal of Economic Perspectives*, **11** (1), Winter, pp. 93–108.

Gordon, Robert J. (1997), 'The Time Varying NAIRU and its Implications for Economic Policy', *Journal of Economic Perspectives*, **11** (1), Winter, pp. 11–32.

Holden, Benjamin A. (1997), 'Edison International Puts Energy into Defending Base', *The Wall Street Journal*, 13 March.

Lawson, Tony (1994), 'The Nature of Post Keynesianism and its Links to Other Traditions: A Realist Perspective', *Journal of Post Keynesian Economics*, **16** (4), Summer, pp. 503–38.

Levy, Frank and Richard J. Murnane (1992), 'US Earnings Levels and Earnings Inequality: A Review of Recent Trends and Proposed Explanations', *Journal of Economic Literature*, **30**, September, pp. 1333–81.

Lipin, Steven (1997), 'Many More Utility Takeovers are Expected that Marry Electric and Natural-Gas Suppliers', *The Wall Street Journal*, 20 March.

Milberg, William (1994), 'Market Competition and the Failure of Competitive Enhancement Policies in The United States', *Journal of Economic Issues*, **28** (2), June, pp. 587–96.

Miller, Edythe S. (1990), 'On Public and Private Control in a "Reasonable" Society', *Journal of Economic Issues*, **24** (1), March, pp. 239–48.

_____(1993), 'The Economic Imagination and Public Policy: Orthodoxy Discovers the Corporation', *Journal of Economic Issues*, **27** (4), December, pp. 1041–58.

Naik, Gautam (1996), 'Going Long', *The Wall Street Journal*, 16 September.

Peterson, Wallace C. (1994), *Silent Depression*, New York: W.W. Norton & Company.

Rappaport, Steven (1996), 'Abstraction and Unrealistic Assumptions in Economics', *Journal of Economic Methodology*, **3** (2), December, pp. 215–36.

Robinson, Joan (1972), 'The Second Crisis of Economic Theory', *American Economic Review*, **62** (2), May, pp. 1–10.

Stiglitz, Joseph (1997), 'Reflections on the Natural Rate Hypothesis', *Journal of Economic Perspectives*, **11** (1), Winter, pp. 3–10.

Trebing, Harry M. (1994), 'The Networks as Infrastructure – The Reestablishment of Market Power', *Journal of Economic Issues*, **28** (2), June, pp. 379–89.

Veblen, Thorstein [1898] (1961), 'Why is Economics not an Evolutionary Science?' in *The Place of Science in Modern Civilization and Other Essays*, New York: Russell & Russell.

Wilke, John R. (1997), 'New Antitrust Rules May Ease Path to Mergers', *The Wall Street Journal*, 9 April.

3. Normative Macroeconomics: Conjoining Keynes and Institutionalism

Philip A. Klein[1]

INTRODUCTION

The theme of this paper is that while American institutionalism began as a dissent from orthodox microtheory it has much in common with the macroeconomics of Keynes. I will here argue that Keynesianism is essentially normative economics, as is institutionalism. It is surely true that Keynes preferred to dwell on the actual economy and to strive to find ways to improve economic performance, rather than to spin out the implications of a perfectly functioning macroeconomic system. He began by denying that either full employment or the operation of Say's Law of Markets could be assumed. In his macroeconomics he struggled to develop ways to improve a flawed macroeconomic system quite as institutionalists had earlier insisted that the task of the discipline was to improve the performance of a flawed price system rather than to contemplate the implications inherent in Smith's invisible hand. Thus both Keynesian and institutional economics converge in their normative insistence on judging the imperfect performance of flawed economies.

I will indicate that despite the great overlap between institutionalism and Keynesian macroeconomics, many institutionalists after Ayres failed to appreciate the commonalities and some were, erroneously in my judgement, even hostile to Keynes.

Finally, I will argue that conjoining Keynes and institutionalism would enhance both traditions in providing for the promulgation of the most useful criteria for assessing macroeconomic theory and policy.

Although the macroeconomy has presumably been with us as long as human beings have had an economy, it was not the focus of much attention before Keynes, certainly not if by 'focus' one means that serious problems were seen to arise therein, requiring the formulation of public policy. (Recall that, by assuming full employment along with Say's Law of Markets classical economists assumed away most macroeconomic problems.)

Marshall, as the pivotal neoclassicist, distinguished 'national income' from national wealth but was unremittingly focused on the microeconomy for in-depth analysis (Marshall 1949, p. 80). In the pre-fallacy of composition world of 1890 little attention was paid to the determination of national income and the implications thereof. The microeconomic determination of output (therefore income), market by market, was presumably satisfactory. We tend, therefore, to forget what Keynes did for (and to) the discipline. Today all of the new classical economists are eager to help us forget, but institutionalists should guard against being unduly influenced by their presumptive claims.

THE MICROECONOMIC ORIGINS OF INSTITUTIONALISM

American institutionalism was originally developed in connection with what we now call microeconomics. It was the disagreement of early institutionalists about the role of prices in resource allocation in general, and the emphasis on living with the results of market allocation in particular, which gave Veblen, Commons, and perhaps even Mitchell, their original unity in opposition to mainstream economics. Of the three, Mitchell was the only one who ventured toward what we now call macroeconomics, but he seems not to have extensively tied his work in institutionalism to his empirical work in business cycles.[2]

A significant bridge between microeconomics and macroeconomics[3] may be derived by assessing the impact which concentrated power has on economic activity. This impact can be analysed, as it is in microeconomics, as concern about how large corporations dominate and shape both consumer demand and firm supply. More broadly, one asks, how does concentrated power impact on the total value system of the society? Institutionalists would argue that concentrated power plays a major role in generating the disjunction between the instrumental deployment of resources in the provisioning process, and the ceremonial deployment.[4] The latter, of course, at any given time is the actual deployment, and from this perspective power concentrations play a defining role in how total resource allocation occurs in the economy. How power and its impact affect the emergent value system is,[5] we shall argue, reflected in the macroeconomy, perhaps there more clearly and completely even than it is in the microeconomy. Accordingly, total allocation must ultimately be examined not merely bit by bit (more accurately, market by market), but for the whole economy.

KEYNESIAN ECONOMICS: INSTITUTIONALIST MACROECONOMICS

The value system defines the character of total resource allocation.[6] There have been, in the United States, federal statutes dealing with various aspects of economic activity since the founding of the republic. But a distinctive and comprehensive role for the public sector arrived only in this century. The Great Depression in the US spawned a ready-made laboratory for macroeconomic experimentation under Roosevelt's New Deal. Keynes's *General Theory* (1936) provided theoretical underpinnings for what today we call macroeconomics. Indeed, a major theme of the present paper is that Keynes gave a major impetus to the institutionalists' longstanding concern with economics as a 'science of valuation' rather than mere 'allocation'. Keynes in effect abandoned the normative meaning of equilibrium; he reduced equilibrium (often regarded as 'good' in classical economics) to the 'mere equilibrium' stressed by Ayres (Ayres 1944, pp. 66–7). After all, the major impact of Keynes's analysis was to suggest that the economy could gravitate to 'underemployment equilibrium' (or for that matter an inflationary 'over-employment equilibrium') quite as – or more readily than that rarity – a 'full employment equilibrium'. The notion that equilibria need not be 'good' was, therefore, at the heart of Keynes's macrotheory and quite at variance with the implicit good that is at the heart of classical economics' microequilibria. The major difference, of course, is implicit in what has been said. When institutionalists refer to 'mere equilibrium' – neither good nor bad *per se* – they have customarily followed Ayres in focusing on equilibrium in individual markets, whereas Keynes was referring to the macroeconomy. But by putting the stress on assessing the performance of the actual – therefore flawed – economy, Keynes asked questions quite compatible with the institutionalist view of the actual economy as a provisioning instrumentality.[7] Is it capable of providing jobs for all? Is it providing for all in an acceptable way, or does the private sector performance need augmentation by the public sector and if so how and to what extent? These Keynesian questions are, we assert, also institutionalist questions. It is for this reason that we shall be concerned here to view Keynes as a contributor to the institutionalist perspective – that economics is concerned with 'valuation' rather than mere allocation. Keynes was thereby, we assert, a major contributor to that profoundly institutionalist concern with valuation.

As a public policy illustration of this perspective in the US, the Employment Act of 1946 contains an explicit statement from the Congress that the federal government in this country has a direct responsibility to further the macroeconomic goals of 'maximum employment, production, and purchasing power'.[8] In the intervening years there has been debate about amending this act in various ways, but it is still on the books essentially as passed in that year. As such the Employment Act of 1946 established for the US a macroeconomic environment which was broadly comparable to that set forth for Britain by William Beveridge in his *Full Employment in a Free Society* (1944).

Beyond all this, of course, the recognition of the existence of a macroeconomy and its serious malfunctioning opened the door for consideration of the entire question of the relationship between the individual and the larger society in economic affairs. What should be the legitimate obligations of the state to the individual? The stage was set for a debate about what standards of general welfare were to be implemented in the economy.

Given their interest in both public sector and private sector performance, institutionalists can work more conveniently within a macroeconomic than in a microeconomic framework. Their instrumental valuation has always pertained to the implications of total resource allocation not just market allocation. Macroeconomics has long been an area in economic theory in which there is a continuing and distinctive inclusion of the public sector. Accordingly, institutionalists should have embraced macroeconomics as an approach that requires inclusion of all resource allocation in judging economic performance. As we shall see, they really did not do this.

To help correct for this deficiency, I shall argue that institutionalism can be related analytically to macroeconomics in a way that furthers many objectives of special concern to institutionalists.

MACROECONOMICS AND THE FOUNDERS OF AMERICAN INSTITUTIONALISM

Veblen

Ultimately Veblen was concerned with how the institutions of society, replete with various built-in invidious processes, acted through the market to distort the allocation of resources. That is, he distinguished between the actual operation of the system and how it would have operated had it been the product only of what emerging instrumental valuation would have produced (for example, Veblen 1904). For Veblen it was market behaviour that reflected the pivotal distinction between industrial standards and pecuniary standards. Because the public sector was relatively small, the question of the extent to which pecuniary valuation in the market caused the entire economy to diverge from the requirements of instrumental valuations seemed adequately comprehensive in Veblen's day. The market and the economy were far more coterminous in Veblen's time than since. The rise of the nonmarket economy, before Keynes, occurred without much analytical consideration from classical and neoclassical economists. In any case, modern macroeconomics is customarily attributed to the impact of John Maynard Keynes on economic thinking. The Keynes who had this impact emerged sometime after the publication of his *Treatise on*

Money (1930); modern macroeconomics is dated from the 1936 publication of his *General Theory of Employment, Interest, and Money*. Veblen, who died in 1929, is the only one of the founders of American institutionalism, therefore, who was gone before modern macroeconomics was introduced.

Commons

John R. Commons died in 1945 and so lived in the Keynesian world for the last nine years of his life. Neither his *Institutional Economics* in 1934, nor Kenneth Parsons's editing of his *Economics of Collective Action* (1950) makes reference to Keynes. However, since Commons's inquiry focus was on 'collective action', bargaining powers and conflict resolution, he envisioned a large and continuing role and responsibility for government. But there is little to suggest that he had much to say about macroeconomics *per se*.

Mitchell

Of the Founding Fathers of institutionalism then, the one to whom we must pay most attention in this context is Wesley Clair Mitchell. During the last twelve years of his life (1936–48) the *General Theory* and its implications for macroeconomics were being widely debated by economists and others.

Alvin Hansen has argued that as Mitchell learned more and thought more about important problems in economics he became less certain of himself and was less willing to take positions on current issues or on 'scientific controversies relating particularly to his field of interest, namely, the vast issues raised by Keynes's *General Theory*' (Hansen 1949, p. 319). To Hansen this uncertainty is a natural part of recognizing the complexity of the world as one gets older.

There is some evidence supporting Hansen's hypothesis. The most likely place for Mitchell to comment on Keynes was in his famous Columbia University course in the History of Economic Thought. The notes from this course, taken by one of Mitchell's students originally in 1935, were meticulously recorded. The notes were updated periodically between 1935 and 1949 and were published in 1967 (Mitchell 1967). This publication indicates that he never focused much direct attention on Keynes, even though Appendix VI entitled 'Some Notes on J.M. Keynes' has nothing but admiring comments, being far more accepting than his colleague, Arthur Burns.[9]

Ayres

In Ayres's *The Theory of Economic Progress*, there are perhaps a dozen references to Keynes. In the first, concerning the 'single-minded' concern of mainstream economists with price analysis, Ayres comments, 'This is true notwithstanding the flurry induced by the writings of Mr. J.M. Keynes' (Ayres 1944). That accurately suggests the degree of importance which Ayres at that time attached to Keynesian economics. Today even the most ardent new classical economist would credit the impact of Keynes as having been more than a 'flurry'. Most of Ayres's other references to Keynes relate to Ayres's interest in underconsumption ideas. But he does not discuss Keynes's break with classical economic findings. Keynes is not central to Ayres's argument in *The Theory of Economic Progress* (compare Ayres 1944, pp. 267–82).

At the end of his life, Ayres did a virtual about face and, to his credit, gave evidence that he not only had come to appreciate the significance of what Keynes had done, but saw that Veblen's concerns and those of Keynes had a large overlap.

Both, for example, were concerned with the value implications of an evolving economy. Said Ayres, in one of his last essays,

> In a very basic sense, . . . what we now call macroeconomics is Veblenian economics, notwithstanding the fact that Keynes did more than anyone else to establish macroeconomics as a distinct discipline . . . Macroeconomics is Veblenian in precisely the sense that it turns away from the sterilities of price equilibrium theories to the realities of the community's efforts to feed and clothe and house itself. This is what Keynes prevailed upon us to do, pointing out that in such an affluent society as ours people go hungry not because of any inexorable laws but only because we choose to do as we do in respects that are quite amenable to alteration. (1964, p. 61)

In the last analysis this is the ultimate challenge of institutionalist economics to the mainstream position. Keynes, to be sure, got there by a different route (possibly even, as Mitchell thought, a more orthodox route). But an important part of the institutionalist challenge is arguably also ultimately the Keynesian challenge. In the final analysis both institutionalist economics and Keynesian economics assess the operation of the flawed economy which in fact we have, rather than admire, via deductive reasoning, the operation of a flawless, beautiful, elegant and precisely functioning system which, alas, we do not have.

Keynes would say the challenge is not to settle for equilibrium if it comes at the expense of either an inflationary or a deflationary gap. In the process of eliminating these gaps we come closer as well to enhancing the life process.

INSTITUTIONALIST REACTIONS TO KEYNES, 1947–80

If Ayres eventually saw Keynes as a major agent for the institutionalist perspective, his institutionalist contemporaries most rarely saw the light. Early on Allan Gruchy had some sympathy for Keynes. He wrote, for example, that Keynes

regarded economics as an aid in the establishment of a partially controlled economy
in which the government would assume responsibility for the goodworking of the
investment process . . . although the shell of his economics may still be described as
orthodox, its contents are largely a contribution to novel twentieth-century thinking.
(Gruchy 1949, p. 244 and pp. 249–66)

More to the point, in perhaps his only extensive comment on Keynes, the early
Gruchy asserted, 'John Maynard Keynes and the American institutionalists
have fundamentally the same general view of the nature of economics' (Gruchy
1950, p. 96). At the same time, however, Gruchy argued that institutionalists
worried about the quality of what was produced (for example, the mix of public
and private goods) while Keynes worried only about the quantity of output
(Gruchy 1950, pp. 106–26).

After this early period in which Gruchy found things to admire in Keynes he
mostly ignored Keynes.[10] On those rare occasions when he referred to him at
all, he began criticizing Keynes severely – mostly for his failure to explicitly
embrace national economic planning. For this reason principally, he continued
to the end of his life to pillory Keynes. Suffice it to note here that in the
General Theory Keynes shows how his views paralleled early institutionalist
thought. He refers to the theory of value and the theory of price as the 'double
life' of economics and comments: 'One of the objects of the foregoing chapters
has been to escape from this double life and to bring the theory of prices as a
whole back to close contact with the theory of value' (Keynes 1936, p. 293).
Mainstream economics to this day scarcely ever recognizes that there is such
a dichotomy.[11] While Gruchy is right that Keynes is not really dynamic, Keynes
never argued that the *General Theory* was genuinely dynamic, but it did (and
does) provide a crucial link to dynamic theory. Moreover, Keynes clearly
makes what I regard as the critical institutionalist assertion, writing:

> I shall argue that the postulates of the classical theory are applicable to a special case
> only and not to the general case, the situation which it assumes being a limiting point
> of the possible positions of equilibrium. Moreover, the characteristics of the special
> case assumed by the classical theory happen not to be those of the economic society
> in which we actually live, with the result that its teaching is misleading and disastrous
> if we attempt to apply it to the facts of experience. (Keynes 1936, p. 3)

Gruchy's contemporaries, with the exception of Foster (see below), took
varying positions, but in the end failed, in my judgement, to appreciate fully the
large degree of overlap between their perspective and that of Keynes. This
group would include John Gambs, Wendell Gordon and Marc Tool. Gambs in
his book has no reference to macroeconomics (Gambs 1946). His only
reference to Keynes is vividly recalled by Fagg Foster: 'Veblen would have felt
a moral obligation to reduce Keynes to a cinder' (quoted in Foster 1981, p.
954). Wendell Gordon, in his *Institutional Economics*, admired Keynes – 'a

fine, healthy antidote to some of the stereotypes of price theory' (Gordon 1980, p. 124) – but ultimately concluded, as did Gruchy, that 'the theory was depression theory, and its chief useful insights had to do with depression and depression unemployment' (Gordon 1980, p. 125).[12] Marc Tool (Tool 1979) makes few references to Keynes, and they are all approving. It is fair to say that Tool never focuses a great deal of attention on Keynesian macroeconomics in his analysis of institutionalism.

J. Fagg Foster: An Exception

J. Fagg Foster was the major institutionalist of the pre-1980 period (other than the 'late' Ayres) to appreciate the relevance of the Keynesian argument for institutionalism. In 1966 Foster considered the relationship between institutionalism and Keynesian economics directly (Foster 1968). He wrote, 'The institutional economics and the Keynesian economics conjoin in relation to the questions asked, the philosophical foundations of economic theory, and the identification of the dynamic factors in the economic process. But the integration of these two bodies of theory still required integration in the professional literature' (Foster 1981, pp. 949–57). A major assertion of this essay is that the work of 'conjoining the two', the need for which Foster recognized so long ago, was done neither by institutionalists nor by Keynesians until relatively recently (compare, for example, Arestis and Eichner 1988 and Eichner 1985). Arguably the compatibility of the two is not fully appreciated by either side to this day.

As early as 1969 Foster called Keynes's *General Theory* 'the most notable application of the institutional approach to a fundamental economic problem'. Seeing beyond the well-known view (both among mainstream economists and institutionalists like Gruchy) that Keynes's approach was 'merely comparative static' and not genuinely dynamic, Foster suggested that Keynesian theory was a theory of economic process, or at least pointed in that direction (Foster 1981, pp. 865–7). Foster recognized early that 'Generality is attained by identifying income as the instantaneous commitment of any particular variables' (Foster 1981, p. 953). Therefore, Foster appreciated that there was a whole range of plausible relationships among the three independent variables (the propensity to consume, the rate of interest and the marginal efficiency of capital). This suggests that in Keynes it was really true that 'equilibrium is merely equilibrium' and could be accompanied by inflation, unemployment or inadequate growth. For institutionalists moreover, he also realized that for these key Keynesian variables, 'each is determined by the mores and folkways and the institutional structure of the community. That is why the Keynesian theory appears as an application of the more general institutional theory of the economic process' (Foster 1981, p. 866). Foster's view is thus almost diametrically opposite to the Gruchy view of Keynes. Foster goes on to note that 'by treating institutional structures as adjustable instead of assuming they are given data, the Keynesian thesis dictates the general conclusion that whatever is technically feasible is financially possible (Foster 1981, p. 866)'. This echoes Ayres's final evaluation. Communities which fail to provide the material wherewithal to enhance human life to the full extent that technology and resources make possible are failing by choice. We shall return to this because it has special relevance for the challenge of the late 1990s.

Foster saw economic progress as a consequence of what he called institutional adjustment. In this process, Keynesian insights were valued. But Foster was right when he concluded: 'With some exceptions, among all the post-Keynesian economists the institutionalists seem to have been the least affected by Keynes's theory' (Foster 1981, p. 954). Today, alas, one would have to amend this to note the explicit, if dubious, rejection of Keynes offered in various ways by the new classical economists – supply siders, rational expectation adherents, monetarists – all of whom have found their own way to defang Keynes in a process which I once referred to as 'reinventing the square wheel' (Klein 1986).

By seeing that the Keynesian variables were components of a process of institutional adjustment, Foster saw beyond the simultaneous adjustment of independent variables determining a unique 'equilibrium income'. This equilibrium income is the *ex post* income on which mainstream economics focuses. Foster was able to focus on the gap between the income that is called 'equilibrium' and the income that would employ all resources. That is, he stressed the implications of inflationary and deflationary gaps, formerly employed by the mainstream to denote departures from full employment equilibrium in the Keynesian model before the emphasis moved to the aggregate demand and supply diagrammatic in which the Keynesian model was restricted to real income analysis.[13]

Both deflationary and inflationary gaps, if one thinks about it, have significance only if one looks at economic activity in processual terms. Keynes pointed in this direction even if he did not develop a theory the mainstream could call dynamic or institutionalists would call 'processual'. But Foster saw early the inherent dynamism in Keynes and its essential compatibility with the institutionalist perspective. Thus he noted, 'The dynamic quality of the Keynesian theory is attained by considering the rate of change in income in terms of the concurrent rates of change in the components of income, which are in turn determined by constantly changing patterns of the mores and folkways and by institutional adjustment' (Foster 1981, p. 953). This is a more accurate view of the character of Keynesian theory than is the mainstream conventional view that Keynes is 'merely comparative static' theory. The significant conclusion, therefore, one which Foster saw, is that 'equilibrium' as an ideal end result of economic activity is as unacceptable for Keynes as it always has been for institutionalists. Keynes notes at the end of the *General Theory* that 'in some respects the foregoing theory is moderately conservative in its implications' (Keynes 1936, p. 377). It is well to remember, nonetheless, that he goes on to suggest a role for the state of which even Allan Gruchy ought to have approved: 'The state will have to exercise a guiding influence on the propensity to consume partly through its scheme of taxation, partly by fixing the rate of interest, and partly, perhaps, in other ways . . . I conceive, therefore, that a somewhat comprehensive socialization of investment will prove the only means of securing an approximation to full employment' (Keynes 1936, p. 378).

Gladys Parker Foster

Finally, an institutionalist of the present generation who has devoted a good deal of attention to Keynes is Gladys Parker Foster. One aspect of her work has addressed the question of whether the money supply in Keynes's *General Theory* is exogenously or endogenously determined (G. Foster 1986). This question is central to the debate which has gone on in the past forty years between 'Keynesians' and monetarists, led by Milton Friedman. The latter, of course, has long argued that the money supply is exogenous; hence monetary policy could and does directly affect the level and rate of real economic activity. G. Foster argues that, while Keynes was not infrequently ambiguous in the *General Theory* about the origin and impact of the money supply, ultimately the money supply has to be endogenously determined in the Keynes system so that the chain of causation can run from real economic activity to the money supply. This in turn means that the chain of causation in Keynes is from investment to saving whereas orthodox economics assumes the reverse. Accordingly, the savings theory of capital formation is undermined: a debt creation theory of capital formation is introduced. Public policy to stimulate investment in a deflationary context is a proper Keynesian *and* institutionalist recommendation. Increasing savings of the rich produces no such stimulus.

In addition, Foster has considered the commonalities which exist in both Keynes's work and in institutionalism which are derived from the perspective of John Dewey. She has noted that Keynes 'had no need to reconcile morals and economics; as he saw it they were already in the same philosophical and logical category' (G. Foster 1991, p. 566). She would place Keynes squarely among those who regard economics as a normative science. While she does not dwell on the overlap between institutionalism and Keynesian economics *per se*, she does explore convincingly the commonalities between Keynes and Dewey. In recognition of the seminal influence of Dewey on institutionalism her work supports the general argument of this paper.

In sum, as far as I can tell, Ayres and the two Fosters are the major institutionalists prior to the present generation of institutionalists who recognized the essential compatibility of institutionalism and Keynesian macroeconomics.

RECASTING THE RELATIONSHIP BETWEEN INSTITUTIONALISM AND KEYNESIAN ECONOMICS

I have long held that in most important respects Keynesian macroeconomics was highly compatible with institutional economics (compare, for example, Klein 1994, p. 106). It is perfectly true that in some ways Keynes stayed within a conventional mainstream perspective, but arguably, as we have already noted, his suggestion that equilibrium might not necessarily be 'good' meant taking a giant step in the direction which institutionalists have from the beginning insisted was critical. If Ayres had microeconomic equilibria in mind when he denigrated their significance, Keynes took precisely the same view of macroeconomic equilibria. If equilibrium is questionable as a good 'end result' for individual markets, why is this not an equally inappropriate way to examine the end result of macroeconomic activity? Because the macroeconomy comprehends more than market activity, institutionalists should have seen this as a big help in moving from the mainstream restriction of economics to the study of market allocation to economics as the study of societal provisioning with resources. In effect this Keynesian perspective provided a major step forward in developing economics as a science of valuation. It is, therefore, unfortunate that so many institutionalists joined mainstream economists in denigrating what Keynes did as being 'merely comparative static', or as 'depression economics'.

If as Fagg Foster reminds us, Keynes focused on the determinants of real income and output, it was only because in the 1930s inflation was not a major problem. In the 1950s the Keynesian system was presented in such a way that 'inflationary gaps' could be depicted quite as readily as 'deflationary gaps'. The key idea was that the level of effective demand did not lead to any ideal level of income (real or nominal) but it did lead to a unique level, one at which widespread unemployment (or unacceptable rates of inflation) could be present.

In logic, therefore, as we suggested at the outset, the likelihood that aggregate demand would lead to 'underemployment equilibrium' as it did in the 1930s could be rearranged to show that 'overemployment equilibria' are also possible. For all economists, including institutionalists, the devastating conclusion from Keynes is that the forces which determine the level of economic activity have no particular affinity leading to precisely the level required to utilize all the productive forces available. What Keynes did, therefore, we repeat, was to agree with Ayres's view of equilibrium as a state without normative implications. As Ayres said in a microeconomic context,

A remark . . . by . . . Lionel Robbins that 'equilibrium is just equilibrium' has been widely quoted. It betrays consciousness if not of guilt at least of general suspicion. Few physicists take the trouble any longer to clear their use of equilibrium of taint of beneficence, since their context implies no such beneficence. That of economics does – hence the denial – if equilibrium is just equilibrium, why are economists so much concerned about it? (Ayres 1961, p. 67)

In a macroeconomic context this is precisely what Keynes means. Macroeconomic equilibrium is simply what any particular level of aggregate effective demand produces, and it is neither good, bad nor indifferent *per* se. Its only importance enters when it is related to pressures of inflation and of unemployment. Both Ayres and Keynes give vivid credence to the notion that in economics one cannot accept, even for purposes of analysis, 'what is' without blurring the distinction between what is and what ought to be in precisely the ways that institutionalists directly confront. Acceptance of 'what is' is as normative a position as to advocate an alternative to 'what is'.

This realization gives the lie to the mainstream assertion that it is the operation of some inexorable laws of positive economic analysis that brand a living wage as out of market-clearing reach because it will produce intolerable inflation. At the same time these economists assert that million dollar bonuses for corporate executives are not only not inflationary but reflect the 'true' inelastic demand we have for these people. The full implications of supply and demand, both for markets and in the aggregate, thus involve what lies behind both. Economists deploy their 'positive analysis' in the pursuit of their normative agendas. At the back of their equilibria is a world of normative assumptions, and ultimately conclusions. That is, when we teach our students (if we do) that the 'natural rate of unemployment' explains low wages and the necessity to keep them low, while the inexorable but value-free laws of supply and demand, reflecting as they do the natural law of the jungle, explain the high bonuses, economists are trying to give their normative assumptions a positive cast.

What Keynes did was to debunk the notion of a macroeconomic 'invisible hand', that is, an equilibrium adjustment in the market, leading via price changes to a balance between aggregate demand and aggregate supply at precisely the level of output (hence income) at which all the productive forces would be employed.

It is, after all, the misbehaviour of the pricing process, viewed in aggregate terms, which makes modern macroeconomics important. And by the same token it was the presumed success of macroeconomic policy (a bit overrated) which was going to bring the original meaning and significance back to the equilibria of price theory in what Samuelson used to call 'the grand neoclassical synthesis'[14] (Samuelson 1955, p. 11 et seq.).

THE CONTAMINATION OF 'POSITIVE' MACROECONOMICS: REVISING THE CIRCULAR FLOW

What has happened in the recent past to macroeconomic theory represents, in my view, a contamination of economic theory by the normative views of our self-proclaimed positive mainstream fellow economists. Consider, for example, 'the circular flow of economic activity'. This is the customary point of departure for explanations of how the macroeconomy functions. If one thinks about it, the evenhandedness of the circular flow has been significantly altered during the 'new classical' effort to restore the attractive ideal qualities to macroeconomic 'equilibrium' which Keynes stripped away. Traditional mainstream explanations always begin by noting that households play two roles – as sellers of the factors of production and as buyers of goods and services from firms. Today, it is clear that new classical economists assume that the role of households as sellers of productive services is the commanding role. It is here that households influence the firms' costs of production. Macroeconomic analysis, in modern mainstream hands, invariably tilts toward keeping production costs down so that profit rates will stay up and firms will be encouraged to produce. But the original circular flow makes it perfectly clear that higher returns to factors can also be interpreted as increasing the ability of households to buy, and this in the original explanations derived from Keynes was also designed to increase the willingness of firms to produce. The prospect of sales, in the most conventional early explanations of how a market system operates, leads to increased investment. The circular flow was not originally an application of 'underconsumption' theory – it was a straightforward explanation of how capitalist production systems are designed to work. Finally, it is important to recall that in considering the 'underconsumption controversy'– that is, whether we should pursue policies designed to encourage consumption or to encourage investment – Keynes states that 'the wisest course is to advance on both fronts at once' (Keynes 1936, p. 325). So much for the view that Keynes was hopelessly fixated on underconsumptionist theory.

THE FRAGILITY OF INVESTMENT INCENTIVES

In addition to the revision of the circular flow, the incentive to invest has become very fragile in modern macroeconomic theory. It is arguably the lynch-pin of the theory of production in capitalist economies. Its new-found fragility has very pernicious implications. It causes mainstream economists, in pursuit of their positive economics, to place a far greater emphasis on keeping inflation down than on keeping employment up. One might argue that the likelihood that households with unemployed heads will buy at lower prices is only slightly better than that they will buy at higher prices. So viewed, raising employment might be viewed as a better way to guarantee the prospects that firms can sell their output than merely keeping down inflation, if the result of that effort is accompanied by high unemployment.

IMPLICATIONS

The asymmetric view of the circular flow and the accompanying view of the incentive to invest as fragile are both self-serving for the existing financial power systems. They are accompanied by a number of subsidiary implicit theorems; large bonuses to corporate executives are fine if they feed the incentive to invest and produce. Higher wages for workers in the same corporation, however, are definitionally inflationary and therefore clearly bad. Capital gains tax reductions (or better their elimination) are wonderful because they, too, encourage investment and production. 'Middle-class tax cuts', except insofar as they represent 'smaller government' – definitionally good – are far less stimulative.

What all this suggests is that current macroeconomic debate makes it far clearer than our microeconomic debates did that economic analysis is normative, whether its practitioners wish it so or not. If the ultimate implication of Keynes was to justify interventionism, neoclassical economists consistently seem to reject it and miraculously to develop an explanation to justify the rejection. Thus interventionist monetary policy, for example, is bad (monetarism) or irrelevant (rational explanations). It does not much matter so long as it is clear that it cannot successfully affect the level of employment in the economy. Ask yourself which came first: the non-interventionist predilections of those who developed the rational expectations approach, or the approach itself? How 'positive' can economic theory be if it is developed in response to a request: 'Find me a theory that will lead to these policy positions?'.

KEYNESIAN ECONOMICS AND INSTITUTIONALISM

The implications of Keynesian economics for the traditional concerns of institutionalists are, therefore, myriad.

We are, for example, suggesting that the distinctive price–value disjunction, a focus of institutionalist attention since Veblen, but still largely ignored by the mainstream, has a counterpart in macroeconomics where it is revealed in the national accounts. Actually it shows up in several ways: first, it is a macroeconomic commonplace nowadays to note that not all goods and services of 'value' are included – for example, work in the home (that is, it has economic value but no price). Second, a distinction is usually made now between a change in gross domestic product and in what Samuelson calls 'net economic welfare' (Samuelson and Nordhaus 1995). The latter includes the attendant consequences of bigger output, both good and bad. Third, one can examine the allocation of resources to various purposes in the national accounts with a view to asking what they reveal about national priorities (reflecting the prevailing societal value system).

The social value principle requires that we ask how is the provisioning process working? What is the relationship between the actual deployment of resources in the economy and that which would fully reflect the prevailing societal value system?[15] Institutionalists insist that all modern societies in actuality subject resource deployment, whether through the market or otherwise, to societal monitoring.

Adam Smith got around the value problem very cleverly. The invisible hand transmogrified private greed, selfishness and self-centredness into a public virtue. It probably did not hold even in Smith's time, because there were surely great disparities in wealth and income, an underclass and great poverty. Pareto optimality would scarcely have been meaningful even then, but at least there were not yet huge and powerful firms, high concentration, and all the other possible sources of resource allocation distortions which have been brought into being with the creation of modern corporate economies. Whether Adam Smith would have urged laissez-faire in the modern world is an interesting question. We should not overlook Smith's famous comment, 'People of the same trade seldom meet together, even for merriment and diversion, but the conversation ends in a conspiracy against the public, or income contrivance to raise prices' (Smith 1776, p. 128). Moreover, he did after all also write approvingly about moral sentiments.

All this means that the fallacy of composition, which forms an essential underpinning for modern macroeconomics, has become a good deal more pervasive than perhaps it once was. We have here argued that the disjunction between price and value, traditionally examined by institutionalists in microeconomic contexts, today shows up as well or perhaps even more starkly in the macroeconomy. The traditional institutionalist concern with the economy as the institutional complex devoted to the provisioning process, is not just the allocation process. But it must be appraised in a macroeconomic context. The evolving economy has always been more than emergent markets, or perhaps better, it has always been more than the sum of all emergent markets. The evolving economy encompasses the dynamic creation and deployment of all resources, human and nonhuman, in conjunction with energy to produce goods and services in the cause of enhancing human life. This process is necessarily dynamic because the knowledge base is always expanding and human wants are always in flux. It is from Veblen that institutionalists learned to look at evolving economic activity in this holistic way as a cultural manifestation of an aspect of human activity.

Institutionalists in general have failed to appreciate, or at least to note in writing, that this bedrock institutionalist perspective is far more readily assessed in macroeconomics than in microeconomics. The macroeconomy is the instrumentality representing at any given time how *all* resources are being used. Institutionalists ask how actual creation and deployment compares both to what is technologically feasible and what enlightened participants in economic activity would democratically vote to do. The disjunction can be assessed market by market, but ultimately it is the collective disjunction which summarizes the inadequacies of the price system.

This means that finally we come to the direct relationship between the value system and the macroeconomy. What are the value implications of total resource deployment in the economy? Unlike microeconomics, which tends to focus only on market allocation via prices, macroeconomics (thanks to Keynes) even in mainstream economics presents a framework within which all resource use can be considered. For institutionalists this means that one can ask, 'What are the value implications of C + I + G?'. No one has ever suggested that prices in markets can totally explain that.

SOCIETAL VALUES AND THE NATIONAL ACCOUNTS

I have always maintained that the National Accounts in effect constitute a current statement about societal values. They provide a running account of the results of societal review of the results of market allocation and of the priorities that prevail for supplementing market allocation with other resource deployment. In this sense the continuing debates in Washington concerning the budget have been debates about societal values.

I offer evidence from the 1994 data. All the talk about our 'gigantic' federal welfare system ignores the fact that we spend on education, training, employment and social services, plus health and Medicare, *less* than we spend for National Defence plus interest on the debt.[16] I say how we spend shows our true priorities. The role of the government, what can legitimately be expected of individuals, and to what degree society should provide a 'safety net' for all are fundamental aspects of this debate, which as shown often ignores what the true expenditures reflect. It is important to note, moreover, that the debate about what constitutes evidence of 'market failure' has never been symmetrical. The current mood is such that it is easy to argue that 'the welfare system has failed'. Failures are not treated as individual cases. We do not generalize other kinds of failure. The savings and loan scandals of a few years ago, the indictment and conviction of a number of businessmen involved in financial chicanery, and so on – these were never discussed as evidence that the financial system or the market system as we know it were failures. Our view of failure is thus asymmetrical: as one moves down the income distribution the likelihood increases that individual cases of various sorts of dishonesty will be generalized to the whole income group from which they come. A Michael Millken is merely an unfortunate aberration; a cheating welfare mother, on the other hand, exemplifies the norm to be expected from a soft undisciplined system.

We have argued that how a society in fact creates and deploys its resources is a statement of what that society's values are. That resources are deployed in ways other than the market should not be difficult to grasp in the United States in the late 1990s. The newspapers are full of reports of the latest daily rounds in the seemingly endless debate about whether the federal government should spend on this or that, whether other levels of government should be permitted to spend, or whether the decisions should be left to private individuals. Anyone who thought Thorstein Veblen was not being adequately rigorous when he suggested that the function of economic activity was to enhance human life need only tune in on any chapter in the discussions emanating from our nation's capital. Resource deployment in the final analysis cannot all be done by prices; prices are not even necessarily available. Values (family or otherwise) are clearly germane, as all agree. The quality of the information on which we debate these matters is also critical (a point institutionalists have long underscored). How we view the economy is germane. The appropriateness of the institutionalist perspective is attested to by the character of the economic debate, as much from non-interventionists and interventionists. Republican leadership may be willing to leave much to the market, but one critical matter they will not leave to the market, namely what we should leave to the market.

That the value debate is not fundamentally about whether to leave things to the market but only about what things not to leave to the market is clear. 'Believers in the market' would not leave to the market the allocation of resources to be devoted to underwriting prayers in school, abortion, the collection of taxes on capital gains, the disallowance of taxes for oil depletion, assistance for large companies in financial difficulties (that is, Lockheed some years ago), and so on. All these activities involve governmental decisions related to resource allocation. They are governmental activities (either directing that resources be devoted to or withdrawn from the public sector) which market lovers do not want to leave to the market. As institutionalists say, all decisions involving resource deployment (in or out of the market and with or without prices) involve value judgements.

In passing, an interesting aspect of all the debates just alluded to is the virtual non-existence of any comment from the nation's economic theorists.

CONCLUSIONS

Early institutionalists had little or nothing to say about macroeconomics, concentrating on microeconomics in general and the price–value disjunction in particular. Later institutionalists (post-1936) mostly ignored Keynes or misunderstood him. Few earlier institutionalists appreciated that Keynesian insistence on developing theory from 'real world facts' and the stripping of any normative implications from equilibrium were two critical aspects of Keynesian macroeconomics which paralleled traditional institutionalist concerns.

Three exceptions to the general indifference to Keynesian macroeconomics were Mitchell, Ayres and Fagg Foster. Mitchell's few comments on Keynes were all admiring, but he never saw the enormous significance of Keynes for the institutionalist position. Ayres ultimately came to appreciate the significance of Keynesian macroeconomics (but after he had done virtually all his important writing). Foster appreciated Keynes but wrote little about him.

Arguably many of the critical controversies about social value theory in action today can best be illustrated with macroeconomic examples. That is, virtually all the debates about value which present themselves in the form of the public versus the private sector, can be comprehended only in a world in which 'G' exists along with 'C plus I'. The value conflicts present themselves here in vivid form. Some questions to ponder:

Why is it appropriate to suggest that investors need special consideration as the buyers of labour, but workers can bear virtually the entire burden of containing inflation even though they are the buyers of goods?

Why is it appropriate to regard higher unemployment as the price of containing inflation but inappropriate to regard higher inflation as the price of containing unemployment? (Actually, I have argued elsewhere (Klein 1990), both are shortsighted.)

Why is it appropriate to regard dishonesty, inefficiency and corruption as peculiarly characteristic of both the poor and those who labour in the public sector whereas the rich and those who invest in the private sector are (by implication) invariably honest, hard working and efficient?

Why are taxes regarded as a form of robbery from 'us' to 'them'? Similarly why are transfer payments undeserved and wasteful?

Should it really be true that banks are too big to let fail, but poor people are invariably too small to save?

Why is special economic consideration based on race or gender 'wrong' but based on income class (the rich) 'productive'?

Why is it sound economics to facilitate production so as to stimulate consumption but not to facilitate consumption so as to facilitate production?

These and myriad other questions crowd in as one contemplates the relationship between macroeconomics and institutionalism. Mainstream economics permits us seriously to lose our way in sorting out the economic challenges. The degree to which the richest economy in the world permits the have nots to suffer, and even more, the degree to which the economics establishment cooperates in turning this result into something to accept and perhaps even to be proud of, is the ultimate distortion of our discipline. At least, as we noted earlier, when we passed the Employment Act of 1946, for one brief moment the profession appeared to understand its obligations after Keynes. Denigrating Keynesian underemployment equilibrium via 'the new classical economics' represents the major accomplishment of the post-war generation of mainstream economists. The institutionalist challenge has never been more pertinent than it is today.

NOTES

1. The author wishes to thank Marc R. Tool and Sasan Fayazmanesh for helpful comments on an earlier draft.
2. That the two can be related, I have tried a number of times to demonstrate. Here I try to do so again.
3. I use the terms in their conventional sense. That is, macroeconomics deals with the whole economy and focuses on national income and output, the aggregate level of employment and the overall price level. Microeconomics focuses on the economy, market by market, and is concerned with the interaction of individual firms and households.
4. The two can be related. Compare, for example, P.A. Klein (1987), pp. 1341–77; P.A. Klein (1980), pp. 871–96.
5. In considering emergent values I noted in 1974, 'An adequate theory would constitute a mechanism through which emergent values are recognized, transmitted, and reflected in the ongoing operations of the economy. More important, economists then could judge both the accuracy and the sensitivity with which the political economy expressed society's emerging values' (P.A. Klein (1974), pp. 785–811. Reprinted in P.A. Klein (1994), pp. 3–25). Many other institutional economists have considered the impact of concentrated economic power on economic performance, including the contributors to Warren Samuels's volume (1979), William Dugger (1980), J.K. Galbraith (1973), and many others.
6. There was public provision for education, tariffs, acquisition of land for railways, public investment in canals and roads, defence, internal security, and so on (compare Book V of Smith's *Wealth of Nations*, 1776).
7. Keynes underscores his basic perspective in his withering comment on Pigou's assertion:

   > Throughout this discussion, . . . the fact that some resources are generally unemployed against the will of the owners is ignored. *This does not affect the substance of the argument*, while it simplifies the exposition. (Quoted in Keynes 1936, p. 6, emphasis in original)

   Keynes deplores the fixation of his predecessors on the 'volume of available resources', and the consequent fact that 'the pure theory of what determines the actual employment of available resources has seldom been examined' (Keynes 1936, p. 5). Full employment equilibrium was not very common in the world. At the macro level, therefore, Keynes's equilibria, like those discussed by Ayres, are also 'mere equilibria'.
8. Edwin G. Nourse, first Chairman of the Council of Economic Advisors, which was established by the Employment Act of 1946, called that Act a 'capstone' and noted, 'The distinctive character of the Employment Act was that it accepted responsibility on the part of the Federal

Government to make systematic study of its several policies and programs to see that they move consistently toward maintaining the health of the economy and continuous high-level utilization of the nation's resources' (Nourse 1953, p. 67). In this Act, therefore, the Congress embraced intervention, and modified the laissez-faire perspective prominent again today. As such, the Employment Act was profoundly institutionalist in approach and in its implications.

9. For a full discussion of Burns's basic rejection of Keynes see his two essays, 'Economic Research and the Keynesian Thinking of Our Times' (1946) and 'Keynesian Economics Once Again' (1947).
10. In his *Modern Economic Thought: The American Contribution* (Gruchy 1947) there is one reference to Keynes, none to macroeconomics. In his *Contemporary Economic Thought* Gruchy (1972) castigates Keynes and the Keynesians because for Gruchy the theory presented is 'essentially static', it is not 'holistic', the interdisciplinary approach is 'wholly lacking' and it 'cling(s) to a narrow view of the nature and scope of economics' (Gruchy 1972, p. 334).
11. After this passage was written I discovered that Gladys Foster noted the same distinction in Keynes and commented that making the money supply endogenous would lead to the reconnection between the Theory of Value and the Theory of Money and Prices. Whether it would eliminate the institutionalists' concerns is problematical (compare G. Foster 1986).
12. This appraisal of Keynes was subsequently taken over almost verbatim in the revision Gordon wrote with John Adams (Gordon and Adams 1989, p. 161).
13. This point can be illustrated with Samuelson's well-known principles text which some years ago used to discuss the Keynesian model in terms of inflationary and deflationary gaps. Now (in recent editions) the 'C plus I' equilibrium is restricted to real income. See Paul Samuelson and William Nordhaus (1995), p. 450.
14. The term appeared by the third edition (Samuelson 1955, p. 11) and did not disappear until the ninth edition (1973).
15. A word of clarification is necessary. I argue that the 'prevailing societal value system' would result in a divergence of resource deployment from the manner of their actual deployment to the extent that information channels are clogged; power is concentrated; choices are, in consequence, presented to participants in the economy in inadequate or incomplete fashion, and so on.
16. *Economic Report of the President* (1996), pp. 370–71.

REFERENCES

Arestis, Philip and Alfred S. Eichner (1988), 'The Post-Keynesian and Institutionalist Theory of Money and Credit', *Journal of Economic Issues*, **21** (4), December, pp. 1003–21.

Ayres, Clarence E. (1944), *Theory of Economic Progress*, Chapel Hill: University of North Carolina Press.

_____(1961), *Towards a Reasonable Society*, Austin, TX: University of Texas Press.

_____(1964), 'The Legacy of Thorstein Veblen', in Joseph Dorfman, Clarence E. Ayres, Neil W. Chamberlain, Simon Kuznets and Robert A. Gordon (eds), *Institutional Economics: Veblen, Commons, and Mitchell Reconsidered*, Berkeley, CA: University of California Press.

Beveridge, William (1944), *Full Employment in a Free Society*, London: G. Allen and Unwin.

Burns, Arthur F. (1946), 'Economic Research and the Keynesian Thinking of Our Times', NBER's Twenty-sixth Annual Report, June, reprinted in *The Frontiers of Economic Knowledge*, New York: John Wiley and Sons, Inc., 1954, pp. 3–25.

_____(1947), 'Keynesian Economics Once Again', *Review of Economic Statistics*,

November, pp. 252–67, reprinted in *The Frontiers of Economic Knowledge*, New York: John Wiley and Sons, Inc., 1954, pp. 207–35.

Commons, John R. (1934), *Institutional Economics*, New York: The Macmillan Company.

_____(1950), *The Economics of Collective Action*, Kenneth H. Parson (ed.), New York: Macmillan.

Dugger, William M. (1980), 'Power: An Institutional Framework of Analysis', *Journal of Economic Issues,* **14**, December, pp. 897–907.

Economic Report of the President (1996), Washington, DC: US Government Printing Office (February).

Eichner, Alfred S. (1985), *Towards a New Economics*, Armonk, NY: M.E. Sharpe Inc.

Foster, Gladys Parker (1986), 'The Endogeneity of Money and Keynes's General Theory', *Journal of Economic Issues*, **20** (4), December, pp. 953–68.

_____(1991), 'Keynes's Ideas and Institutionalist Philosophy', *Journal of Economic Issues*, **25** (2), June, pp. 561–8.

Foster, J. Fagg (1968), 'Understandings and Misunderstandings of Keynesian Economics', abstract for paper, paper originally read in 1966 at the AFEE meeting, subsequently published in the *Rivista Internazionale di Scienze Ecionomiche e Commerciali*, quoted in introduction to article, reprinted in *Journal of Economic Issues*, **15** (4), December, pp. 949–57.

_____(1981), 'Economics', The Papers of J. Fagg Foster, *Journal of Economic Issues*, **15** (4), December, pp. 853–1012.

Galbraith, J.K. (1973), *Economics and the Public Purpose*, Boston: Houghton Mifflin.

Gambs, John S. (1946), *Beyond Supply and Demand*, New York: Columbia University Press.

Gordon, Wendell (1980), *Institutional Economics*, Austin, TX: University of Texas Press.

_____ and John Adams (1989), *Economics As a Social Science*, Riverdale, MD: The Riverdale Company.

Gruchy, Allan G. (1947), *Modern Economic Thought: The American Contribution*, New York: Prentice-Hall Inc.

_____(1949), 'J.M. Keynes's Concept of Economic Science', *Southern Economic Journal*, **15** (3), pp. 244, 249–66.

_____(1950), 'Keynes and the Institutionalists: Some Similarities', and 'Keynes and the Institutionalists: Important Contrasts', in C.L. Christianson (ed.), *Economic Theory in Review*, Bloomington, Indiana: Indiana University Publications, pp. 106–26.

_____(1972), *Contemporary Economic Thought*, Clifton, NJ: Augustus M. Kelley Publishers.

Hansen, Alvin (1949), 'Wesley Mitchell, Social Scientist and Social Counselor', *Review of Economics and Statistics*, November. Reprinted in Arthur F. Burns (ed.), *Wesley Clair Mitchell, The Economic Scientist*, New York: National Bureau of Economic Research, Inc., 1952.

Keynes, John Maynard (1930), *A Treatise on Money*, New York: Harcourt, Brace and Company.

_____(1936), *The General Theory of Employment, Interest, and Money*, New York: Harcourt, Brace and Company.

Klein, Philip A. (1974), 'Economics: Allocation or Valuation?', *Journal of Economic Issues*, **8** (4), December, pp. 3–25, p. 16. Reprinted in P.A. Klein, *Beyond Dissent*, Armonk, NY: M.E. Sharpe, Inc., 1994, pp. 3–25.

_____(1980), 'Confronting Power in Economics: A Pragmatic Evaluation', *Journal of Economic Issues*, **14**, December, pp. 871–96. Reprinted in P.A. Klein, *Beyond Dissent*, Armonk, New York: M.E. Sharpe, 1994, pp. 125–46.

_____(1986), 'Reinventing the Square Wheel: A Behavioural Assessment of Inflation', in Stanley Kaish and Benjamin Gilad (eds), *Handbook of Behavioural Economics*, Greenwich: JAI Press. Reprinted in P.A. Klein, *Beyond Dissent*, Armonk, New York: M.E. Sharpe, 1994, pp. 81–104.

_____(1987), 'Power and Economic Performance: The Institutionalist View', *Journal of Economic Issues*, **21**, September, pp. 1341–77. Reprinted in P.A. Klein, *Beyond Dissent*, Armonk, New York: M.E. Sharpe, 1994, pp. 147–78.

_____(1990), 'What's Natural About Unemployment?', in P.A. Klein (ed.), *Analyzing Modern Business Cycles, Essays Honoring Geoffrey H. Moore*, Armonk, New York: M.E. Sharpe Publishers. Reprinted in P.A. Klein, *Beyond Dissent*, Armonk, New York: M.E. Sharpe, 1994, pp. 273–80.

_____(1994), *Beyond Dissent*, Armonk, New York: M.E. Sharpe.

Marshall, Alfred (1949), *Principles of Economics*, Eighth Edition, New York: Macmillan Company.

Mitchell, Wesley Clair (1967), *Types of Economic Theory*, edited by Joseph Dorfman, vols. I and II, New York: Augustus M. Kelley.

Nourse, Edwin G. (1953), *Economics In The Public Service*, New York: Harcourt Brace and Company.

Parsons, Kenneth (1950), Supplemental Essay contribution to J.R. Commons, *Economics of Collective Action*, New York: Macmillan.

Samuels, Warren (ed.) (1979), *The Economy as a System of Power*, New Brunswick, NJ: Transaction Books.

Samuelson, Paul (1955), *Economics: An Introductory Analysis*, New York: McGraw Hill Book Co.

_____(1973), *Economics*, Ninth Edition, New York: McGraw Hill.

_____ and William Nordhaus (1995), *Economics*, Fifteenth Edition, New York: McGraw Hill.

Smith, Adam (1759), *The Theory of Moral Sentiments*, Edinburgh: A. Miller, A. Kincaidy and J. Bell.

_____(1776), *An Inquiry into the Nature and Causes of the Wealth of Nations*, Modern Library, New York: Random House, 1937.

Tool, Marc R. (1979), *The Discretionary Economy*, Santa Monica, CA: Goodyear Publishing Company, Inc.

Veblen, Thorstein (1904), *The Theory of Business Enterprise*, New York: Charles Scribner's Sons.

4. Financial Dominance in the US Economy: The Increased Relevance of Veblen's Analysis in a Post-Keynesian Structure

James M. Cypher[1]

FINANCE, FRAGILITY AND STAGNATION

This chapter analyses the contemporary structure of credit and finance through the prism of Thorstein Veblen's *Absentee Ownership,* first published in 1923. The opening section critically explores his dissection of the system of absentee ownership in order to concentrate on his highly original and ultimately quite current theoretical formulations regarding the centrality of the credit system and the financial structure. With this as background, the following section argues that the relative neglect of Veblen's framework of analysis arises from the brief period of dominance of the Keynesian paradigm of regulation and stabilization. With the decline of this paradigm, Veblen's framework once again becomes of increasing relevance as a means to interpret macro-dynamics. A brief interpretation of the 1991–96 expansion is undertaken in the following section to illustrate the viability of Veblen's perspective. In the final section some of the insights of Hyman Minsky regarding speculation and financial instability, within the context of 'money manager capitalism', are analysed in light of his problematic association with institutional analysis. The purpose of this investigation is to attempt to demonstrate the contemporary applicability of Veblen's ultimate effort to offer a summary analysis of the institutional structure and dynamics of the US economy.

VEBLEN ON THE LARGER USE OF CREDIT

Aside from the work of Dudley Dillard, cited below, until quite recently most institutional economists have paid scant attention to Veblen's work on credit, overcapitalization, financial strategies and crises. Equally surprising, neither

Minsky nor the post-Keynesians seem to have mined Veblen's work on these issues (for example, Dymski and Pollin 1994). In the case of those writing in the 'Minsky tradition', this is more understandable, particularly since Veblen's work may appear to be pre-modern to some and impenetrably opaque to others. Furthermore, many of Veblen's remarks, and indeed his entire framework of analysis in many instances, would appear to be badly off the mark in an economy dominated by Keynesian forms of regulation, stimulants and policy safeguards. Consider, for example, the following typical passage *within the context of a Keynesian framework of analysis*:

> In ordinary times there is always such a running margin of unemployment, both in the key industries and those underlying industries which depend on them for their necessary ways and means. And even in busy times few if any of these industries will ever come up to anything like the volume of production that would result from a free use of the same man-power and material resources under competent technical management with an eye single to production. Sound business considerations will not permit it. The businesslike duties of management turn constantly on a sagacious restriction of output at the point of 'balanced return,' and on the many exacting details of speeding-up and slowing down, of laying-off and taking-on, of hiring and firing, which arise out of this necessary strategy of balanced unemployment. (Veblen 1923, pp. 389–91)

Within the pure Keynesian paradigm of the postwar US economy, the above passage is clearly difficult to understand. Veblen insisted that the dynamics of capitalism were limited to a constant 'sagacious restriction of output' while pervasive and structurally necessary unemployment remained a defining systemic characteristic. Business interests, representing the triumph of credit-manipulating financial sector interests, were actively engaged in the 'sabotage' of industrial efficiency in order to achieve their underlying objective: a balanced return. In contrast, during the 'golden age' period of the long postwar expansion from 1947 to 1970, Keynesian objectives such as full employment, while never fully realized, seemed to be goals within reach. The most dysfunctional attributes of modern capitalism were subordinated and contained via astute macroeconomic regulation and intervention. Post-Keynesians, writing in the Minsky tradition, tend to hold up the 'golden age' period as a 'norm' or standard; a laudable goal in itself. But such an orientation would lead these same analysts *away* from Veblen's *oeuvre* because the assumed underlying characteristics of modern capitalism are hypothesized by Veblen in a manner which radically contrasts those characteristics and potentialities hypothesized by the post-Keynesians.

Since the early 1970s, the Keynesian safeguards and interventions have clearly diminished in power, scope and acceptable usage as the ideological dominance of ultra-laissez faire policy was consolidated. Meanwhile, in many respects (but clearly not all) the US economy, and the EC economies, as well as Japan's, have increasingly performed (or under-performed according to Keynesian percepts) as Veblen would have suggested. Slow, anaemic growth, structural unemployment, dynamic creation of new credit instruments and strategies, frequent and often severe slump periods, inadequate capital formation, meagre growth in productivity, increasing inequality of income accompanied by imaginative forms of conspicuous consumption, and 'downsized' middle management are but some of the major characteristics of the 1970–96 period. Given this, and given further the unstable and speculative financial markets of the current period, some institutionalists have turned to Veblen in their search for an analytical framework which can adequately serve as a point of departure for further investigation into what Veblen would have termed the 'deranged' financial markets (for example, Cornford 1995, Scott 1996, Wolfson 1994).

Yet, while institutionalists have shown considerable interest in the sphere of finance, and while some of their scrutiny of matters pertaining to credit creation has led to a recent incorporation of some of Veblen's analysis into contemporary analysis, such work has focused solely on Veblen's *Theory of Business Enterprise* (1958), ignoring his significant recasting of major theoretical conceptions which appeared in *Absentee Ownership* (1923).

In his comprehensive, and essentially balanced and fair-minded review of Veblen's work, Joseph Dorfman argued that Veblen's last major work, *Absentee Ownership*, was far from his most outstanding effort (Dorfman 1934, pp. 467–85). Dorfman's dour appraisal of *Absentee Ownership* may have contributed to the relative neglect of this work. Perhaps, however, such neglect arose from a misperception that Veblen was merely rewriting and synthesizing much of his earlier work. In any case, *Absentee Ownership* has not served as a touchstone for contemporary work pertaining to the sphere of finance, even for those who explore the institutionalist paradigm. That this is so is all the more surprising as the book leads up to the last major theoretical chapter entitled 'The Larger Use of Credit'. Even Dorfman acknowledged this to be perhaps 'the most important chapter in the book' (Dorfman 1934, p. 480). Yet, having made such an allowance, he quickly suggested that there was really little new or original in the chapter.

The Credit System in Early Monopoly Capitalism

In *The Theory of Business Enterprise* Veblen drew a distinction between competitive capitalism and the finance-driven, monopoly/oligopoly/trust form of economic organization which came to dominate the US economy from the 1870s onward (Veblen 1958). Here Veblen explored the implications of a 'credit economy' where 'capital' had become only distantly linked to tangible capital, or the monetized value of the means of production. The consolidation of the newly dominant monopoly/oligopoly firms had been achieved through rapid financial innovations in investment banking as well as within the financial (stock and bond) markets. The accumulation of quick profits and historically unprecedented fortunes had arisen primarily as a result of new and ever more creative uses of credit, and only tangentially – if at all – to organizational and technological improvements achieved through economies of scale and scope in the fused and combined financial/industrial monoliths of the late 19th century. Capital had become 'capitalized putative earning-capacity' arising from both the monetary expression of the value of the tangible assets of the corporation and the intangible capital (Veblen 1958, p. 67).

The monetized value of *tangible* assets was normally represented through the face value of corporate bonds and the selling price of preferred stock. But the *greater part of* the capitalized value of the modern corporation came from *intangible* capital. Such capital represented the discounted present value of such items as 'goodwill', patents, market share, anticipated future growth and earnings. It also commonly included fictional entries such as the capitalized 'value' of the promoters profits taken in creating/financing megacorporations by financial agents. Veblen viewed virtually all intangible capital as being subject to and arising from the creative manipulations of investment bankers and other 'captains of finance'. The chief objective of the economic system was to expand, manipulate, lend to and sell from the fictitious heights created through the new schemes employed to inflate capitalized value (Veblen 1958, p. 75).

The underlying purpose of the credit economy was to systematically redistribute the ownership and profits of assets heretofore linked to, and arising from, industrial activities to the financial sector. He maintained that capitalism had reached a major turning point during the period 1895–1905 (Veblen 1923, pp. 210–14). The captains of finance, whether operating in the financial markets, lending to non-financial businesses, or originating promoters profits for mergers and acquisitions, all specialized in buying, selling and innovating in the markets for 'vendible capital' (to be contrasted with activities wherein a 'vendible product' was created and traded). The truly great fortunes of the Gilded Age arose not from sharp trading in vendible products, but from 'manipulations' in the markets for 'vendible capital'. As such, the focal point of the economic system had shifted: 'this traffic in vendible capital is the pivotal and dominant factor in the modern situation of business and industry' (Veblen 1958, p. 83).

Absentee Ownership

Absentee Ownership sought to describe and analyse an economic system which had substantially evolved from that described in *The Theory of Business Enterprise*. Of the many differences which Veblen found between the late 19th century and the first decades of the 20th century, three were of the most fundamental nature: First, business cycles, while far from absent, were of a more *moderate* nature compared to those of the 19th century when the 'inflation of capital and prices' ran 'riot' ending in a 'headlong liquidation' inducing panics and crisis.[2] Second, the tendency toward chronic depression which served as a dominant backdrop to *The Theory of Business Enterprise* no longer dominated. Third, the Veblenian dichotomy of 'industry' and 'business', which might be found in his earlier distinction between the 'Captains of Industry' and the 'Captains of Finance' no longer existed. Industrialists had been shouldered aside; industry was now run with an eye to financial opportunities. Investment bankers who dominated the financial sphere intermingled with those who operated the key industries. A co-mingling of interests, rather than dichotomous tensions and potentialities, predominated.

Thus, to Veblen it was fundamentally inaccurate to divide the economy into 'monetary' (or financial) and 'real' (or goods producing) spheres. The sphere of finance had totally interpenetrated the rest of the economic system. In the following quotation, where Veblen drives home this point, his term, 'chief client', is utilized to define the 'borrower' or industrial arm of the interlocking matrix of owners:

> in great part the chief banking-houses and their chief clients are now identical in point of their business interests; to a very appreciable extent identical in point of ownership. So that the same 'Interest' – that is to say the same group of absentee owners working together as a team in pursuit of gain – will not infrequently be found to be the dominant owners on both the debit and credit side of a given account. (Veblen 1923, p. 362)

Veblen utilized the case of Standard Oil, with its vast holdings in petroleum production and distribution systems and its extensive investment bank holdings. The shares of Standard Oil were held in immense amounts by certain banks, whose share capital was, in turn, held in huge amounts by the Standard Oil shareholders. One gigantic interlocking financial–industrial behemoth sought to maximize the return on its capitalized assets. And the Standard Oil–financial interlock was the norm of the new structure formed early in the 20th century. Thus, while Veblen continued to employ a 'bifurcation' of absentee owners as either industrial or financial businesses, he insisted that this 'bifurcation' was for illustrative purposes only. Absentee ownership constituted, in 'essence', a '*conjugation*' (emphasis added) of the owners of capital. The owners existed in a new environment of 'collusive moderation' of live-and-let-live (Veblen 1923, pp. 376, 383). Yet, 'the seat of the new order . . . [was] to be found on the financial ground' since both debtors and creditors were deeply engaged in methods to trade on an ever thinner margin of equity via 'new extensions of credit' (Veblen 1923, pp. 381, 332 and 346).

Veblen's *Theory of Business Enterprise* reflects his, quite impressive, interpretation of the US economy from roughly 1873 through the first years of the 20th century. The system, he then argued, was prone to chronic depression. In *Absentee Ownership,* however, Veblen argued that a 'new era' was under consolidation: 'The pivotal factor in the business enterprise of this new era is the *larger* use of credit which has come into action during the last few decades' (Veblen 1923, p. 326, emphasis added). The new order was one wherein absentee owners (stock and bondholders who were also often corporate directors) utilized 'business agents' such as investment bankers and corporate officials to achieve their objectives. These objectives particularly included: (1) trading on an ever thinner margin of equity, (2) the artful use of imaginary capital (that is, intangible capital) via the credit system to appropriate an ever-greater portion of the tangible output, and (3) frequent resort to new and creative forms of finance (financial innovation). Thus investment bankers were '*creators* of capitalised intangibles'(Veblen 1923, p. 381, emphasis added).

Where, then, was the US economy headed? Veblen sketched three possibilities:

- Reversion to the situation prior to 1905 where the giant trusts in each key industry sought their own advantage at the cost of the other major industries (that is, 'anarchy').
- Dominance of a coalition of interests arising from the major investment banks acting in close alliance with the Federal Reserve which would guide the system of absentee ownership.
- The vested interests which controlled and dominated the key industries and the natural resources might 'draw together on a concerted plan of common action and set the pace for the country's industry as a whole by limiting output and service to such a rate and volume as will best serve their own collective gain' with the full support of the banking interests. (Veblen 1923, p. 227)

Veblen maintained that the second trajectory was the most likely, in order to:

safeguard the interests of absentee owners at large, maintain a steadily rising overcapitalisation of absentee assets, and assure an indefinitely continued increase of net gains on investments and credit commitments. The drift just now appears to set in that direction. These agencies may be able to maintain such a balanced and stable progressive expansion of assets and earnings. In any case, the dominant position of this community of 'investment-bankers,' moving in concert under the steady surveillance of the Federal Reserve, will exercise an influence of this kind and will greatly affect the outcome. (Veblen 1923, p. 226)

In contrast to the dynamics leading to depression which he sketched in *The Theory of Business Enterprise*, Veblen's scrutiny of the systemic forces of monopoly capitalism led him to argue that a precarious stability had been introduced via institutional change:

there has . . . gone forward a sweeping progressive reorganisation of the business community, which has placed the country's business affairs on a footing of credit and corporate ownership. With the result that toward the close of the century the financial community, who command the country's solvency and dispense the country's credit, found themselves in a position to take over the control and the usufruct of the country's industrial system by taking over the ownership of those strategically dominant members of the industrial system that are known as the 'Key Industries'. Since then the key industries have been progressively taken over into the absentee ownership of the country's *credit institutions*, and this absentee ownership has progressively been consolidated and arranged in manageable shape. The arrangement has now been brought to a manageable degree of stability. (Veblen 1923, pp. 231–2, emphasis added)

Unlike his analysis in *Theory of Business Enterprise*, Veblen emphasized in several passages that the new era was one of increasing macroeconomic stability, wherein there would be a particular distaste for debt-deflation crises of the type which prevailed in the 19th century. The 'interests' in finance and industry would co-operate on this point, as would the Federal Reserve which served as an administrative extension of these interests. But the creation of the Federal Reserve in 1913 was merely one of many significant changes in the underlying structure of the economic system which Veblen took into account in *Absentee Ownership*.

The 'progressive era' (1900–1920) had been marked by many changes which served to add to the stability of the underlying socioeconomic system, while simultaneously strengthening the position of the 'interests'. William Greider made this point regarding the Federal Reserve (an institution which Veblen stressed at several points in *Absentee Ownership*):

The money reforms enacted in 1913, in fact, helped to preserve the status quo, to stabilize the old order. Money-centre bankers would not only gain dominance over the new central bank, but would also enjoy new insulation against instability and their own decline. Once the Fed was in operation, the steady diffusion of financial power halted. Wall Street maintained its dominant position – and even enhanced it. (Greider 1987, p. 275)

It was not merely the existence of the Federal Reserve which led Veblen to recast his analysis of the modern business system. He took the measure of a new era where a broad range of institutional changes were being consolidated, particularly in the area of state–business relations. Among these changes were the federal income tax (1913), the Clayton Act and the Federal Trade Commission (1914), and state workmen's compensation laws (in all but six southern states by 1920). Veblen's eloquent summary of these major institutional changes were later confirmed by historians who have maintained that the 'progressive' initiatives largely strengthened and consolidated the grip of the absentee owners (Weinstein 1968).

While the new system of absentee ownership did not perpetually hang on the edge of a financial panic, as had the earlier structural configuration of US capitalism described in *Theory of Business Enterprise*, it nonetheless was explicitly fragile:

> Financial peace and stability is a matter of the first consequence to the Interests, and to all those who are concerned in the business of capitalised credits. The fabric of credit and capitalisation is essentially a fabric of concerted make-believe resting on the routine credulity of the business community at large. It is therefore conditioned on the continued preservation of this prevalent credulity in a state of unimpaired tensile strength, which calls for eternal vigilance on the part of its keepers. The fabric, therefore, is always in a state of *unstable equilibrium*, liable to derangement and extensive disintegration in case of an appreciable disturbance at any critical point. (Veblen 1923, p. 383, emphasis added)

At best, then, Veblen describes a new era of 'financial peace and stability' precariously undergirded by a make-believe structure of finance, existing in a perpetual state of unstable equilibrium. He continually insisted that the economic system moved through time in an evolving manner incorporating all sorts of 'discoveries, inventions, adaptations, and short-cuts . . . new ways and means and new uses for the old'. Given this, and his acute knowledge of the emergence of numerous new financial instruments, it is clearly within the central focus of his institutional analysis to anticipate that financial innovation would continue, and would continue to play a major role in working to undermine whatever new tendencies were at work to encourage 'financial peace and stability' (Veblen 1923, p. 419; Veblen 1958, Chapters 5 and 6). Thus while greater macroeconomic stability is a defining characteristic of the new era, it is a 'stability' balanced on a knife-edge.

RISE AND FALL OF KEYNESIAN REGULATION: 1933–96

With the gradual introduction of Keynesian forms of regulation and demand management during the Keynesian era (1933–71) little interest seemed to remain in the themes elaborated by Veblen. From 1947 to 1970, the US economy grew relatively rapidly, productivity growth remained high, business cycles were short and mild, unemployment rates generally were low, inflation was contained and financial factors were not perceived by most observers to be of central importance in understanding the macro-dynamics of the economy. But since 1970 the growth performance of the US economy has been weaker, the benefits of growth have been very unequally shared, recessions have become deeper, with recovery more subdued, unemployment rates have generally remained stubbornly high, and financial factors have moved into the forefront of much contemporary analysis of the economy.

The postwar expansionary wave (1947–70) coincided with the rise and consolidation of Keynesian methods of regulation via macroeconomic interventions such as industrial policy, fiscal policy and monetary policy. During the post 1970 period there was a gradual, but steady, withdrawal from Keynesian forms of intervention and guidance, often led by economic theorists who were, and long had been, hostile to the insights of Keynesianism and anxious to turn back the clock to the heyday of 'savage capitalism' as explored in *Theory of Business Enterprise*, circa 1880 (Heilbroner and Milberg 1995).

Keynes was anxious to reduce the power of financial intermediaries to control and influence the macroeconomy, viewing as he did the financial sector as a source of particularly unsavoury and destabilizing speculative activities. It would therefore seem to follow that the retreat from Keynesianism would entail the subsequent rise of financial speculation and the resurgence of destabilizing and deleterious forces and factors which preoccupied Keynes (and Veblen). Trained and casual observers alike would seem to be in agreement that financial factors, particularly speculation in financial markets, have increasingly played a role, even a dominant role, in the determination of macroeconomic performance.   Volatility in the financial markets had become one of the defining characteristics of the stagnation wave from 1971 to 1996.   In the 1980s, for example, the US dollar's value in relation to the key currencies doubled from its 1970 exchange rate and then fell to one-half the 1970 value. Interest rates soared and gyrated while the stock market reached impressive highs in 1987, tumbled and then leaped into totally unknown levels by 1996. Real estate values soared through most of the 1980s and then crashed. One-third of the Savings and Loan firms were liquidated due to their reckless and unsustainable financial speculations, and bank failures in the late 1980s and early 1990s reached levels unknown since the 1930s.

Among the many excellent studies conducted in recent years to examine the sources of the current stagnation, the work of Robert Pollin and Martin Wolfson offers keen insight into the relationships between speculative finance and economic malaise (for example, Dymski and Pollin 1994; Pollin 1996a, 1996b; Wolfson 1994). Table 4.1 presents a number of macroeconomic data which have been the focus of attention of several studies of the financial structure. First considered are data which show a dramatic drop in the annual rate of growth of investment in the four full cyclical expansions since 1969. Table 4.1 also shows the rapid expansion of new corporate debt in relation to the sale of new equities (representing the capitalization of assets). This ratio (net new equities/non-financial corporate debt) achieved an average negative level of 50.0 per cent in the 1982–90 expansion as corporations borrowed either to: (1) buy already existing assets; (2) seek a capital gain; or (3) cover for declining profits and declining income and to meet the current financial obligations of the corporation.

Table 4.1 *US investment and financial trends: non-financial corporations and financial sector borrowing*

Business cycles	1960–69	1970–73	1974–79	1980–81	1982–90
Gross investment, annual average growth (%)	6.2	4.3	4.1	0.4	2.2
New equities/increase non-financial corporate debt (%)	4.9	14.0	3.8	−1.2	−50.0
Profit on equity, pretax (%)	12.2	4.3	5.9	6.0	8.6
Interest on debt paid out from pretax profit (%)	10.9	27.2	29.7	50.7	51.0
Financial sector borrowing/ total net borrowing (%)	8.6	13.8	12.9	17.3	20.9

Sources: Data compiled from US National Income Accounts, Federal Reserve data and Robert Pollin 1996a, p. 53; 1996b, Table 11.

Note also the rate of profit, which only partially recovered the 1960–69 level. Meanwhile, growing in significance was interest paid from earnings, expressed as a percentage of earnings, which dramatically increased, thereby reducing the profit rate below that expressed in row three. Finally, the last row of Table 4.1 records the very impressive expansion in the share of total debt absorbed by the financial sector. From the 1960–69 expansion to that of 1981–90 the increase in financial sector debt as a percentage of total debt (including household, non-financial business government and foreign debt as well as financial sector debt) was 143 per cent. This growth over the cycle expansion periods far outstripped that of government borrowing, which increased 69 per cent. While borrowing by governments continued to absorb a greater share of total borrowing in 1981–90 (20.9 per cent vs. 26.7 per cent), more than one of five dollars borrowed were utilized by the financial sector itself – presumably to enhance earnings via adroit activities in the burgeoning financial markets.

The strains and pressures on the non-financial sector were such that strong, sustained expansions, as exhibited in the expansionary wave, were supplanted by *instability* wherein the growing burden of debt and failed speculative adventures generated an economic downturn for both debtors and creditors throughout the economy:

> The underlying source of financial instability, at the simplest level of accounting, must be that debt commitments are systematically outstripping the income flows necessary to service them. In turn, the basic explanation for the systematic deviation between debt commitments and income flows is that borrowed funds are used

disproportionately to finance speculative and compensatory spending, that is, borrowing to purchase existing assets with the expectation of capital gain and to compensate for declining income streams . . . Put another way, instability results when debt is used insufficiently to finance productive spending, that is, spending that enhances the income generating capacity of firms and individuals. (Pollin 1996a, p. 55)

Not only does the current environment of financial innovation simultaneously open new venues of speculation, it also debilitates macroeconomic policy interventions. This puts in motion a vicious circle of cumulative causation. Given the enhanced instability, critics of Keynesian policy interventions increasingly were able to make their case that policy interventions 'failed'. Meanwhile, the policy interventions which these critics advocated – more ultra-laissez faire – widened the scope of the vicious circle as less regulation of the financial sphere simultaneously opened up new opportunities for further financial innovations.

Martin Wolfson's *Financial Crises* offers a straightforward confirmation of arguments presented here (Wolfson 1994). He argued that the US had passed through four basic stages in regard to financial crises: (1) Through the early 1930s, when financial crises were severe, and their impact had profound effects on non-financial corporations, bank depositors, farmers and small business.[3] (2) The 1947–66 period, when financial crises were non-existent and presumed to have been eliminated due to institutional changes introduced by the New Deal. (3) The 1966–82 period, when financial crises occurred but their impact on the non-financial sector was quite limited. (4) The period since 1982, when financial crises increased in frequency, became more severe and were more clearly linked to speculative finance (Wolfson 1994, pp. 212–19). Why had this occurred? For Wolfson the reasons were complex, but may be summarized as arising from a disruption of the institutional conditions which provided stability for the banks and the savings and loans in the early postwar period. Under this general concept, Wolfson analysed a number of changes within the financial sector, including the rise of money market mutual funds and the growth of finance companies owned by non-financial corporations which had sidestepped the banks to issue their own commercial paper. Other factors contributing to financial fragility briefly discussed include: (1) the creation of secondary markets for 'securitized' assets allowing lenders to increase their willingness to accept risk because such assets can be resold; (2) the rise of globalized financial markets and instruments; and (3) the diluted impact of monetary policy within the context of a fluid and innovating financial sector (Wolfson 1994, pp. 222–4).

THE UNUSUAL EXPANSION OF 1991–96

By late 1996 the US economy had experienced five years of economic 'recovery' with strange, and apparently paradoxical, results: unlike other recovery periods since the late 1960s, the recovery of late 1991 was overwhelmingly 'investment-led'. 'Business investment – machinery and equipment – has contributed more to growth in the United States . . . in the early stages of the current expansion than during past upswings' (OECD 1995, p. 28). During the first nine months of 1995 investment accounted for a remarkable 56 per cent of total GDP growth (Mandel 1996, p. 30). Leading this surge in investments, computers and related equipment, measured in real terms, have increased from 4.7 per cent of total investment in 1985 to 20 per cent in 1994 (OECD 1995, p. 32). Yet, while the shift in emphasis toward the computer industry would seemingly indicate that the investment-led recovery was sparked by the consolidation of a major industry, thereby boosting growth potential, average economic growth remained at the 'growth recession' level of 2 per cent. Most paradoxical was the exceedingly modest increase in productivity – a 1.1 per cent annual increase from late 1991 to mid 1996, compared to a 2.7 per cent rate from 1950–73 (Koretz 1996, p. 32).

All branches of mainstream economic theory would predict that an investment-led recovery, stimulated by a major industry (computers) should underlie a strong, balanced recovery. Yet, even after several years of recovery, in 1994, real hourly earnings for non-supervisory production workers were *below* the level achieved in the trough of the recession in 1990. The paradox of growth without tangible benefit for the workforce became more striking in the first nine months of 1995 when the economy expanded at a relatively respectable annual rate of 3.5 per cent, while wage and salary earnings (including benefits) rose a mere 0.2 per cent, in real terms (Hershey 1995, p. 1). Wage decline has its counterpart in a profit increase: the return on equity of US industrial corporations increased from an average of 9 per cent in 1992 to 16 per cent in 1995 (Leonhardt 1996, p. 97).

Further signs of imbalance were glaringly obvious. US stock market growth astounded most observers: in 1995 the most widely cited index of stock prices increased by 33.5 per cent. This was followed by a 27.5 per cent increase to November of 1996, resulting in the valuation of all stock traded on the New York Stock Exchange at $6.8 trillion. The total value of all corporate equities rose to 81 per cent of GDP immediately prior to the market crash of 1987. By early 1997 stocks had reached the unprecedented level of 110 per cent of GDP. Leading the run-up in the stock market were the mutual funds which in both January and February 1996 poured more money into the stock market in one month than these funds had spent in any 12 month period prior to 1992 (Norris 1996, p. C6). In 1985 the entire mutual fund industry (including bond and money market funds) held approximately $500 billion. By 31 October 1996, the US mutual funds held over $3 trillion. Stock market mutual funds had increased their assets by 90 per cent since the end of 1994 (Wyatt 1996, p. 1).

What explains the paradox of high profits, high investments coupled with falling earnings for employees, 'growth recession' levels of GDP expansion, and a productivity slowdown of impressive proportions? Pursuit of such a question in any detail is well beyond the scope of this article. Nonetheless, it is hypothesized here that the major characteristics of the current 'recovery' are to be explained through a thorough exploration of matters which Veblen emphasized in his commentaries on macroeconomic dynamics. More specifically, it is argued here that the high profits taken in the industrial sectors have inordinately been diverted to speculative forms of finance, with the stock market and the international currency markets being but two examples. It is further argued that the funnelling of industrial profits into speculative markets, and the direct participation in such markets by the huge hedge funds and other financial institutions, is consistent with an 'investment-led' recovery in that the financial markets and the financial intermediaries have been major buyers of 'plant and equipment' (particularly computers and related equipment) in order to maintain their trading capabilities in the context of a period of unprecedented growth in these financial markets.

The evidence to support this proposition is largely indirect. Table 4.2 records the impressive growth in but one area of the financial markets – the global derivatives market. The absolute size of these markets is impressive. But the purpose of Table 4.2 is to contrast the spectacular growth rate of these financial markets to the near stagnation in the broader economy. Such disproportional growth can be demonstrated in several ways, one being the approach taken by the Bank for International Settlements (BIS) which measured the global derivatives markets' annual value of trading (eliminating double counting) between 1986 and 1991 in relation to the combined GDP of the OECD nations. This ratio rose from 0.10 in 1986 to 0.40 in 1991 (Office of Technological Assessment 1993, p. 153). Given that the growth in the aggregate derivatives markets has only accelerated since 1991, updating of this ratio would clearly indicate a continued rise. Table 4.2 demonstrates the growth in some organized markets, along with two estimates of the size of 'over-the-counter' financial instruments. The growth rate is computed for the time-series compiled by the International Swaps and Derivatives Association. The much larger estimate for these financial instruments compiled by the BIS for 1996 ($47.5 trillion of contracts outstanding after eliminating double counting) arises from a more inclusive methodology employed. In the context of the above discussion of an 'investment-led' recovery, Table 4.2 illustrates the close connection between the growth of the computer industry and the staggering rise in trading. Yet it is unclear how the huge investments in plant and equipment necessary to accommodate the spectacular increase in trading volume has had a wider impact on productivity throughout the economy. (Clearly, a significant portion of the

Table 4.2 Expansion in the financial markets: global trading in derivative instruments (trillions of US dollars*)

Year	1986	1990	1994	1995	Growth (86–95) %
Exchange-trades					
Futures: interest rate	0.370	1.455	5.757	5.863	1,485
Options: interest rate	0.147	0.600	2.623	2.742	1,765
Futures: currencies	0.010	0.017	0.040	0.038	280
Options: currencies	0.039	0.057	0.056	0.043	10
Futures: stock market index	0.015	0.069	0.127	0.172	1,047
Options: stock market index	0.038	0.094	0.238	0.327	760
Over-the-counter swaps					
Bank for International Settlements estimate	n.d.	n.d.	n.d.	$47.500	
International Swaps and Derivatives Association estimate	0.500	3.450	11.302	$17.990	3,400

* Double counting eliminated.

Sources: Data from Bank for International Settlements and International Swaps and Derivatives Association and IMF (1996), p. 19.

trades recorded in Table 4.2 occurred outside US-based markets.) Table 4.3 shows the rapid pace of financial innovations in financial instruments from 1972 to 1992. This illustrates the bewildering pace of overall financial innovation which has served to create vast new markets for the creation of credit and the opportunity to widen the scope of the financial markets. Although the US stock market is but one financial market, its recent evolution is indicative of a larger trend: in 1964 the various brokerage houses trading on the New York Stock Exchange had the capability of transacting 10 million shares per day. By 1991 trading capacity, based on incoming orders from throughout the globe, reached one *billion* shares per day (Kurtzman 1993, p. 30).

The global market in foreign currencies, likewise, followed the general trend: by the early 1990s, specialists in the global financial markets estimated that on an average business day $800 billion dollars worth of foreign currency was traded through a variety of markets and financial instruments. By 1996 $1.2 trillion was exchanged per day (Fuerbringer 1996, p. 1). Meanwhile, in the early 1990s, the daily *commodity* trade in foreign goods and services (that is, tangible products) in international markets amounted to $20 to $25 billion (Kurtzman 1993, p. 64). Thus, far from the conventional idea that the financial markets are merely the 'dual' of the 'real' markets in tangible goods and services, the link between the two had become problematic. Speculation was the main driving force in the gigantic global currency market, as it was elsewhere.[4] Only a tiny fraction of the funds changing hands in the stock market were utilized to raise new issues, and the foreign currency market clearly had little to do with the financing of international production and trade.

Table 4.3   Financial innovation: the creation of new trading instruments, 1972–92

		Type of new trading instrument			
1	2	3	4	5	6
1972 Foreign currency futures					
1973 Equity futures					
1975 Mortgage-backed bond futures	Treasury-bill futures				
1977 Treasury-bond futures					
1979 Over-the-counter options: currencies					
1980 Currency swaps					
1981 Treasury bond futures options	Bank CD futures options	Treasury-note futures	Equity-index futures	Eurodollar futures	Interest-rate swaps
1983 Interest-rate caps/floors	Treasury-note futures options	Equity-index futures options	Futures options in currencies		
1985 Eurodollar options	Muni-bond index futures	Swap options			
1987 Average options	Commodity swaps options	Bond futures	Bond options	Compound options	
1989 3-Month Euro-DM futures		Ecu interest-rate futures	Futures on interest-rate swaps		
1990 Equity index swaps					
1991 Portfolio swaps					
1992 Differential swaps					

Sources: Chase Manhattan Bank data; Phillips (1994), p. 217.

Within the confines of the US economy, financial innovation and credit expansion were moving ahead at an impressive rate in the course of the expansion which began in 1991. Even with employee earnings virtually flat, the financial intermediaries had managed to increase their credit card debt by 47 per cent from 1993 to 1995 (Hansell 1995b, p. C1). Yet, credit expansion via consumer credit was but one of many forms of credit creation, such as new forms of securitization, arising in a context of minuscule real economic growth (Hansell 1995a, pp. C1, C9).

As the financial markets soared and the credit creating capabilities of the financial intermediaries extended into new forms two questions arose: could the expansion be maintained through financial innovations and credit creation? And could the institutions created in the 1930s to counteract downturns and stabilize expansions rise to the task of combatting and counteracting financial forces and factors created, in part, to evade these governmental regulatory and safeguard mechanisms designed for another era?

If past history serves as a guide, the answer to the first question must be: 'certainly not'. The evidence to support an unqualified 'yes' to the second question was difficult to obtain. This was so because the financial markets had become increasingly global, while the regulatory system remained national, with but moderate and insufficient control of the international markets vested in the BIS. And it was also the case because the regulatory mechanisms of the 1930s were in the process of either being eliminated or sidestepped by the financial institutions. Such was the case for the Federal Reserve. The Federal Reserve's power to regulate the economy via control over commercial bank activity was increasingly of limited importance because the banks' share of total assets owned by financial intermediaries fell from 52 per cent in 1950 to only 30 per cent in 1990 (Knodell 1994, p. 142). And, more generally, the financial system had been given much freer rein because the rise of ultra-laissez faire ideology had permitted a silent (partial) deregulation of the financial system of the US.

MINSKY AND THE INSTITUTIONALISTS

Casting the events and tendencies traced in the preceding two sections into a coherent economic analysis is a daunting challenge which is increasingly being undertaken by a creative group of analysts – many working within the institutionalist paradigm. Some institutional economists have long focused on the credit system. Dudley Dillard, in particular, drew strong parallels between the work of Thorstein Veblen and J.M. Keynes (Dillard 1980, 1987). Yet, until recently, the centrality of the credit system and its participatory, if not causal, role in economic crises and cyclical turning points was not a major thematic focus of institutional theory. Dillard's insightful and comprehensive review of the credit system, 'A Monetary Theory of Production' published by the *Journal of Economic Issues* (JEI) in 1980, reappeared, in a lengthened version, in the JEI in 1987 as a solicited paper entitled 'Money as an Institution of Capitalism'. It formed part of the second volume of 'Evolutionary Economics', two special issues of the JEI. The editor, Marc Tool, sought 'definitive' and 'referential' papers on 'how institutionalists explain and appraise the character and performance of the modern economy' (Tool 1987, pp. 1420, 1422). Of interest here is the fact that while Dillard's second paper once again commenced with Veblen in order to initiate a discussion on the centrality of the credit system to issues of growth, crisis and stagnation, it concluded with a summary of Hyman Minsky's work on financial instability (Dillard 1987).

Significantly, Minsky's work increasingly appeared in the JEI, culminating in bestowal of the annual Veblen–Commons Award by the Association for Evolutionary Economics, which publishes the JEI, shortly before his death in 1996 (Minsky 1980, 1995, 1996). Yet Minsky's position within the scope of institutional economics is problematic. Both the institutionalists and the post-Keynesians have argued that Minsky's work lay within the province of their respective schools of thought. However, in Minsky's articles cited above there is no reference to any particular institutionalist view, or theory, of credit.[5] Nonetheless, institutionalists have devoted increasing attention to matters that preoccupied Minsky (for example, Scott 1996; Goldstein 1995; McClintock 1996; Wray 1992). Presently, there is a dense overlapping of themes and analytical explorations among some who claim a post-Keynesian lineage with others who consciously operate within an institutionalist paradigm.

Minsky's work has yielded three major insights which have quite close affinity to concepts employed by Veblen, as discussed previously. First, there is the *Minsky Paradox*: Minsky's research and theoretical observations led him to the conclusion that the US economy was increasingly prone to convulsions arising from the financial sphere as this portion of the economy evolved and underwent institutional change. For Minsky, profit-maximizing financial institutions would be driven to circumvent or sidestep forms of governmental regulation and control in order to engage in increasingly risky financial activities. This would make the economic system ever more prone to financial crises because many of these activities would create new forms of credit and debt which could not be continually financed with the returns which debtors and creditors had anticipated when such financial agreements were originally consummated. But, paradoxically, while forms of speculative finance grew at an accelerating pace as the economy moved from cyclical peak to cyclical peak, Minsky argued that no 'great' depression was to be anticipated because Keynesian-style government intervention would be utilized to stave off a cumulative interlocking chain of bankruptcies which could start in the financial sphere and spread outward in a downward spiral. Lender-of-last-resort capabilities as exercised by the US Federal Reserve, or the US Treasury, and stabilizing institutions such as the Federal Deposit Insurance Corporation could be, and would be, brought into action should the need arise. Confirmation of this Keynesian stabilizing role was not difficult to obtain, as a careful discussion of the stock market crash of 1987 would reveal. Nonetheless, the question continues to arise: have financial innovations and massive speculative activities reached such proportions and complexity that they could overwhelm the stabilizing institutions? And might the shift toward ultra-laissez faire become so sweeping that those who are in charge of the stabilizing institutions will fail to act in a timely and creative manner since their faith in the asserted equilibrating tendencies of markets will overwhelm their pragmatic inclinations? By 1996 Minsky had subtly moderated his position on the 'Minsky Paradox', arguing that the US economy had entered a new stage of heightened instability and uncertainty wherein the established stabilizing institutions might, in fact, be overwhelmed (Minsky 1996).

Interrelated with the Minsky Paradox, and providing part of the basis for it, is the concept of *financial fragility*. Financial fragility defines the condition of the economy at any moment in time. Thus, as a rule, as the economy reaches a cycle peak the degree of financial fragility increases, thereby contributing to an economic downturn and conditioning the length of the slump, or contractionary, period. In turn, the degree of financial fragility is determined by the prevalence, spread and depth of *credit creation and borrowing* relative to income flows received by the various sectors of the economy, including financial institutions and financial markets, non-financial corporations and households. As financial innovation increases, new credit and debt instruments are created. There is a tendency to utilize these new instruments, usually well beyond the level which would appear reasonable given income flows to the sectors of the economy. In short, leveraging can be taken to new heights, thereby creating fragility.

Minsky argued that all sectors speculate, so speculation can be, and normally is, one of the prime motives for the creation and use of new financial instruments. But while lenders are motivated to attempt to maximize underlying capital assets (thereby enhancing risk), borrowers may be driven by uncertainty and expectations which are never realized. Uncertainty, one of the bedrock concepts of the Keynesians, is intrinsic to and a fundamental aspect of capitalism. Another force driving borrowers is compensatory financing, where borrowers use new credit to cover prior obligations and shortfalls in current income. As an expansion proceeds, and/or as previous bad debt is underwritten by government stabilizations and interventions, both lenders and borrowers are prone increasingly to discount the credit crises of the past and the risks of debt-deflation. As the credit build-up proceeds, the system exhibits greater signs of 'fragility' which may be seen in quantitative indicators such as the ratio of debt-to-equity, or the portion of borrowing which is short term in relation to all debt, or by other measures (Wolfson 1994, pp. 213–18).

As financial fragility builds, the likelihood of an episode of *financial instability* grows – this being a situation wherein a small change in asset values, and/or a small change in income flows, or even, perhaps, a change in the *rate* of growth of asset values or income flows, sets off some event in the financial sphere whereby turbulence and losses in the financial system are quickly translated to some goods and services sectors and a recession ensues. The ebb of the economy is inevitable – financial instability is an *endogenous* feature of the economy.

Minsky's theoretical formulation is sufficiently general to encompass a number of dynamic possibilities, many of which he did not explore in any detail. For example, what determines the pace of financial innovation? If financial innovation is relatively rapid, and if opportunities to speculate are rife, will the growth process be undermined relatively faster? That is, will cycles be marked by lower growth, lower rates of increase in productivity, and a stagnation in earnings for the majority? These questions lead into a terrain which is too rarely discussed by the specialists of the financial sphere – the relationships between financial strategies and possibilities and the production of tangible goods and services.

Money Manager Capitalism

Minsky's useful encapsulation of the current metamorphosis of the US economy as operating within an institutional framework dominated by elements of 'money manager capitalism' deserves emphasis (Minsky 1996, pp. 362 –5). Money managers first made their appearance in the early 1970s, gaining new importance with the emergence of self-financed pension plans in the 1980s. Minsky argued that money managers, by controlling the gigantic mutual funds (now in stocks, bonds, indexes and so on) and the secretive hedge funds, had introduced a new 'layering' of financial intermediation.

Under the sway of money manager capitalism, the economy drifts toward financial activities. Capital accumulation, via (1) investments in new technologies, and (2) government-supported infrastructural projects, atrophies. (In money manager capitalism, government policy respects, and therefore reflects, the speculative, short-run ultra-laissez faire priorities of the new institutional structure.) Much of the capital investment which does occur is perverse – capital formation to enable the exploding financial markets to handle ever-greater numbers of trades per day, hour and minute, and 'low-road' investments in facilities designed to raise profits through low-wage, 'flexible' forms of production. Emphasized by Minsky, a new layer of financial intermediation has evolved encompassing aggressive mutual funds (including hedge funds) and pension funds as new participants in financial markets. At the close of 1994, mutual funds (excluding the privately held hedge funds) controlled $2.16 trillion in assets, while the Federal Reserve's data on the largest US commercial banks indicated that they controlled $1.14 trillion in commercial and household loans (Wyatt 1996, p. 1; Hansell 1995a, p. C1). Thus, given that the largest banks operate in a tightly concentrated structure where they account for the overwhelming majority of commercial bank assets, it was the case that, in terms of asset size, money managers at the mutual funds controlled twice the financial capital of the commercial banks. By 31 October 1996, the mutual funds had increased their assets to $3.39 trillion, registering a growth rate of 57 per cent over the previous 21 months, thereby leaving the commercial banks even further behind in terms of assets (Wyatt 1996, p. 1). These data, while not definitive, add some specificity to Minsky's concept while reinforcing his formulations.

Meanwhile, the financial markets are increasingly internationalized, operating as 'stateless' global casinos (Cornford and Kregel 1996). At the same time, there has been a notable shift toward the short term: non-financial corporations are increasingly controlled or influenced by the sway of financial institutions (including banks and insurance companies), which are driven to maximize short-term profits. These institutions now operate within the context of globalized financial markets which offer a growing array of increasingly volatile financial assets, including foreign currencies. These new assets now increasingly compete with the ongoing societal needs for financial funds to be sunk into long-term projects designed to bring forward major innovations in product and process technologies. Funding for such long-term commitments is increasingly unlikely when the focus of financial intermediaries is on the short-term profits to be gained by forays into a burgeoning variety of global financial markets and instruments (Useem 1996). In short, predatory activities increasingly replace productive activities. And, as new financial markets and financial instruments are forged, in a world where knowledge, foresight and prudence are increasingly scarce, the predictable result is increasing financial fragility and 'unexpected' systemic crises arising in the financial sector.[6]

CONCLUSIONS

As Keynesian forms of regulation and intervention have been increasingly (but not entirely) abandoned from 1971–96, the US macroeconomy more and more resembles the system described by Veblen in *Absentee Ownership*. His focus on the centrality of credit as the pivotal factor in the determination of the performance and dynamics of the economic system deserves serious consideration in light of the role which the financial markets and financial innovation now play in the contemporary economy. His analysis of dynamic unstable equilibrium propelled forward by credit creation and bolstered and buttressed by the Federal Reserve conveys the essential concept of the Minsky Paradox. His insistence that the 'volume of credit is more widely detached from all material objects and operations, and increasingly so' would certainly fit well in any serious analysis of the current conjuncture (Veblen 1923, p. 326). Veblen's depiction of an economy in unstable equilibrium resting, in part, on credit innovations which facilitate fictitious capitalizations fits well with the concept of money manager capitalism. And Veblen's framework of analysis is compatible with the endogenous theory of credit, the emphasis on financial innovation and the destabilizing forces of credit financing which are major themes of those writing in the Minsky tradition. In most respects in this area of economic analysis, Veblen's institutional view would seem to fit extremely well with those who are exploring the cutting edges of financial systems and structures. A few institutionalists are incorporating some of Veblen's powerful insights into the structure of finance into their work on the contemporary economy, yet his treatment of the credit system in *Absentee Ownership* does not serve as a touchstone. Outside of institutionalist analysis, only Keynes's formulations on finance vs. industry are taken as a point of departure by most theorists – above all Minsky. Veblen's work, so long neglected, commonly misinterpreted and so thoroughly disparaged, deserves to be incorporated into a modern analysis of credit, financial fragility and financial innovation.

NOTES

1. For nearly 30 years Professor Paul Dale Bush has been a most valued Departmental colleague and an inspiring role model of the outstanding scholar/instructor. I am beholden to him for his unstinting generosity and commitment.

    In preparing this article, an essay in trespassing, several scholars, many with extensive knowledge of the credit system, have provided research materials and/or comments. I thank Andrew Cornford, Doug Dowd, Gary Dymski, Ilene Grabel, Phillip A. O'Hara and Charles Whalen. I am particularly grateful to Professor Robert Pollin. None share any culpability for the analysis presented here.

2. Veblen apparently saw the Panic of 1907 as the last of the old-style crises, and the institutional change which was accelerated by this crisis, including the creation of the Federal Reserve, as indicative of a new era. How then might one account for the stock market crash of 1929 within the context of Veblen's new era? Veblen's emphasis on a more moderated pattern of growth continues to allow for such a downturn. Moreover, it is consistent with Veblen's conceptualization that there followed a rapid evolution of institutions created prior to the Depression, such as the Federal Reserve. Corporate liberalism, in other words, began in the era of 'absentee ownership' and the Depression accelerated and consolidated such tendencies noted by Veblen. In this light, the high Keynesian era of the 'golden age', 1947–70, could be viewed as an 'over-reaction' to the Depression, with the 1971–96 period showing increasing, but not complete, correspondence with Veblen's formulations of mature capitalism. Thus while important vestiges of the 'high Keynesian era' remain, negating the possibility of a literal usage of *Absentee Ownership* as a template to describe the 1971–96 period, the incorporation of Veblen's last major analysis of the structure of modern capitalism adds coherence and insight for a contemporary analysis.

3. Veblen's division between the pre-1905 period and that which followed to 1923 is not presented. Wolfson does not follow Veblen's lead on this point, nor has the important distinction received adequate attention from institutionalists.

4. Unfortunately, like most other terms in economics, speculation carries many meanings: pure speculation has sometimes been defined as buying for resale, rather than for income, in the case of a financial asset. Where commodities or tangible goods are concerned, the motive is to buy for resale rather than use. Sometimes included will be excessive leveraging, or 'gearing', which is borrowing to purchase assets (tangible or financial) with a very thin margin of equity capital. A less obvious form of speculation, overestimation of potential returns, arising from a vitriolic

combination of uncertainty and unfounded optimism, can lead to excessive borrowing as well as lending. For a further consideration of the issue, see Ilene Grabel's article on national financial complexes (Grabel 1997).

5. Dillard received one reference, but for an article which appeared in a collection of 'post-Keynesian' analyses.

6. Mainstream economists have, of course, managed to overlook the transformation of the US economy and/or are convinced that such transformations are efficiency enhancing. Why they have done so is best explained in Robert Heilbroner and William Milberg's insightful text, *The Crisis of Vision in Modern Economic Thought* (Heilbroner and Milberg 1995).

Some of the pathological features, details and results of money manager capitalism are presented in Gordon 1996; Harrison 1994; Hayes 1996 and Phillips 1994, although none use the term, nor do they bridge the gap between an analysis of the so-called 'real' economy and the sphere of finance.

REFERENCES

Cornford, Andrew (1995), 'Inside an Emerging Financial Market', *Journal of Economic Issues*, **29** (3), September, pp. 929–38.

_____ and Jan Kregel (1996), 'Globalization, Capital Flows and International Regulation', Working Paper no. 161, The Jerome Levy Economics Institute Working Papers.

Dillard, Dudley (1980), 'A Monetary Theory of Production', *Journal of Economic Issues*, **14** (2), June, pp. 255–74.

_____ (1987), 'Money as an Institution of Capitalism', *Journal of Economic Issues*, **21** (4), December, pp. 1623–48.

Dorfman, Joseph (1934), *Thorstein Veblen and His America*, New York: Viking Press.

Dymski, Gary and Robert Pollin (eds) (1994), *New Perspectives in Monetary Macroeconomics*, Ann Arbor, Michigan: University of Michigan Press.

Fuerbringer, Jonathan (1996), 'Swapping Money', *New York Times*, 19 December, pp. C1, C3.

Goldstein, Don (1995), 'Uncertainty, Competition, and Speculative Finance', *Journal of Economic Issues*, **29** (3), September, pp. 719–46.

Gordon, David (1996), *Fat and Mean*, New York: The Free Press.

Grabel, Ilene (1997), 'Savings, Investment and Functional Efficiency: A Comparative Examination of National Financial Complexes', in Robert Pollin (ed.), *The Macroeconomics of Finance, Saving, and Investment*, Ann Arbor, Michigan: University of Michigan Press.

Greider, William (1987), *Secrets of the Temple*, New York: Simon and Schuster.

Hansell, Saul (1995a), 'Banks at the Dawn of New Worries', *New York Times*, 21 February, pp. C1, C9.

_____ (1995b), 'A Shaky House of Plastic', *New York Times*, 28 December, pp. C1, C16.

Harrison, Bennett (1994), *Lean and Mean*, New York: Basic Books.

Hayes, Robert (1996), 'US Competitiveness "Resurgence" versus Reality', *Challenge*, March–April, pp. 36–44.

Heilbroner, Robert and William Milberg (1995), *The Crisis of Vision in Modern Economic Thought*, Cambridge: Cambridge University Press.

Hershey, Robert (1995), 'Worker Earnings Post Rise of 2.7%, Lowest on Record', *New*

York Times, 1 November, pp. 1, C2.

IMF (1996), 'Global Financial Markets', *Finance and Development*, **33** (4), December, pp. 19–21.

Knodell, Jane (1994), 'Financial Institutions and Contemporary Economic Performance', in M. Bernstein and D. Alder (eds), *Understanding American Economic Decline*, Cambridge: Cambridge University Press, pp. 114–60.

Koretz, Gene (1996), 'How to Raise US Productivity', *Business Week*, 9 December, p. 32.

Kurtzman, Joel (1993), *The Death of Money*, New York: Simon and Schuster.

Leonhardt, David (1996), 'Corporate Scoreboard', *Business Week*, 4 March, pp. 96–8.

Mandel, Michael (1996), 'Is Business Running Scared?', *Business Week*, 12 February, pp. 30–31.

McClintock, Brent (1996), 'International Financial Instability', *Journal of Economic Issues*, **30** (1), March, pp. 13–34.

Minsky, Hyman (1980), 'Capitalist Financial Processes', *Journal of Economic Issues*, **14** (2), June, pp. 505–24.

_____(1995), 'Longer Waves in Financial Relations', *Journal of Economic Issues*, **29** (1), March, pp. 83–96.

_____(1996), 'Uncertainty and the Institutional Structure of Capitalist Economies', *Journal of Economic Issues*, **30** (2), June, pp. 357–70.

Norris, Floyd (1996), 'Market Place', *New York Times*, 27 March, p. C6.

OECD (1995), 'Investment in the Current Upswing', *OECD Economic Outlook*, **57**, June, pp. 26–32.

Office of Technological Assessment, US Congress (1993), *Multinationals and the National Interest*, Washington: US Government Printing Office.

Phillips, Kevin (1994), *Arrogant Capital*, New York: Little, Brown and Company.

Pollin, Robert (1996a), '"Socialization of Investment" and "Euthanasia of the Rentier": The Relevance of Keynesian Policy', *International Review of Applied Economics*, **10** (1), pp. 49–64.

_____(1996b), 'Financial Intermediation and the Variability of the Saving Constraint', Working Paper in Economics no. 96-26, Department of Economics, University of California, Riverside.

Scott, Peter (1996), 'New Alchemy: Veblen's Theory of Crisis', *Journal of Economic Issues*, **30** (1), March, pp. 1–12.

Tool, Marc (1987), 'Introduction to Evolutionary Economics V. II', *Journal of Economic Issues*, **21** (4), December, pp. 1419–44.

Useem, Michael (1996), *Investor Capitalism*, New York: Basic Books.

Veblen, Thorstein (1923) *Absentee Ownership*, New York: Viking Press.

_____ [1904] (1958), *The Theory of Business Enterprise*, New York: Mentor Books.

Weinstein, James (1968), *The Corporate Ideal in the Liberal State: 1900–1918*, Boston: Beacon Press.

Wolfson, Martin (1994), *Financial Crises*, Armonk, New York: M.E. Sharpe.

Wray, Randall (1992), 'Alternative Approaches to Money and Interest', *Journal of Economic Issues*, **26** (4), December, pp. 1145–78.

Wyatt, Edward (1996), 'Some Worries About the Rush into Mutual Funds', *New York Times*, 27 December, pp. 1, C2.

5. Normative Analysis of Instituted Processes

F. Gregory Hayden

The conventional view with regard to scientific methodology and philosophy has been to emphasize a distinction between the analytical approach, which is based in linguistic or conceptual analysis, and the empirical approach, which lets empirical findings guide science and philosophy as much as possible. The original institutional economics view is that methodology and philosophy should be guided as much as possible by empirical investigations; a view that does not conform to the linguistic or conceptual tradition. Institutionalists usually designate the linguistic or conceptual approach as a formal approach, in which formalized abstractions are laid down as immutable rules of the game (usually axiomatically) without respect to whether or not there is an empirical base for the rules of the game. They usually refer to the empirical approach as a substantive approach by which the results of real-world investigations are used to identify the substance of systems and to change the substance as social and technological changes or new investigations create problems for the systems methodology. Institutionalists agree with Richard Schlagel that: 'Philosophical problems do not arise *primarily* from conceptual or linguistic confusions, but because of the dislocating effects of *our* established beliefs or conceptual linguistic frameworks owing to empirical discoveries or theoretical developments in the sciences and other intellectual or cultural disciplines' (Schlagel 1995, p. 1, original emphasis).

Empirical studies, as they reveal social, economic and technological changes, continuously upset philosophical systems. When the properties of philosophical and methodological approaches are found to be inconsistent with the real world, the approach can be changed to conform to the new findings or it can be treated as a game and continue to perform analytical techniques allowed by the game. For example, when it was discovered that all real-world systems are open systems, it was clear that real-world systems cannot be equilibrium systems. This meant that formalized models based on equilibrium were not relevant analytical devices for analysing real-world socioecological systems. Therefore, institutionalists abandoned equilibrium models while others continued to develop equilibrium models into more complex intellectual games.

Although institutionalists have traditionally termed the linguistic and conceptual approach to methodology and philosophy as formal, such terminology is misleading because empirical studies of substantive socioecological systems are completed according to a formal methodology. The emphasis of institutionalism should be that the methodological form should change as evidence indicates that it is inconsistent with empirical findings or that it is inconsistent with relevant linguistic and conceptual analysis. Paul Dale Bush recognized the need for developing formal methods for institutionalism and contributed significantly toward providing a formal base for institutional theory and methodology (Bush 1983, 1987, 1991). This is important for assisting empirical studies, for theoretical development and for policy applications. Bush has suggested that the future work on his analytical model would require extension and refinement (1983, pp. 61–2).

The purpose here is to refine part of Bush's formalization with the assistance of the ideas, tools and nomenclature of normative philosophy and deontic logic. Bush has given an explication of the concept of a normative system as defined by institutionalists. The explication of the normative world is the method by which abstract concepts are transformed into more exact concepts so they become consistent tools of empirical analysis, thus providing for greater efficiency of research. Some have wondered whether such a method of reconstruction is by its nature incapable of assisting us in grasping reality, because they claim it proceeds by abstraction and leads to an impoverishment of our understanding. Objections of this kind are based on a misrepresentation of abstraction and appear to be unaware of the philosophy of the normative system. All scientific thought is based on abstraction. What is important is that such thought be relevant to understanding real-world systems which are guided by social norms.

Institutionalists have traditionally emphasized the importance of duty and obligation embedded in socioeconomic institutions. Thus, to complete a normative system, it is necessary to turn to deontic logic, the logic of duty and obligation. Decisions within a normative system provide for a range of possible actions, called the normative range. Deontic logic provides the tools to define the extent of duty and obligation. Bush's work has provided a general framework for the concerns of institutionalists. With the assistance of normative system philosophy and deontic logic, analysis can be refined to allow for enhanced empirical analysis, decisions and action.

The intent here is to take us a step closer to fulfilling a statement of purpose made by John Groenewegen of Erasmus University at a professional meeting. During a panel discussion he said that, since there is not evidence of universal models, our goal should be to have well-developed models on the shelf for different types of institutional structure. Then, as investigations are undertaken to study different kinds of problems, institutionalists can retrieve the most appropriate model from the shelf. The intent here is to begin with the foundations laid by Bush, in order to discuss a methodology for building toward Groenewegen's 'shelf' models.

It was stated above that this work would depend on the ideas, nomenclature and tools of normative systems. Let me emphasize, however, that normative philosophers will not agree with some of the applications that will be made of their tools; although dependent upon, the applications will not always be consistent with. In an Ayresian sense, the work here is a new combination of normative technology for an alternative use. The purpose is to articulate a methodology to guide normative description and empirical investigation. The normative system of the real world does not always fit the normative requirements of normative philosophy. This is not meant as an adverse criticism; rather, it is to clarify the different purpose. Normative philosophers have been interested in logical systems based on axioms from philosophy, while institutionalists are interested in tools for articulation and evaluation of real-world socioecological systems.

Some normative philosophers emphasize that for a system to be valid, it must not contain contradictions or tautologies. Yet social systems contain numerous contradictions and tautologies. For example, the powerful ideology of supply-side economics is based on neoclassical methodology, which is constructed with the assistance of numerous tautologies. Supply-side economics cannot be ignored as an important normative force just because it is based on tautologies; its impact on social, economic and ecological components has been too significant for social scientists to ignore. As another example, tautologies are the base of computers because computers are based on boolean mathematics which is, in turn, based on a series of tautologies. We cannot exclude the computer world and its social, economic and ecological impacts because it contains tautologies. The tools of normative and deontic philosophers are important; the purpose here is to bend them toward the needs of institutionalism.

With regard to contradiction, Bush clarified with the axiom of transience the difference between the axioms of logical systems and the axioms of the real world. Neoclassical methodology assumes transitive relations. Yet Bush pointed out that empirical investigations have found dominance relations that are not transitive. He demonstrated a nontransitive dominance system based on graph theory from mathematics (Bush 1983, pp. 44–5).

FOUNDATION OF NORMATIVE SYSTEMS AND DEONTIC CATEGORIES

Karl Polanyi explained that the norms of a social situation include (1) prohibitions, (2) obligations and (3) permissions. This was consistent with his advice that socioecological analysis should be centred on and guided by process, norms and policy (Polanyi 1957, pp. 248–50). To focus on process, norms and policy, it is necessary to define the normative prohibitions (Ph), obligations (O) and permissions (P) that provide the rules for socioecological transactions. (A symbolic reference is provided at the end of the text for the reader's convenience.) These are the norms that guide the actions taken in an ongoing social process. They determine the patterns of institutional activity that give institutions correlative capability and statistical regularity. Polanyi emphasized the constant motion of social processes; thus, normative components are action oriented. John R. Commons had completed a particular application consistent with Polanyi's general theory prior to Polanyi's writing the general theory. In Commons's *Legal Foundations of Capitalism*, he described the normative criteria in a capitalist social system as the working rules of going concerns that specified what individuals (1) must do, (2) must not do, (3) may do, (4) can do with the aid of collective power, and (5) cannot expect from the collective power (1924, p. 6). The first three are consistent with Polanyi's obligation, prohibition and permission. The last two can be deleted because all social norms are collective.

Although it will not be discussed here, Polanyi and Commons needed to add optional to their deontic categories of prohibition, obligation and permission in order to include their respective concerns for privilege in socioeconomic situations. Both scholars explained that some actors may have the status and power to be indifferent toward a normative rule. That deontic modality allows that the norm-subject may either perform or not perform the act.

Walter C. Neale and Georg H. Von Wright are two scholars who have emphasized the question 'why?' and provided answers to it in explaining the relationship between norms and human action. The most important aspect of their emphasis on that question is paradigmatic. Their paradigms explain that institutional action is completed for a reason or reasons. The answer to the question 'why?' is the reason. In explaining institutional activity, Neale wrote that belief norms are a set of ideas or representations explaining or justifying the activities and the governing rules and are answers to questions starting with 'why?' (Neale and Pearson 1962, p. 1). The reason includes the norm that orders, permits or prohibits the doing of an action and the necessary connections that make (or do not make) the doing or forbearing of the action a practical necessity (Von Wright 1983, p. 74). Paradigmatically, institutional action has an end in view with normative statements to the effect that something ought to or may not be done. Neale and Von Wright have both clarified that persons involved in an institution can neither be depended upon to know the social belief criteria nor be depended upon to be truthful about them. Beliefs are social and are not necessarily known by all the different agents involved in a process. 'Conscious awareness of the function of an institution is not necessary and in part will often be absent' (Neale 1987, p. 1196).

THE SOCIAL FABRIC MATRIX OF SOCIAL, TECHNOLOGICAL AND ECOLOGICAL CRITERIA

The literature of normative philosophy, although emphasizing social systems, has not developed a whole-system approach. The emphasis has been on particular logic rather than the transactional whole. The task here is to explain the analysis of normative systems within the context of the overall social fabric matrix. Figure 5.1 is a simple overall view of the social and cultural components and how the fabric of a social system is reticulated.

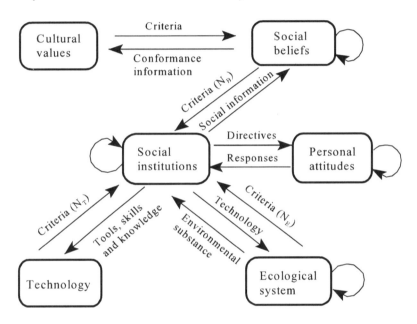

Figure 5.1   *Relationships among values, beliefs, attitudes, institutions, technology and the environment*

The components are cultural values, social beliefs, social institutions, attitudes, technology and ecological systems. With respect to Figure 5.1, the analysis and discussion below will concentrate on the criteria that are concomitant with social institutions; the three normative sets are social belief criteria (N_B), technological criteria (N_T) and ecological system criteria (N_E). These norms are the standards for judging whether institutional patterns are appropriate. Since normative philosophy does not take a whole-system approach to normative decision making, N_T and N_E are seldom of concern in that literature, while the institutionalist tradition makes them apparent. N_T and N_E are not defined in any anthropocentric sense. Technology, which is the combination of tools, skills and knowledge, does not think about and decide upon normative criteria. Technological norms are the criteria conveyed to society as a result of the combination selected by societal units such as corporations. Likewise, no assumption is being made that an ecological system is reflective about values and beliefs. N_E, instead, represents the normative criteria consistent with the maintenance of a particular kind of ecological system as institutions apply technology to that system.

The three sets of criteria (N_B, N_T and N_E) are the first components entered in the simple social fabric matrix (SFM) in Figure 5.2.

Delivering Components / Receiving Components	Social norm (N_B)	Technological norm (N_T)	Ecological norm (N_E)	Authority institution (I_{A1})	Authority institution (I_{A2})	Processing institutions (I_p)
Social norm (N_B)				1		
Technological norm (N_T)				1		
Ecological norm (N_E)				1		
Authority institution (I_{A1})					1	
Authority institution (I_{A2})						1
Processing institutions (I_p)						1

Figure 5.2   Social fabric matrix of norms and institutions

The SFM is an integrated process matrix designed to express the attributes of the parts as well as the integrated process of the whole (Hayden 1982, 1985). The rows represent the components which are delivering, and the columns represent the components which are receiving. The participle form serves to denote that the SFM is designed to model an action process. The SFM is 'a systematic attempt to identify the relevant set of influences that shape the behavior of a system' (Gill 1996, p. 169). If the SFM in Figure 5.2 were complete, it would include all the components in Figure 5.1. The SFM in Figure 5.2 does not contain all components of a full SFM, nor does it indicate all deliveries among the components. It is limited to normative concerns. Deliveries made among matrix components (from rows on the left to columns on the right) are indicated by a 1 being placed in the cell where the delivery is made. If one wanted to complete boolean manipulations on the matrix, 0 could be placed in the cells where deliveries are not indicated. Below, when particular deliveries in the matrix are discussed, the cells of interest will be laid out in digraph format, with the deliveries in the cells indicated on the edge (directed line) between cells. The designation of the cells will be included in the textual discussion, designated as the *i*th row that is delivering to the *j*th column. The numbers of the rows and columns are indicated in Figure 5.2.

Normative Criteria and Institutions

Each major norm that applies to numerous institutional settings has a number of subcriteria (n_B, n_T and n_E) that apply to particular institutional situations or cases. Thus, N_B obligates the application of n_{B1}, n_{B2} and n_{B3} under the conditions of the institutional authority of I_{A1}; N_T obligates the application of n_{T1} and n_{T2} under the conditions of I_{A1}; and N_E obligates the application of n_{E1} and n_{E2} when applied to institution I_{A1}. The first row of Figure 5.3 informs us that N_B directs ($\supset$) an obligation (O) of n_{B1} & n_{B2} & n_{B3} given institution I_{A1}.

	SFM cells
$N_B \supset O\ (n_{B1}\ \&\ n_{B2}\ \&\ n_{B3})/I_{A1}$	(1,4)
$N_T \supset O\ (n_{T1}\ \&\ n_{T2})/I_{A1}$	(2,4)
$N_E \supset O\ (n_{E1}\ \&\ n_{E2})/I_{A1}$	(3,4)

Figure 5.3   Norms and obligations for institutions

The conjunction (&) means that the subcriteria are to be applied *together*. This is the delivery in cell (1,4) of the SFM. The second statement in Figure 5.3 is similar in that the technological norm, N_B, directs an obligation for n_{T1} and n_{T2} to be applied together to institution I_{A1}, and the third row contains a statement about a similar delivery for the subcriteria of N_E. The delivery in an SFM digraph format between norms, N_B, N_T and N_E and institution I_{A1} is found in Figure 5.4 with the deliveries indicated on the edges (directed lines) from the norms to the institution I_{A1}. Normative criteria deliver instructions for subcriteria to be applied with other subcriteria in order to complete the respective super criterion. In turn, the designated subcriteria outlined above become the criterial standards to be applied by institutional authority I_{A1}, as indicated in Figure 5.4.

As John R. Commons emphasized, institutional authorities come in many forms. They may be explicitly designated as government agencies or judicial branches. However, institutional authorities are also designated by those agencies within other kinds of institutions. For example, a used car salesperson may be given the authority (obligated) to make sure that safety requirements are met on automobiles before they are sold. Thus, we do not attempt to find an authority institution within a particular kind of agency. As Bush has explained, institutions are patterns of correlated behaviour (Bush 1987, p. 1076), so the authority patterns of an institutional authority can be correlated across different kinds of agencies.

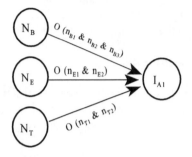

Figure 5.4   SFM digraph: norm delivery of conjunctive subnorms to institutions

From the array of criteria delivered to the authority institution, rules (r), regulations (re) and requirements (rq) need to be articulated in order for the norms to influence and guide action. In the normative philosophy literature, r, re and rq are often used interchangeably, and sometimes inconsistently. Here, we will designate rules as the broader and more authoritative code that guides regulation to achieve particular conduct or establish a pattern with regard to particular institutions. Regulations are completed to control or govern the action of an institution through action requirements. Requirements are required responses to symbols. They usually take the form of orders, requests and questions. Requirements are given externally. If requirements are consistent with the regulations and rules, they are instituted to carry out action to achieve the purpose of regulations. As instituted and presented to the agents, requirements exist, so to speak. Although agents undertaking the action often do not know the reasons for the required action, actions can still be consistent with a normative end (Von Wright 1983, p. 54). The human agent may have an end quite different than the normative reason for the requirement. A worker may be following order requirements for a paycheck without reflection on the normative end for which the requirement exists.

An example of a rule statement could be as follows: to permit maximum utilization of sources of radiation consistent with the health and safety of the public. A regulation consistent with that rule could be as follows: the calibration should be performed under the direct supervision of a radiological physicist who is physically present at the facility during the calibration. Requirements regarding calibration would be numerous, with precise instructions about when and how to calibrate and exactly what instruments to use.

Regulations are usually justified and explained, especially when codified in an operations manual. There are *reasons* given for carrying out the regulations. The reasons for carrying out regulations appeal to normative rules in the discourse. It is an action discourse because it emphasizes the actions the regulations are aiming to accomplish. In a corporate setting, managers, attorneys, directors and executives are expected to know and be accountable to the reasons given for the regulations. Without the reasons, administrative personnel will not know how to adjust requirements as situations change in order to achieve the intent of rules.

Rules are made in order to fulfil norms and are usually explained in discourse similar to norms discourse. Great effort usually goes into explaining the norms and the reason the rules are necessary in order to fulfil normative beliefs. Such rules are found in court decisions and legislation. An example is when the courts give trees standing in the courts to bring lawsuits in order that courts can make rules to protect trees in a manner consistent with ecological system norms.

For the purposes of explaining normative systems, two types of authority systems are described with regard to carrying norms to the action field. The higher (meaning most authoritative) authority was designated as I_{A1} above. These are institutions that interpret norms for a particular situation and the particular properties of a situation and then frame, structure and explain the rules for the situations in which the rules are to be applied, which rules are to be applied and the acceptable reasons for applying the rules. I_{A1} authorities are institutions like courts and legislative bodies, and they 'lay down the law' to other authoritative institutions, such as corporate authorities, designated as I_{A2}. I_{A1} represents authority as rule maker, while I_{A2} represents authority as regulator and enforcer.

Corporations are divided between authority institutions and processing or production institutions. The latter will be designated as I_p. The authority I_{A2}, often referred to as 'headquarters' for a corporation, promulgates the numerous regulations that are utilized to determine the requirements of the corporate production process, I_p.

Rules of Institutional Authority

I_{A1} authorities deliver, as indicated in cell (4,5) of the SFM, a number of rules, $r_1 \ldots r_n$, to I_{A2} authorities. Rules come in the form of rulings with regard to properties of a situation (S). Therefore, where r represents rules of obligation, prohibition or permission with regard to situations, in general $I_{A1} \supset O(r_1 \ldots r_n)/S_1 \ldots S_n)$. I_{A1} obligates the application of an appropriate rule or rules given a particular situation or situations. We can think of numerous different possibilities. For example, $I_{A1} \supset O(r_2 \& r_3)/S_1$ states that I_{A1} obligates rules r_2 and r_3 to be applied together to situation S_1.

Alternatively, cell (4,5) of the SFM can be expressed in digraph format as in Figure 5.5, where I_{A1} delivers an obligation to I_{A2} to apply rules, $r_1 \ldots r_n$ to situations $S \ldots S_n$ as those situations are formulated in rulings by I_{A1}. In a more complete SFM, each of the relevant situations in the series, $S_1 \ldots S_n$, would be included in the SFM with its own row and column under I_{A2}.

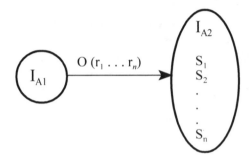

Figure 5.5   SFM digraph: institutional delivery of rules to another institution

Regulations of Institutional Authority

A major task for those studying a problem area is to identify the convergence of various rules, socioecological properties and situations. Social life is never so simple as to have set rules and regulations that obligate or prohibit the same action in all situations within the same institution. We do not observe rules being applied to an institution as a whole. Rather, what can be observed are such activities in situations (see Neale 1987, p. 1184). The situations are made up of properties. As the deontic content of social properties changes, the deontic status of particular action changes.

This can be demonstrated with a simple example of a real-world problem. It is the issue of whether waste from a production process, I_P, can be spread on farm land in the region near the production centre in order to minimize production costs. This action issue can be called U. Under what conditions should I_P workers be obligated to spread the waste and under what conditions should this action be prohibited? To simplify, assume there are three properties that make up situations that are relevant to the corporate leadership's decision making. The properties are: the river has a high volume of water, so the waste would be diluted and dissipated quickly if rainfall washed the waste from the land before being absorbed by the soil (F); the soil temperature is high enough to allow high rates of waste absorption (G); and the waste is spread (H). The compound of the properties (F, G, H) defines the socioecological situations. A simple technique from deontic logic for discovering the potential number of situations is 2^n where n is the number of properties. Given the three properties, there are eight possible situations, as demonstrated in Figure 5.6.

Situation	Properties	Action Solution/re
S_1	F G H	OU/F $\vee$ G
S_2	~F G H	OU/F $\vee$ G
S_3	F ~G H	OU/F $\vee$ G
S_4	~F ~G H	
S_5	F G ~H	
S_6	~F G ~H	
S_7	F ~G ~H	
S_8	~F ~G ~H	

Figure 5.6   Properties of situations and consequential action, given a regulation

We see in Figure 5.6 that property F is negated (~) in situation S_2, which means the volume of water in the river is low. Which situations provide for what deontic requirement? That depends on the normative rules which, as explained above, depend on normative criteria. If the normative rule is that pollution of the river should be a concern, a regulation, re, could be promulgated that would obligate the spreading of waste whenever either F or G exists. This means situations S_1, S_2 and S_3 are situations obligating action U, or OU. The action solution is indicated in the right-hand column, given the regulation re. The solution content of situation S_4 is Ph U $\leftrightarrow$ ~F & ~G, or action U being prohibited is equivalent ($\leftrightarrow$) to a situation where the properties, F and G, are negated.

Although the paradigm here differs from that in the book, *Normative Systems* (Alchourron and Bulygin 1971), the book is very helpful, in general, and especially with regard to formulae (beyond the simple 2^n used above) for various combinations of properties and situations. There are more than three properties in most institutional situations, and there may be more properties in some situations than others in a specific institution. Or, the number of properties may change on different occasions. For example, the religion of human agents may become a property in situations when persons of that religion become involved in those situations. Let us assume that Irish Catholics, for example, are not allowed to have jobs in a region and the rented trucks (from another region) that arrive to haul waste (property H) are driven by Irish Catholics, then that special property comes into play when such truck drivers enter the situation. The above advice to consult property and situation techniques in *Normative Systems* is not to suggest that such techniques be used to determine what is happening in a society. Rather, it is that such techniques can serve as tools to help identify potential possibilities that researchers should look for in institutions being investigated.

In the SFM digraph format, regulations are delivered to the processing institution, for example, a corporate production centre, as in Figure 5.7. Figure 5.7 is the delivery in cell (5,6) of the SFM in Figure 5.2. I_{A2} delivers the regulation that I_p is obligated to undertake action U if confronted with situation S_1 or S_2 or S_3, and I_p is prohibited from undertaking action given situation S_4 or S_5 or S_6 or S_7 or S_8.

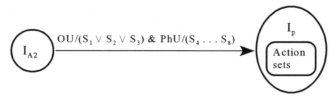

Figure 5.7   SFM digraph: institutional delivery of action solution to another institution

Requirements of Processing Institutions: Action Agents and Temporal Events

S_1, S_2 and S_3 are known by the condition of their respective properties. How are they known? By monitoring, indicating, measuring, auditing, observing, gauging, accounting, producing, storing, loading, hauling, spreading, supervising, and so forth. These are actions accomplished by requirements being delivered to agents that are in action settings. The relevant situations to which the process, I_p, are to direct agents have been defined by more authoritative institutional settings. As situations develop, and are recognized, agents are sent into action settings through requirements to accomplish their required action, that is, to fulfil their roles. 'Whenever ends and necessary connections justify a normative statement to the effect that a certain thing ought to (may, must not) be done then a command (permission, prohibition) to somebody to do this thing, given by somebody in pursuit of these ends, has a teleological foundation in the ends of the norm-authority' (Von Wright 1983, p. 74). The agents necessary to fulfil the requirements of any process are varied and numerous. They can be categorized as human agents (h), technological agents (t) and ecological agents (e), which are sometimes difficult to separate neatly. (Humans are biological as well as thinking and working beings.) To accomplish the action solution, say of spreading waste, the action solution U is divided into several subactions (W, X, Y, Z) that must be coordinated around an event or events (E). Thus the subactions are equivalent to U or U ↔ [W &

X & Y & Z]. The requirements (rq$_1$ . . . rq$_n$) prohibit, obligate or permit the subactions by directing the human, technological and ecological agents to perform some act or acts depending on the action the normative system has formulated as appropriate.

Events, happenings and occasions make the state of affairs temporal. Agents ought to act in conjunction with the appropriate events, happenings and occasions. 'For it is the act and the state of affairs which, together with their consequences do or do not make the world preferable, not the mere presence of obligation. Thus we should restate all "ought statements" so that whatever falls within the scope of an "ought" operator receives an explicit temporal index' (Forrester 1996, p. 214). Requirements are given to agents to act on certain events, happenings or occasions. Therefore, the delivery in SFM cell (6,6) would be as indicated in Figure 5.8.

Figure 5.8   SFM digraph: internal delivery of requirements by an institution

In Figure 5.8, the production institution I_p directs, with requirements rq$_1$ to rq$_n$, to produce actions W, X, Y and Z with agents h, t and e on the occasion of event E to sustain the situation S_1 or S_2 or S_3. The coordinated action [W & X & Y & Z]$_{h\&t\&e}$ can be performed only on the condition that the combination of properties of a situation is present. S_1 as a whole, for example, ceases to exist unless some institution such as I_p maintains it because property H of S_1 is an institutional action.

CONFLICT IN THE MODERN WORLD

This explanation of how to organize the analysis of a normative system is not presented in order to suggest that all real-world normative systems are harmonious or continuous, or that they maintain commonality of normative criteria, avoid excess or inadequate redundancy, and are without gaps and conflict. Quite the contrary. This holistic approach to normative discourse is intended to encourage studies to be completed to find the gaps, discontinuity, disharmony and conflicts. Given the fragility of the modern social world, the adequate redundancy of institutional patterns that assure conformance to ethical norms, and concomitant rules and regulations, is a paramount concern; likewise the concern for providing for such redundancy through policy when institutional patterns are changing. The current global economic system has very much gained the upper hand in defining institutional patterns, regulations and requirements and, in turn, in creating global chaos. This is all the more reason why holistic studies of normative systems need to be completed in order to define the characteristics of the current system, so that we will have an opportunity to find the system particulars that lead to deleterious consequences and, in turn, recommend policy alternatives. However, system completeness, that is, creating redundancy, closing gaps, resolving conflicts and so forth, is not sufficient if the teleological beginning is flawed. That issue, which is a major issue in the modern world, is one that has been very much ignored by social scientists.

Conflict of Normative Ends

The teleological ends of the normative system were defined above as being made up of three sets of normative criteria. They were defined as social belief criteria (N_B), technological criteria (N_T) and ecological criteria (N_E). What has not been of much concern for either normative system philosophers or social scientists is whether these criteria are consistent. The concern for consistency of the normative criteria is not just a deontic concern for logical completeness and consistency. It is a real-world concern of major importance. Society has lost the institutional ability to make N_B, N_T and N_E consistent with each other and consistent with an instrumental flow of events and actions in its processing institutions. The dominant norms are in conflict; therefore, the subnorms, as well as the consequent rules, regulations and requirements for directing action, are conflicted.

Such conflicts lead to results that have left some agents destitute or destroyed, and others frustrated, when they learn of the resulting degradation and destruction. An example is the removal of peasant farmers from their land in South America so European-based corporations can denude and intensely cultivate the land for soybean production, so the soybeans can be shipped to the United States to produce plastic used in weapons that are exported to Africa, so different tribal groups, whose traditional societal patterns have been hopelessly disrupted, can slaughter each other. The peasant families move into a destitute status in slum areas, the numerous species that occupied the wetlands and woodlands of the peasant farms are destroyed as the wetlands and woodlands are destroyed, the soil becomes eroded by the agribusiness-selected technology utilized for cultivation, and water sources are polluted because of chemical runoff from the corporate farms and because of the waste byproducts of plastic production in the first world. The weapons lead to more dislocation and destruction in Africa. In addition, the whole process of production, involving overland hauling and oceanic and air shipping, is extremely energy intensive. Volumes could be filled with similar examples. We deplore this system. No one could call such a world efficient. Yet those kinds of examples continue to escalate at the community, regional and global level. Why? Mainly because institutional structures have not developed to enforce the coordination of N_B, N_T and N_E, nor has much effort gone into investigating how such coordinating institutions should be structured.

Conflict between Bureaucracies and Institutions

What has happened is that more and more of our decisions are made by goal-oriented bureaucracies that have a narrow focus on what their goals ought to be. Lives in the modern world are dominated by bureaucracies rather than by broader-based institutions. An increasing proportion of the lives of decision makers is spent in bureaucracies, and they think increasingly in terms of bureaucratic goals. The automatic impulse to fulfil bureaucratic goals has replaced social reflection of social norms. Those in academic communities watch their colleagues race after research funds to fulfil bureaucratic goals of money acquisition rather than reflecting on what kind of research is consistent with social needs. How can professors most easily acquire research money; by following the research goals of multinational corporate bureaucracies. Those in homes watch marketing bureaucracies define consumption impulses via television. How do family members learn how they will be most admired by others; by following the marketing bureaucracies' goals. How can corporate executives stationed around the world by global corporations get promoted; by following corporate goals. Societal decision making becomes a series of impulses to bureaucratic goals rather than a reflection of consistent social, technological and ecological norms. Bureaucracies are overpowering social institutions, especially democratic institutions. In addition, given the power of modern technology, impulses can cause immense damage, first, because the impulsive decisions direct powerful technology and, second, because modern communication technology quickly transmits bureaucratically designed goals into reality across the globe.

We can use Figure 5.1 to help conceptualize the magnitude of the issue. As displayed, a set of institutions is at the centre. The information processing and decision making of those institutions are, increasingly, determined by bureaucracies and, increasingly, those bureaucracies are not guided by transcendental norms or transactional analysis. Some of those institutions are important in defining the combinations of tools, skills and knowledge that define technology. As demonstrated in Figure 5.1, the kind of technology utilized defines criteria (N_T) for how institutions are to function. Thousands of years of human history have demonstrated that new technological combinations can improve and sustain social and ecological life and can be coordinated and adjusted to fit other socioecological components. Numerous examples exist to the contrary, especially recently. We know of new technological combinations that have depleted and contaminated water supplies, poisoned wildlife and people, and made the expression of important social norms impossible. We should not expect otherwise if those making decisions about technological combinations are not being guided to provide for criteria commensurate with appropriate social and ecological criteria.

Figure 5.1 indicates a relationship between institutions and ecological systems. This connection has become increasingly important in determining the functioning of ecological systems. Nature is not as natural as in the past. The application of technology establishes the relationship between the ecological systems and social institutions that establishes normative criteria (N_E) for society to follow. For example, the combination of technology for growing peanuts (to provide peanut oil to Europe) in Africa imposes a set of criteria upon society requiring it to convert land into deserts. A different technology would direct a different set of criteria.

Currently the matrix of social institutions, technology and ecology creates criteria that, in turn, direct the formation of rules, regulations and requirements to function which further erode commitment to social beliefs. Societies are falling apart because institutions that carried and enforced norms across different organizations have become less important to people. Those institutions are increasingly ignored in some cases, and despised in other cases. A society that has the basic criteria by which it lives dissolve and disintegrate is neither pretty nor predictable, and it often loses its ability to recognize authority that is not authoritarian. Without strong commitment to consistent norms, the only real authority in a society is the one with a monopoly on weapons. We learn this in reports about cities in Russia where a mafia-type fascism is providing authority and in similar reports from all around the world. The new world disorder brought about by the attempt to rapidly replace legitimate social processes (often with bureaucratic market processes) is creating authoritarian systems which are not at all concerned about the coordination of the normative components of society, technology and ecological systems. Those closest to the environment (for example, workers and managers in African peanut fields) may be able to see the damage caused by the criteria directing societal action. Yet there is seldom a social means for those observations to change the ecological criteria (N_E) or to direct a change in technological criteria (N_T) or social beliefs (N_B) in order to bring about a change in the normative system.

The social belief (N_B) connection in Figure 5.1, beyond needing to be coordinated with N_T and N_E, needs to be protected and slowly adjusted when change is needed. Beliefs cannot be coordinated or their adjustment paced if analysis does not identify an institutional means for such control. The importance for coordination has been made above in the discussion about technological and ecological criteria. Pacing change is even more important with regard to social beliefs. Karl Polanyi explained in the *Great Transformation* the fragility of social institutions if change is too rapid, and the suffering of humans if institutions break down. If an attempt is made to change social beliefs too quickly, human society loses its ability to know its own social norms and to recognize legitimate authority; therefore, institutions cease to function to provide for human needs. This is a current problem because rapid deviations from social norms, in order to fulfil bureaucratic goals, have become a dominant trend across the globe.

CONCLUDING REMARKS

The normative systems approach explained above clarified the importance of normative belief criteria, along with technological and ecological criteria, for the maintenance of authority and the working of socioecological processes. Professor Bush devoted much of his work to the understanding of evolutionary change and the process of instrumental decision making. As world affairs are revealed to us today, it would be difficult to find two more important concerns. Consistent with Professor Bush's leadership, the work here has attempted to utilize the assistance of normative philosophy and deontic logic to refine the description of normative processes. The approach is more holistic than that found in normative philosophy, yet the suggested way to describe normative relationships calls for more precise description than has been practised in institutional economics. If this kind of description can be used to more precisely define normative systems, data bases can be created consistent with the description; normative gaps and inconsistencies can be identified; and research agendas can be refined to determine the way that social, technological and ecological system norms should be structured to provide for a more instrumental instituted process.

We need to become precise in the modelling of requirements in institutions in order to know whether the consequences of the requirements are consistent with the normative standards, because it is through requirements being placed on the human, technological and ecological agents that beliefs and value criteria are manifested in reality. A small change in a requirement with regard to radiation exposure can lead to results quite different than were expected. A change of a few degrees in water temperature in a river due to industrial activities can render a species extinct. Which requirements regarding radiation and temperature levels are consistent with normative standards? We cannot know without precise modelling that connects requirements to the normative system through the instituted process.

APPENDIX: SYMBOL REFERENCE

This symbol reference is included for the convenience of the reader. The symbols in the text are:

SFM – social fabric matrix
Ph – prohibited or forbidden
O – obligation or obligatory
P – permission or permitted
N_B – social belief norms or criteria
N_T – technological norms or criteria
N_E – ecological norms or criteria
n_{B1}, n_{B2} and n_{B3} – subnorms or subcriteria of N_B
n_{T1} and n_{T2} – subnorms or subcriteria of N_T
n_{E1} and n_{E2} – subnorms or subcriteria of N_E
I_{A1} – authority institution for making rules
I_{A2} – authority institution for making regulations
I_P – processing institution for delivering requirements
r – rules
re – regulations
rq – requirements
E – event, happening or occasion
F – situational property of a high volume of water in the river
G – situational property of high soil temperature
H – situational property of spreading waste
S – situation
U – action to spread waste to solve a problem
W – subaction of U
X – subaction of U
Y – subaction of U
Z – subaction of U
h – human agents
t – technological agents
e – ecological agents
n – number
$\sim$ – negation
& – conjunction
$\vee$ – disjunction
$\supset$ – directs or necessarily implies
$\leftrightarrow$ – equivalence
/ – given

REFERENCES

Alchourron, Carlos E. and Eugenio Bulygin (1971), *Normative Systems*, New York: Springer-Verlag.

Bush, Paul D. (1983), 'An Exploration of the Structural Characteristics of a Veblen–Ayres–Foster Defined Institutional Domain', *Journal of Economic Issues*, **17**, March, pp. 35–65.

_____(1987), 'The Theory of Institutional Change', *Journal of Economic Issues*, **21**, September, pp.1075–116.

_____(1991), 'Reflections on the Twenty-Fifth Anniversary of AFEE: Philosophical and Methodological Issues in Institutional Economics', *Journal of Economic Issues*, **25**, June, pp. 321–46.

Commons, John R. (1924), *The Legal Foundations of Capitalism*, Madison: University of Wisconsin, 1968.

Forrester, James Wm. (1996), *Being Good and Being Logical: Philosophical Goundwork for a New Deontic Logic*, New York: M.E. Sharpe.

Gill, Roderic (1996), 'An Integrated Social Fabric Matrix/System Dynamics Approach to Policy Analysis', *System Dynamics Review*, **12**, Fall, pp. 167–249.

Hayden, F. Gregory (1982), 'Social Fabric Matrix: From Perspective to Analytical Tool', *Journal of Economic Issues*, **16,** September, pp. 637–61.

_____(1985), 'A Trans-disciplinary Integration Matrix for Economics and Policy Analysis', *Social Science Information*, **24,** September, pp. 869–903.

Neale, Walter C. (1987), 'Institutions', *Journal of Economic Issues*, **21**, September, pp. 1177–1206.

_____ and Harry W. Pearson (1962), 'Institutions and Economics', unpublished paper, pp. 1–12.

Polanyi, Karl (1957), 'The Economy as Instituted Process' in Karl Polanyi et al. (eds), *Trade and Market in Early Empire*, Glencoe, Ill.: The Free Press, pp. 243–70.

Schlagel, Richard H. (1995), unpublished letter to author, pp. 1–2.

Von Wright, Georg Henrik (1983), *Practical Reason*, Oxford: Basil Blackwell.

6. Changes in the Institution of Corporate Governance: The Case of the Dutch Market for Corporate Control

John Groenewegen

INTRODUCTION

With growing internationalization national institutions are under pressure; competition policy in the Netherlands is for instance changing towards European standards (Groenewegen 1994); conjunctural and structural policies are becoming more and more alike (see for instance the French case during the 1980s); and more recently such a development seems also to be taking place with respect to the institutions of corporate governance. By 'corporate governance' we mean the internal and external disciplining mechanisms which together govern the corporation. So corporate governance has to do with internal procedures of decision making, the involvement of different stakeholders in that process, as well as with external pressures coming from financial markets, external markets for managerial labour and the like. Within the system of corporate governance distinctions can be made among the governance of human resources (internal and external labour markets), the governance of technology (private and public R&D as well as joint ventures), the governance of intermediate products (vertical integration and sub-contracting) and the governance of capital (debt and equity). In this paper we focus on the way management is disciplined by the stock market known as the market for corporate control.

The question is raised whether changes in the system of corporate governance are such that different systems are converging towards one model. The argument is that globalization forces corporations to adapt to the most efficient model and it is often suggested that this is the Anglo-Saxon model. This convergence question has a deeper meaning: if through global competition the most efficient system of corporate governance survives, then presumably its underlying economic theory can be applied in which 'economizing behaviour, rational spirit and efficiency' is the only analysis of importance. Differences in institutional context and especially the relation between that context and the behaviour of economic actors are then considered of marginal importance. If on the contrary it is shown that the institutional context is important in explaining differences between systems of corporate governance, then the one-sided universal theory should be replaced by an approach in which the uniqueness of institutional structures is emphasized.

In analysing recent developments in the Dutch system of corporate governance, it is argued that the evolution of a national institution largely depends on its specific history and the culture in which it is embedded. This implies that not one efficient system will survive, but that different systems – each with its own strengths and weaknesses – evolve along their own unique path.

This chapter is organized as follows: first, two models are discussed, the Anglo-Saxon model and the Continental European/Japanese model. Second, using the characteristics of the latter, the Dutch institutional structure and the Dutch system of corporate governance are considered. Third, a description of recent developments in Dutch corporate law follows. Fourth, in order to make a broader comparison, an overview of systems of corporate governance in Germany, France and Japan is provided. Fifth, empirical evidence about the performance of different systems of governance is presented. Finally, conclusions are drawn about the process of institutionalization and the issue of convergence.

TWO MODELS OF CORPORATE GOVERNANCE[1]

Systems of corporate governance are embedded in broader economic systems, which consist of values, government regulations, the way labour unions and employer associations organize markets, and the like. Chalmers Johnson (1982) distinguished two types of market economies: the regulatory and development state. The former is the ideal type of an economic system, in which the market process is central; in the latter structural objectives about the economic development are explicitly formulated by a public agent that guides the market process. This fundamental difference in orientation has implications for the role of government and firms, the nature of policy instruments and the characteristics of corporate governance.

In the regulatory state, government is at arm's length from the firms. Macro conjunctural policy together with a strong competition policy (is supposed to) create a favourable environment for firms. The idea is that firms are put under pressure in the product market, that managers are put under pressure in the market for managerial labour and that management is further disciplined by the capital market, where takeovers are not hindered by technical and structural barriers. In this system transactions are governed through classical contracts and disputes are solved in public court.[2]

In the developmental state government is heavily involved in the structural development of the economy through a system of indicative planning and industrial and technology policies. Close links existing between government and corporations aim at long-term strategies which focus on the realization of structural objectives at macro, meso and micro level (growth of BNP, specific sectoral developments, size and clustering of firms). Competition is important, but competition is organized by private and public actors. Such private ordering is not only allowed, but often stimulated when considered in the interest of desirable long-term structural developments. In such an environment it can be considered efficient if firms can protect themselves against takeovers, especially when long-term relations are purposefully nurtured. Markets, then, are not anonymous blunt selection mechanisms, but well-managed governance structures in which competition, domination and cooperation co-exist. In such an economic system transactions are governed through relational contracts and disputes are solved in private as well as public courts.

The regulatory state is the Anglo-Saxon model, also called market model, of which the US and the UK are good examples. The role of shareholders is dominant in the firm and management is internally, as well as externally, controlled by the suppliers of capital. The developmental state is the Japanese model, also called the network or relational model, in which different stakeholders play a role, which is shown in the internal organization of the firm and the role of external disciplinary mechanisms. The Continental Europe model, also called the social market economy, is also characterized by organized markets, but there labour unions and employer associations play an important role.

THE DUTCH INSTITUTIONAL STRUCTURE

The Dutch economic system – that is, its institutional context of values, norms, rules and structures – can be characterized as an 'organized market' (Groenewegen 1994). Private ordering is not only allowed by government, but in many cases government stimulates self-regulation, monitors it and guides it in a direction considered in line with the 'general interest'. In the Dutch system many associations of interest groups can be found, which regulate their own markets and which do so in close consultation with government. This results in norms of behaviour in which information exchange, consensus building and cooperation are highly valued. This also results in formal advisory bodies in which different interest groups are represented; these groups become part of the decision-making process which helps to produce adequate information and increases the legitimacy of public policies. They make rules and regulations with respect to quality standards, entry to the industry, vocational training, participation in the results of public R&D, and so on. Socio-political structures exist in which labour unions, branch organizations, technological institutes and the like, have a well-defined place and role. In market structures competition and cooperation co-exist and in micro structures firms are not a nexus of classical contracts, but coalitions of stakeholders in networks with intensive economic, financial and personal relationships.

Historians point to the value of stability in Dutch society. Change is necessary, but shocks have to be avoided. Security is precious and the securities of others should be respected. The Netherlands is a country with a high 'insurance density' and the social security system is a well-developed one. The Netherlands is not an individualistic society where risk-loving individuals constantly try out new things in uncertain markets; the Dutch are more group-oriented and nurture the sheltering of stability through regulation and structures. The group-orientedness is reflected in the organizational structures in politics, as well as in corporations and in all kinds of associations and foundations. In politics groups have their own party; cabinets are always coalitions where the prime minister is the leader among equals. The same holds for the board of directors of corporations, of labour unions, of universities, of associations and foundations. The groups are formally organized with detailed statutes, democratic elections and the like. The groups help to identify the interests of individuals; the rules of the game are clear as well as the duties and responsibilities. The Netherlands is not a society of informal structures in which individuals must find their own way.[3] In the history of the Netherlands, democratic organization and administration of cities, guilds and corporations have formed an institutional structure in which groups and associations in close cooperation with government play a central role. Illustrations are to be found, among others, in the corporation with limited liability, which organized the trade with the Far East in the 17th century, in Dutch competition law which was based on the abuse system[4] and in the way many branch organizations have public ordering powers to organize vocational training, create establishment rules for new firms, regulate investments and even set rules for price policies.

The way corporations are governed and the role of the capital market as a market for corporate control should be understood within the Dutch institutional structure.

The Dutch Institutions of Corporate Governance

The system of corporate governance consists of internal and external disciplinary mechanisms. How is the firm internally organized and what kind of pressures come from external markets?

In the Anglo-Saxon model shareholders delegate power to the management, which consists of a board with the Chief Executive Officer (CEO) at the top. The separation between owners and management raises well-known agency problems. Owners and managers have different objectives and information is unequally distributed. Generally management is better informed which calls for mechanisms to discipline management. Examples are regulations and institutions dealing with information, monitoring and disciplining. With respect to the information issue, several regulations in the Anglo-Saxon model aim at transparency of the market and equal access to information. Management is legally obliged to inform shareholders in detail about the accounts of the corporation and the misuse of inside information is heavily fined. With respect to the monitoring issue, independent non-executive directors can be appointed as members of the board of directors, which monitors management on behalf of the shareholders. Because the CEO is often also chair of the board of directors and other executive managers are also members of the board of directors, the independent role of the latter is doubtful. Management is mainly disciplined by the threat to be taken over by competitors or raiders, who can restructure the corporation and replace management. An efficient market for corporate control is assumed to operate.

The Dutch corporate system is different. In the Netherlands the monitoring role of the shareholders is delegated to a supervisory board (Raad van Commissarissen: RvC), which monitors and disciplines the management board (Raad van Bestuur: RvB). The shareholders in their general meeting appoint both the RvC and the RvB, and approve the annual accounts. For large corporations (so-called 'structure corporations') with limited liability,[5] Dutch law provides special regulations which limit the power of the shareholders in favour of the supervisory board. The supervisory board is very powerful, because it appoints the management board and approves the accounts. Moreover, the members of the supervisory board are appointed by co-option: new members are elected by existing members.[6]

It is clear that the Dutch view of the firm differs from that of the Anglo-Saxon. In the Netherlands the firm is considered to be a system functioning in the interest of several stakeholders; the corporate governance should not serve only the interest of the shareholders, but also the interests of the employees. The supervisory board is responsible for the continuity of the firm in general, which implies an optimization of a diversity of interests. This view is expressed in the limitation of the power of the shareholders, in the view of management as a team with shared responsibilities and the chairman as the 'first among equals', and finally in the decision-making process. That is based on consensus building with the workers' council and the labour unions as important partners. The supervisory board is considered to be responsible for the long-term view and the stability in the relationships. The co-option system exists to secure stability. Often the members of the supervisory board are not very familiar with the special capabilities of the firm and the special characteristics of the sector and markets the firm operates in; running the firm is the responsibility of the management. Members of the supervisory board are often chosen because of their more general knowledge and their relations with politics, research institutions and the like. Members of the supervisory board are consulted about major investment decisions and decisions concerning the internal and external organization of the firm. Also a crisis in the board of management can be solved by the supervisory board, whose decisions may result in the dismissal of members of the management team.

DUTCH MARKET FOR CORPORATE CONTROL

The Dutch system provides instruments through the use of which corporations can often avoid buyouts and takeovers. Because of the limited power of the shareholders, the interest in taking over a Dutch firm is reduced. It is, however, possible in specific conditions to overrule the structural model and to give in to the wishes of a raider (Voogd 1989). In order to protect themselves more effectively, Dutch firms can make use of an additional set of protection measures. Consideration of anti-takeover devices is the heart of any discussion about the Dutch corporate governance.

Until recently firms could make cumulative use of several protection barriers:

1. Preference shares: These shares give holders specific voting rights, as well as a right to a fixed dividend percentage before the ordinary shareholders can claim their rights. These shares are not traded on the stock market. Mostly management is mandated by the General Meeting to issue preference shares. Usually the preference shares are held by a friendly foundation.
2. Priority shares: Priority shares give the holders exclusive rights in major decisions like the proposing and dismissal of board members, changes in the statutes, the issue of new shares, the liquidation of the firm, and the like. These shares are also mostly concentrated in a friendly foundation.
3. Certificates of an administrative office: In this case the shares are sold to an administrative office, which issues in return tradeable certificates. The voting power remains in the hands of the administrative office. In an extreme version, the certificates cannot be exchanged for ordinary shares.

4. Small firms with limited liability which are not subject to the special 'structural regime' can make the rule that the general meeting elects the members of the boards out of a binding nomination of at least two persons for every seat. Such a binding nomination can only be overruled by a two-thirds majority.
5. Restrictions on the total number of votes are allowed in the Netherlands, but this protection device is mostly not very effective, because it can be circumvented by straw men at the general meeting.

Well-known anti-takeover measures from Anglo-Saxon countries like the 'poison pill' and 'crown jewels' are not so common in the Netherlands.[7]

Recent Developments in the Dutch Market for Corporate Control

In its annual report of 1985 the board of the Association of the Amsterdam Stock Exchange (Vereniging van Effectenhandelaren) suggested a relation between the limited numbers of shares traded and the relatively low prices on the one hand and the existence of many well-protected firms in the Netherlands on the other. In the discussion that followed also the more general relation between efficiency and protection measures was debated. In 1987 that theoretical discussion mirrored reality when for the Netherlands an unusual takeover fight developed in the publishing industry (Elsevier and Kluwer). In the meantime a committee was established and reported in a majority decision that the existing protection measures should be maintained. The argument was that Dutch firms should be able to prevent the sale of important parts of the Dutch industrial structure, because such a sale runs the risk of 'asset stripping', the transfer of highly valued parts of the firm, such as R&D facilities, to other countries, with significant negative consequences for Dutch industrial networks and well-educated employees. However, a minority of the committee did not agree with the positive view on protection measures and saw good reasons to forbid a limitless cumulation of protection devices. Interesting was the fact that the board of the Amsterdam Stock Exchange made clear that it agreed with the minority. From their point of view the function of protection measures in the Dutch institutional structure provides the possibility for management to weigh the interest of the different stakeholders. For that function it is not necessary to protect the firm with a cumulation of all kinds of protection measures, but a maximum of two protection devices should be sufficient.

In reaction to the position of the board of the Amsterdam Stock Exchange, the firms listed on the stock exchange organized themselves in 1988 into the 'Association of Listed Firms' (Vereniging van Effecten Uitgevende Ondernemingen). The firms feared a breakdown of protection measures, which was considered a real danger, especially for the medium sized, relatively cheap, but well-performing firms.

Meanwhile Dutch politicians had received a request from the European Union to come up with a proposal about how to harmonize Dutch law with the more Anglo-Saxon model.[8] The Dutch Minister of Finance favoured, in line with the Dutch institutional context, a form of self-regulation and invited the two parties (the Amsterdam Stock Exchange and the Association of Listed Firms) to come up with proposals in which their conflicting views would be harmonized. After difficult discussions a temporary compromise was reached: in the so-called Annex X of the stock market regulations it was stated that a firm could not have more than two protection devices and the certificates that could not be exchanged for ordinary shares (so-called 'ncrs') were forbidden.

At the Ministry of Finance politicians could not make up their mind about the compromise and ordered the two parties involved to produce a more detailed form of self-regulation to be approved by government before 1 April 1995. The Minister added as a general guideline that the agreement should not offer management of firms 'the possibility to protect themselves permanently from the majority of the shareholders'. After discussion the idea of an independent panel turned out to be acceptable to both parties. Such a panel should be created according to the British example. An independent panel of arbitrage should decide about the continuation of the protection measures. The discussion between the board of the Stock Exchange and the Association of Listed Companies concentrated on three issues: the number of shares a majority party should have before it could ask the panel's arbitrage, the duration of the period after which that majority could involve the panel ('cool down period') and the criteria of evaluation the panel should apply. A little bit later than the deadline, a compromise was reached and made public on 8 May 1995. It specified that:

1. A shareholder with a majority of 70 per cent can after 18 months ask a specific takeover panel, consisting of independent experts, to forbid the protection devices of the firm.
2. The panel has to take into consideration not only procedural issues, but also issues of business policy such as: what is the identity and reputation of the bidder? What are her/his intentions with the firm? What are the strategies of incumbent management? What are the possibilities of implementing their policy statements? What are the consequences of the different policies for the different stakeholders?

The Minister of Finance was not completely satisfied yet and asked for more details about the independence of the panel members and the criteria they should apply. In general the Minister seemed to be in favour of the possibility of takeovers, unless it was proven that such action should be prevented because of negative consequences for the 'General Interest'. He expected an answer by 1 October 1995. The answer arrived at the Ministry on 29 September: The parties held to their earlier proposal but were more specific about the responsibilities of the 'panel'. The existing *Ondernemingskamer* (a unique Dutch institution which is a chamber where conflicts within and between firms are settled) has to evaluate the procedural aspects of the issue; in addition a new committee of this chamber has to evaluate the elimination of protection measures. It is expected that such a procedure will take seven to eight months. As of December 1996, the Minister of Finance has not sent a draft law to parliament; the necessary consensus is still not reached.

Before evaluating the Dutch case from an evolutionary institutional perspective, we put things in a wider perspective with consideration of the status of corporate governance in Germany, Japan and France.

A COMPARISON: GERMANY, JAPAN AND FRANCE

The Netherlands fits well into the Continental model, but like every country it has its own specific characteristics. In order to get a better idea of the Continental model (also called the 'Organized' or 'Network Model', see Moerland 1995) we discuss in this section the situation in Germany, Japan and France.

In Germany historically the banks have played a pivotal role in the economy. In the system of *Universalbanken*, banks can undertake all kinds of different financial activities in the commercial, investment and insurance business (Schulz 1995). Banks in Germany hold shares of individual corporations and have representatives on the supervisory boards of the firms. Banks as lenders, as well as shareholders, strengthen the long-term nature of relationships. Banks have access to strategic information, are involved in strategic decision making and create a stable financial environment for management. The financial relationship is reflected in the banks' voting power based on their own shareholding, as well as on the shares deposited with them by their clients. Moreover, the representative of the bank is often appointed as chairman of that board. The close relationship between banks and firms makes hostile takeovers exceptional in Germany.

The role of banks in Japan has similarities with Germany: cross-stockholding, loans and interlocking directorates of the 'group bank' make the bank an important 'lender of last resort' and responsible for the reconstruction process of the firm in case things go wrong. The bank plays an important disciplining role for management and replaces the market for corporate control in that respect. Because of these close relationships and the minor importance of the equity market, hostile takeovers are very rare in Japan (Groenewegen 1995). However, internal and external developments are forcing the Japanese to question their system of corporate governance. Is it not necessary to introduce elements of the Anglo-Saxon model into the Japanese system? Signs which point in that direction can be found in recent policy measures. The position of shareholders has been strengthened and the possibility of selling firms has been improved. In 1989 the tax law was changed: proceeds from sales of firms are taxed at 29 per cent of the sale price (before 1989 the proceeds had to be added to income). The Ministry of International Trade and Industry (MITI) promoted foreign investment by allowing foreigners (owning more than one-third of the stock) to carry forward losses in the first three years to set off against taxable income for seven years. Since 1 August 1992 foreigners are no longer banned from buying shares of partially privatized utilities to a maximum of 20 per cent. MITI launched a consulting company to advise foreign firms on takeovers. The costs of lawsuits by shareholders against management decreased to 8200 yen per case. Large companies were obliged to appoint an independent auditor. Many more measures to improve the position of the shareholders are expected, but what does that really mean?

These developments should be evaluated in the institutional structure in which the industrial groupings play an important role. If cross-stockholding continues to exist, and if banks continue their supervisory role, then the underlying structures of the Japanese system of corporate governance remain intact. Recent research of the Fair Trade Commission shows a stability and increase in the cross-stockholdings among group members, which indicates continuity in the relationships among the firms in the Japanese groups. In other words, the basic disciplining mechanisms remain.

Also the other relations among Japanese firms (loans, intermediary goods, interlocking directorates, members of President Clubs) show a strong stability. This does not mean that no changes occur, but it does show that the fundamental characteristics remain intact. The existing system serves the interests of the main actors well and there is no reason to change the fundamental institutions. The changes listed above are first of all signals to the outside world (especially the US), but they are largely cosmetic.

To understand why the need for an Anglo-Saxon market for corporate control is not felt in Japan, one needs to study the total system of disciplinary mechanisms in its historical setting. Kester (1991) explains the absence of the need for takeover pressure as a consequence of the existence of other disciplinary mechanisms in the Japanese system. Kester points to two objectives of takeovers. One has to do with 'trading hazards' (uncertainty, opportunism in the supply of intermediary products) and the other with shirking of management (so-called 'downward opportunism'). Vertical integration through takeovers aims at avoiding these 'moral hazards', which the Japanese corporate governance system efficiently reduces with the subcontracting relations and the exchange of intermediate goods between firms belonging to the same group. The second issue of agency problems can be controlled with a market for corporate control, but the Japanese system provides for business groups as a substitute disciplining mechanism. Information exchange inside the business group and informal control mechanisms provide for an effective pressure on management. That is not to say that Japanese firms perform efficiently in the same sense as the American ones. On the contrary: 'efficiency is contextual' (Goldberg 1980), which means that within the specific institutional context of Japan, stakeholders look for disciplining mechanisms which result in an efficient allocation of resources. So in the Japanese context, government regulations and organizational business structures can be very efficient in organizing the transaction of an intermediate product in a subcontracting relation, whereas the same transaction in the US is efficiently organized in a vertically integrated firm. But there is more: the contents of the concept of efficiency can differ from one context to another. It is a well-known fact that in the Japanese context long-term dynamic efficiency prevails over the short-term static one. In other words, institutional context, efficiency and pressure to change the institutional context are interrelated.

In the Latin countries of Europe often a combination of state ownership, financial holdings and cross-stockholding can be found: stock markets are underdeveloped. Also here interesting developments take place and France is a case in point.

In France the fundamental concern is to make the capital market more attractive for foreign investors without giving up specific French characteristics. The French system is often characterized as '*capitalism sans capital*' (capitalism without capital), that is to say, management is autonomous and independent of shareholders. One speaks about management as a '*conception monarchique*' (the president of the firm is a king). The independent position of the 'President-Directeur Général' (PDG) is based on the law of 1966 which creates the possibility of countervailing powers, but these have never materialized. Close relations between top management and civil servants, as well as politics through the *corps d'état*, make the state a disciplining force which has been successful in some 'Grands Programmes' (nuclear energy, telecommunications, transport), but has been a complete failure in others (machine tools, consumer electronics, computers). The discussion in France[9] focuses on the question of whether it is necessary and possible to integrate part of the Anglo-Saxon model into the French one in order to make French firms more attractive for foreign capital. In short, is it possible to give shareholders a more dominant position so they are willing to supply risk capital? Then the dominant role of the state, the close links between the state and large industrial groups, the cross-stockholding between the nucleole of the economic system are all questioned. The internal control of corporate governance would be supplemented or complemented with external control from the capital market. Proposed is a *conseil d'administration* which consists of three parties: one part executive directors (the management), one part non-executive directors appointed by the shareholders and one part independent non-executive directors elected on the basis of their expertise. The PDG is responsible to the council.

Also new committees which monitor and control management are suggested: one that controls the accounts and another that makes the nomination for the successor of the PDG. Clearly, this new structure is intended to give stake-holders more information about the firm and performance of management and more power to control. Also in the French case we observe the introduction of elements from the Anglo-Saxon model, but actors are very well aware of the blessings of their own system. So instead of a convergence we suggest a divergence thesis; the different systems import elements from each other, but their fundamental characteristics remain the same.

EMPIRICAL EVIDENCE ABOUT PERFORMANCES OF DIFFERENT SYSTEMS OF CORPORATE GOVERNANCE

In the discussion about the need for changing existing systems of corporate governance, the performances of the different systems should play a central role. However, measuring performances is not the thing economists do best. Measurements are difficult because firms provide very distorted information in their annual reports (how to lie with statistics about profit) and because of the diversity of criteria that can be used for measuring performances. De Jong (1995) has published interesting figures showing the differences between Continental and British firms as representatives of the models presented above. As one criterion of comparison, net value added per employee (NVA/E) was calculated for 100 of the largest European firms. Net value added is revenue from sales minus costs of inputs. This gross value added minus depreciation results in net value added and divided by the number of employees gives a good indication of the performance of firms. The results are: 60 per cent of Continental firms and 27 per cent of Anglo-Saxon firms had higher than average NVA/E scores in 1991 and 1992, that accordingly the Continental firms show much better performances than the Anglo-Saxon firms. The share of Anglo-Saxon firms in the 500 largest firms worldwide has fallen drastically in the last 25 years. What is striking is that the number of British firms that do not do well using the NVA/E index is sector-wide; only very few UK-based firms meet the Continental performance: British Airways, Glaxo, Smith-Kline Beecham and Shell do well in their respective sectors.

With respect to the criteria of profitability and dividends to capital suppliers, the British firms score much higher than the Continentals: British firms pay 20 per cent on average to shareholders whereas the Continentals pay 10 per cent. There seems to be a clash between profitability and value added. The system of Anglo-Saxon corporate governance maximizes profitability and value for shareholders, whereas the Continental system stimulates growth and value added. The Continental system takes the interest of more stakeholders into account whereas the Anglo-Saxon system is really capitalistic in the sense that shareholders are the primary beneficiaries.

THE ART OF INSTITUTIONALIZATION

Elsewhere we have discussed the need for an interdisciplinary approach for
understanding, explaining and managing corporate systems (Groenewegen and
Vromen 1996). From the insights of the theory of institutional change as
presented by Bush (1987) we learn that an interdisciplinary understanding of
the characteristics and developments of institutions, such as the Dutch system
of corporate governance, is an extremely complicated matter. Internal as well
as external pressures are involved as well as rigidities due to existing interests
and structures. For example, external pressures to change the Dutch system are
generated by the EU and are resisted by important actors in the Dutch economic
and political system. In understanding the character and significance of these
pressures the distinction between ceremonial and instrumental functions in
institutions is helpful. By ceremonial institutions Thorstein Veblen referred to
arrangements that served the interests of specific power groups; instrumental
functions in institutions serve the progress of society generally. The concept of
the 'institutional space' becomes relevant: in employing this distinction what
is the room for manoeuvring within the existing or modified institutional
structure? Actors can mobilize internal pressures and explore the institutional
space available. But whose interests do those pressures serve? Narrow private
interests or broader public concerns? For what decision purposes is the
institutional space being used? Important for understanding changes in existing
institutions, like the proposal of the arbitrage panel in the Dutch case, is first
of all an understanding of the complexities of existing organizations, the
coordinating mechanisms, the pressures and structures, as well as the purposive
interests of the main actors involved. From that understanding a recognition of
the growth of society's knowledge fund (Bush 1987) permits the drafting of
needed changes in our system of corporate governance in order to maintain our
competitiveness, to achieve the instrumental value of such change to demolish
the ceremonial practices involved and finally to use the institutional space
available to act to implement the institutional changes so designed and justified
(Tool 1985).

Analysing the information about the existing Dutch institutional structure,
the system of corporate governance, its performances, the discussion among the
board of the Amsterdam Stock Exchange and the listed firms, we come to the
conclusion that the Dutch independent panel is an institutional solution that fits
well into the existing structure yet enhances prospects for decision making that
serves instrumental public purposes.

The Dutch system of organized markets is under heavy attack from
ideologists. The phantom of deregulation, privatization, strong competition or,
in short, more market, is the normative cliché. The argument is that the

institutional structure of norms, rules and structures hampers competition and entrepreneurship. The message to government is simple: create markets with structures that guarantee strong competition (many suppliers, independent decision making) and forbid regulations which distort flexible pricing. Then automatically the performance will be economically efficient.

This view is contested by the institutional-evolutionary approach: markets are not neutral selectors, but filter the interests of different actors. Markets can be effective, but whose goals are served? Markets can be efficient, but whose means are used? In other words, markets are embedded in an institutional structure which makes efficiency 'contextual'; different values and norms, formal and informal rules and different structures, all result in different behaviour of actors and different economic processes of production, distribution and consumption; the processes result in different performances in terms of allocative and dynamic efficiencies. The idea that a neutral selection mechanism exists is something to be proven; in the real world such markets are exceptions instead of the rule.

All this is not to say that markets and competition cannot be efficient: competition between rivals with equal power struggling in more or less stable environments forces entrepreneurs to look for production cost minimization through new combinations of inputs, for improvements of the product and service, to lower prices and to organize production so that transactions costs are reduced. Regulations and structures which hamper such 'healthy competition' should not be allowed in market economies.

However, such corrected markets can also easily fail: political scientists and neo-institutionalists point to the role of interest groups, of ideology and of limited knowledge, which all make it plausible that efficient institutions do not emerge.

Instead of assuming an efficient process of institutionalization based on maximizing individuals being controlled by an anonymous competitive selection process, neo-institutionalists point to the necessity for careful analysis of the process, an understanding of the interests of the actors involved, and a grasp of the complex interdependencies in specific situations. Only with a better understanding of the process of institutionalization that actually explains the behaviour of the parties involved, can recommendations be made for effective government policies. Such governmental policies should reflect the 'art of institutionalization'. A government that wants to increase instrumental efficiency by means of, for instance, a change in the legal rules, ought to be well aware of the existing institutional context, the objectives of the different actors involved, and the interdependencies of the economic system.

It is our understanding that the Dutch system of corporate governance described above is a good example of efficient institutionalization. The draft law fits well into the existing Dutch institutional structure, and introduces elements from the Anglo-Saxon model that reduce rigidities without disturbing the basic instrumental features of the Dutch model. The decision-making process has been and still is efficient, not in the sense that decisions are quickly taken, but in the sense that all stakeholders are involved and that no interest group dominates the process. That nature of the decision-making process is fundamental to 'instrumental valuation' and deserves to be called 'civilized capitalism' (see Groenewegen 1997).

NOTES

1. H.W. de Jong (1995) distinguishes between three models: the Anglo-Saxon (free market capitalism), the German type (social market capitalism) and the Latin type of capitalism. In the latter family control, state enterprises and financial groupings are important characteristics.
2. In classical contracts the conditions, rights and obligations are specified in detail contrary to relational contracts.
3. This has probably to do with the first associations responsible for water control. Polders need a very precise regulation of the water system and all participants must obey the rules strictly. That is literally a matter of life and death. These associations ('Waterschappen') still play an important role although their legislative powers are reduced. In Japan group-orientedness also plays an important role which could be traced back to the management of the rice fields.
4. Dutch competition law will be changed from an abuse system (agreements are allowed, unless . . .) to a system which forbids certain agreements between firms. It is an attempt to harmonize policies in Europe (see Groenewegen 1994).
5. A firm is large when subscribed capital amounts to at least 22.5 million guilders, the firm employs at least 100 persons and the firm has a so-called workers' council, which advises the management board on behalf of the employees. When these conditions are fulfilled the firm is called a 'structure corporation' (*structuurvennootschap*) and is then subject to the special legal regulations.
6. Although the Dutch system has many similarities with the German one there are also important differences. First the German system does not have the co-option system; second the German system has a legal division of seats in the supervisory board between representatives of employees and shareholders; and third the appointment of the members of the management board in Germany is limited to a specific period, typically of five years.
7. With a poison pill, management tries to make the takeover less attractive, for instance by the right of incumbent shareholders to buy new shares at a low price, which then have to be bought by the raider for the high market price. A crown jewel is the part of the firm with most value added; that jewel can be sold separately to a friendly firm (the so-called 'white knight').
8. In the past Margaret Thatcher had urged EU commissioner Bangemann to start the process of harmonization of the laws concerning protection measures. It was considered unacceptable that British firms could be easily taken over by German, Dutch or Swiss firms, which themselves were protected against foreign takeovers.
9. See, for instance, *Le Monde* 28 March, 1995: 'Un rapport patronal vante les mérites du "capitalisme a la française"'. *Le Monde*, 27 April, 1995: 'Le débat sur "le pouvoir dans l'enterprise" partage le monde patronal'. See also: Christian Saint-Etienne 1995 and Ezra N. Suleiman 1995.

REFERENCES

Bush, Paul D. (1987), 'The Theory of Institutional Change', *Journal of Economic Issues*, **21**, pp. 1075–116.

De Jong, H.W. (1995), 'European Capitalism: Between Freedom and Social Justice', paper delivered at the F. de Vries Lectures, Erasmus University Rotterdam.

Goldberg, V. (1980), 'Relational Exchange Economics and Complex Contracts', *American Behavioural Scientist*, **23** (3), pp. 337–52.

Groenewegen, J. (1994), 'About Double Organized Markets: Issues of Competition and Cooperation', *Journal of Economic Issues*, **28** (3), September, pp. 901–8.

_____(1995), 'A Changing Japanese Market for Corporate Control', in J. Groenewegen, C. Pitelis and S.E. Sjöstrand (eds), *On Economic Institutions*, Aldershot: Edward Elgar.

_____(1997), 'Institutions of Capitalism: US, Europe and Japan Compared', *Journal of Economic Issues*, **31**, June, pp. 333–47.

_____ and Jack J. Vromen (1996), 'A Case for Theoretical Pluralism', in J. Groenewegen (ed.), *Transaction Cost Economics and Beyond*, Boston: Kluwer Academic Publishers.

Johnson, C. (1982), *Miti and the Japanese Miracle*, Palo Alto: Stanford University Press.

Kester, W.C. (1991), *Japanese Takeovers: The Global Contest for Corporate Control*, Boston: Harvard Business School Press.

Moerland, P.W. (1995), 'Alternative Disciplinary Mechanisms in Different Corporate Systems', *Journal of Economic Behaviour and Organization*, **26**, pp. 17–34.

Saint-Etienne, C. (1995), *Le Combat de la France*, Paris: Editions ESKA.

Schulz, C. (1995), 'Towards a Compound Approach of Internal and External Capital Markets', mimeo, Erasmus University Rotterdam.

Suleiman, E.N. (1995), *Les Ressorts Cachés de la Réussite Française*, Paris: Editions de Seuil.

Tool, M.R. (1985), *The Discretionary Economy: A Normative Theory of Political Economy*, Boulder: Westview Press.

Voogd, R.P. (1989), *Statutaire Beschermingsmiddelen bij Beursvennootschappen. Monografieën vanwege het van de Hijden-Instituut*, Deventer: Kluwer.

7. Science, Ethics and Democracy: Towards an Institutional Version of Ecological Economics

Peter Söderbaum

Most actors in society associate science with objectivity and value neutrality. The scientist seeks truth and stands outside the phenomena observed. However, an increasing number of scholars, and perhaps especially in the social sciences, have begun to understand that this is only part of the story. According to one line of reasoning, values and ideology influence research work in a variety of ways. The reasons why one scholar believes in a particular theoretical perspective or paradigm, such as neoclassical economics, while another regards a different theoretical outlook as fruitful, say institutional economics, may reflect differences in ideology, moral preferences – even opportunism. 'Reality' is perhaps not out there, apart from the observer; rather, 'reality' can be perceived as socially constructed where ethics and ideology to some degree influence what is constructed and made visible.

Some role will remain for objectivity. But traditional ideas of only one truth or true paradigm will have to be abandoned. Pluralism and a degree of humility seem to be warranted. Truth can be regarded as relative to the chosen perspective and there are typically more perspectives than one in relation to a particular phenomenon.

Environmental problems, the focus of this essay, exemplify an area where many ideologies and theoretical perspectives meet. To single out one ideology or ethical standpoint with connected paradigm as the 'correct' one seems to me to contradict prevailing ideas of democracy. Science can illuminate and expand our understanding of a societal issue, but it should not seek to point out a single solution for issues which are in part political and ideological.

If the idea of value neutrality is abandoned in some respects, the whole issue of the scholar's role will change. It then becomes natural and even necessary to openly declare one's position with respect to values and ideology. For example, a single scholar or a group of scholars affiliated to a university department, research institute or international research association may take a stand in favour of ecological sustainability, for instance by choosing to work in the spirit of the 1992 United Nations Conference in Rio de Janeiro and its Agenda 21. According to this view, mission statements are as relevant for universities and research institutes as for business corporations or environmental organizations.

In this chapter, I discuss issues of epistemology and paradigm in relation to environmental problems, suggesting that our ideas of Man as a scholar and of Man in other roles are of importance in attempts to develop a more productive conceptual framework than that of mainstream neoclassical microeconomics.

PROBLEMS OF ENVIRONMENT AND DEVELOPMENT

The evolution of science and of universities has long been characterized by specialization and compartmentalization. Connected with this development is the strengthening of a belief that not only scientific problems (in some limited sense) but even societal problems can be solved within the scope of a single discipline. What is now becoming increasingly understood is that most societal issues – and environmental problems belong to this category – are multidimensional and multifactorial by nature. They require transdisciplinary approaches rather than single discipline approaches.

One aspect of this recognition that environmental problems span different disciplines is the understanding that problems do not reside exclusively 'out there in the fields'. While the measurement of environmental parameters, such as the pH value of a lake at a particular place for succeeding points in time, is important, it is at the same time increasingly understood that there is a human side to the problems observed. Human beings, our organizations and society at large, all influence what goes on in the lake and in the environment more generally and human beings are led by their world views, ideologies and ethical considerations. This means that world view, ideology, ethics and related scientific perspectives have to be considered as part of any attempt to alleviate pollution of lakes and rivers or improve the state of the environment at large. It can no longer be assumed, for instance, that there is a consensus in society about the objectives of macroeconomic development or that these objectives can be condensed to growth in GNP terms. Scholars are becoming increasingly sensitive to the many ethical and ideological issues involved.

Related to values and ideology are the institutional circumstances, that is issues of law, organization, power relationships and conflicts of interest. Is it enough to modify present institutions in order to deal with the environmental problems that we now face, or are radical institutional changes required? While encouraging minor changes that can improve the state of the environment, we should not exclude the possibility of more fundamental institutional reforms. In contemplating such possibilities, some degree of pluralism would appear to be required.

WHAT IS ECOLOGICAL ECONOMICS?

Ecological economics can be described as a field of study rather than a single discipline. Problems related to environment and development are the starting point. As the term suggests, it is an area for transdisciplinary studies where the more traditional disciplines of ecology and economics meet. In addition to the disciplines mentioned, a number of other social, humanistic, natural and engineering sciences as well as law can contribute to an understanding of environmental issues and ways of dealing with them. In the specific version of ecological economics emphasized here, economics and management sciences are at the heart of an interdisciplinary analysis.

As alluded to in the introduction to this essay, ecological economics is value-driven. Although there may be differences in interpretation and definition, scholars taking part in this project are committed to an ecologically sustainable development.

Pluralism with respect to epistemology and paradigm is a further characteristic of ecological economics, meaning that different, even conflicting, theoretical perspectives can exist side by side. In his *Ecological Economics* article, Robert Costanza, as editor of the journal, maintained that a large measure of 'conceptual pluralism' is warranted. There is probably not one right approach or paradigm. This point was further elaborated as follows:

> Environmental and resource economics, as it is currently practised, covers only the application of neoclassical economics to environmental and resource problems. Ecology, as it is currently practised, sometimes deals with human impacts on ecosystems, but the more common tendency is to stick to 'natural' systems. Ecological Economics aims to extend these modest areas of overlap. It will include neoclassical environmental economics and ecological impact studies as subsets, but will also encourage new ways of thinking about the linkages between ecological and economic systems. (1989, p. 1)

Neoclassical economics represents the mainstream at most departments of economics in Europe, the USA and perhaps more generally in the world. Neoclassical environmental economics – or 'resource economics' as in the above quotation – is simply an extension of the neoclassical paradigm to cover a specific set of environmental problems.

Neoclassical economics can be described as a paradigm or theoretical perspective where the idea is to imitate physics and other natural sciences as faithfully as possible – more precisely the state of these disciplines at the time when the neoclassical paradigm was first articulated – with respect to epistemology, equilibrium thinking and an ideal of mathematical modelling. This theory furthermore relies on a specific version of ethics connected with utilitarianism and hardly raises the kind of moral issues that will be addressed here.

Institutional economics, on the other hand, which is the preference of the present author, strives to incorporate knowledge from other social disciplines such as sociology, psychology, educational science, political science, business studies and so on. Though a minority current within economics, it can – and should – be seen as part of a mainstream within social sciences as a whole. Institutional economics is more sensitive to different kinds of ethical reasoning and the spectrum of political ideologies in our societies. For this reason 'political economics' is more informative as the name of the discipline.

Briefly, institutional economics: (a) emphasizes historical, evolutionary patterns of events (rather than equilibrium analysis); (b) is thereby more related to biology, ecology and social sciences (outside economics) than to physics; (c) is more open-ended in its logic and relies partly on fragmentary patterns and images (rather than closed mathematical models); (d) emphasizes 'institutions' defined as 'rules of the game', power relationships, resource endowments and organizational factors as important objects of study; and, finally (e) is more sensitive to valuational and ideological issues than are colleagues in the neoclassical camp.

Here, I will only elaborate on the final point by quoting one of my favourite institutional writers, Gunnar Myrdal:

> Valuations are always with us. Disinterested research there has never been and can never be. Prior to answers there must be questions. There can be no view except from a viewpoint. In the questions raised and the viewpoint chosen, valuations are implied.
>
> Our valuations determine our approaches to a problem, the definition of our concepts, the choice of models, the selection of our observations, the presentations of our conclusions – in fact, the whole pursuit of a study from beginning to end . . .
>
> In this context I have argued for, and in my own research from *An American Dilemma* onward have tried to observe, the necessity in any scientific undertaking of stating, clearly and explicitly, the value principles which are instrumental. They are needed not only for establishing relevant facts but also for drawing policy conclusions. (Myrdal 1978, pp. 778–9)

In what follows, I will emphasize this valuational or ideological orientation not only of the scholar but also of the individuals in society that we observe and interact with in various ways. Contrary to Myrdal, I will often use the word 'ideology' rather than speak generally about values. A simple definition of ideology is 'ideas about means and ends' or 'means–ends philosophy'. Ideology, then, is not limited to the usual established political ideologies like socialism, liberalism, conservatism and the more recent ecologism and feminism (Eccleshall et al. 1994), but includes ideas about means and ends in more limited areas of application such as health care ideologies (differing with respect to centralization/decentralization, for instance) or environmental ideologies (where degree of technological optimism can be a distinguishing characteristic). This view is broadly in accordance with Douglass North's definition: 'By ideology I mean the subjective perceptions (models, theories) all people possess to explain the world around them' (North 1990, p. 23).

PLURALISM, DEMOCRACY AND 'PARADIGM CO-EXISTENCE'

It has already been suggested that monism, that is reliance on a single perspective, may be an important part of the problem. If that is the case, movements in the direction of pluralism can be part of a solution. Most neoclassical economists believe firmly in monism even though much of their message – applied at a meta-level – ought instead to point in the direction of pluralism. I am thinking of the opportunity cost principle, meaning that alternatives should always be considered and be systematically compared. Similarly, arguments among neoclassicists in favour of competition rather than monopoly as means of improving efficiency suggest that views that compete with the neoclassical paradigm should be encouraged. Related to the idea that competition is a good thing is the idea of the consumer's sovereignty. At a meta-level one may think of 'supply' and 'demand' of concepts and theories. If economists supply ideas in this 'market', men of 'practical affairs' may appear on the demand side as consumers of ideas. But again, if only one commodity (neoclassical economics) is supplied and if there is an interest in alternative ideas, our consumer will not be 'free to choose', to use the language of Milton Friedman.

Epistemology in Table 7.1 refers to 'theory of science'. It includes a view of the scholar in relation to the subject matter that represents his interest of study and how he relates to other individuals. Paradigm is equivalent to 'theoretical perspective' and 'ideology', as already indicated, to means–ends relationships at a societal level, or in specific areas of human concern. Ethics in turn is concerned with values, 'oughts', purposes and so on concerning relationships between individuals and with Nature. Epistemology, paradigm and ideology in

Table 7.1   There is an epistemological as well as paradigmatic and ideological side to the debate about monism versus pluralism

Aspects	Monism	Pluralism
Epistemological	I	II
Paradigmatic	III	IV
Ideological/ethical	V	V

Table 7.1 should be understood as aspects of human perspectives and not as categories that can be readily separated. One of the main arguments of this essay is that neoclassical economics as a paradigm is connected with, and indeed in many ways is inseparable from, ideology and epistemology. The three concepts of epistemology, paradigm and ideology are overlapping. If one desires to emphasize the completeness of a perspective, including all three elements, the term 'world view' can be used.

Thomas Kuhn's idea of 'paradigm shift' (Kuhn 1970) is basically connected with monism (compare I, III and V). At a point in time, only one theory of science, paradigm and related ideology is regarded as the correct one or as representing the truth. Anomalies may appear in the sense that certain facts are incompatible with the prevailing model. This in turn may lead to a search for a new explanatory model which can accommodate these new facts. If such a model is devised and accepted, it replaces the previous one and a paradigm shift has occurred.

I think that this view of the world, where one paradigm completely replaces another and where only one perspective is seen as correct at a time, has to be modified. At times it can even be a dangerous idea, leading to tensions and confrontations within the scientific community and elsewhere, which may actually hinder progress. Regarding economics for example, neoclassicists who hear about institutionalism may become unnecessarily alarmed. As part of a monistic view of science, only one paradigm can be correct: 'If they (the institutionalists) are right, we must be wrong. Since our knowledge is useful in many ways, they must be wrong'.

Pluralism and 'paradigm co-existence' seems to me to be a much more fruitful basic principle (compare II, IV and VI). Georg Henrik von Wright observes that there is a role for complementarity even in the natural sciences. Light as a phenomenon can be interpreted as part of a theory of particles, but also as part of a theory based on waves (von Wright 1986). Each of these two perspectives – which (according to present knowledge) are logically incompatible – contributes to an understanding of light as a phenomenon. The wave theory adds to the understanding offered by the particles theory and vice versa. Relying exclusively on one of the two theories will limit our understanding of light as a phenomenon. Von Wright refers to Niels Bohr, who argued that both models have to be accepted. They are at the same time mutually exclusive and complementary. Bohr pointed to a number of examples and suggested a more general theory of the complementary aspects of reality.

Moving now to the social sciences, there are additional reasons for keeping an open mind. The history of economic thought or the history of sociology, psychology or political science over the past century suggests that there have always been competing perspectives. In economics, a Marxist version has played a role of challenger to neoclassicism. In the industrialized 'western' countries, the German Historical School and later the Institutionalism of

Thorstein Veblen and others were influential for long periods. In the USA, the latter had a substantial impact on New Deal policy in the 1930s. So, complementarity and paradigm co-existence seems to be a rule in social sciences rather than an exception.

In understanding the history of economic thought, an evolutionary perspective is useful. Theories and paradigms are born and survive for a time and may then fall into oblivion. The number of adherents to a particular paradigm may grow or decrease between two points in time. This means that the idea of 'paradigm shift' can still be used but only in a more limited sense of referring to a change in the 'dominant paradigm'. Paradigms are sometimes modified or may merge with other paradigms, as suggested by Alan Randall, a neoclassical environmental economist:

> The ultimate convergence of resource economists on the single true theory is an entirely false hope. The synthesis of the alternate schools of thought – a fond hope of many – is precluded for exactly the same reasons that preclude the climactic test (or series of tests) that eliminates all rival theories but one. Disagreement will be the norm, now and indefinitely, although the proximate foci of disagreement may change over time.
>
> It may be possible to misread this line of argument as implying that resource economics will be characterized, into the indefinite future, by endless disputes between institutionalists and neoclassicals with little change or progress in either paradigm and no generally applicable standards of excellence by which to make intra-paradigm or cross-paradigm evaluations of particular contributions. To the contrary, there will be intra-paradigm testing, leading to progress or degeneration in each paradigm. One or both schools may eventually be abandoned. Alternatively, paradigm shifts may occur as new evidence and novel argument lead to abandonment of some avenues and expansion of others. Institutionalism or the neoclassical school (or both) may achieve a partial synthesis with some newly emerging and not incompatible paradigm. Excellence will be pursued ubiquitously. However, some dimensions of excellence are universal (logical rigour, for example), for other dimensions the standards of excellence will be internal to the paradigm. (Randall 1986, p. 213)

One reason for a large measure of pluralism in the social sciences will be added here – the role of ideology. Since economics is coloured by values and ideology, the only way to prevent economics from becoming a one-sided propaganda force in society is pluralism. Monism in a social science which plays such a central role in public debate, can hardly be compatible with democracy.

Pluralism does not mean that all perspectives are equally valid or command the same number of advocates. The dynamism referred to by Randall rather means that the number of researchers associated with each paradigm changes over time. At a specific point in time, paradigm A may predominate, or two paradigms, A and B, may be of equal importance in terms of adherents. This means that Kuhn's argument in terms of paradigm-shift is still relevant, but only with respect to changes in 'dominant paradigm'.

With pluralism and paradigm co-existence as leading principles in the scientific community, truth becomes multi-faceted. Perspectives may be complementary, or contradict each other for logical and/or ideological reasons. This may stimulate further research, help clarify ideologies and provoke dialogue about values.

The need for pluralism and tolerance is further strengthened when one considers epistemology in relation to economics and social science in more general terms (compare I versus II in Table 7.1). A number of epistemological tensions can be identified (Table 7.2). Such tensions should not be understood

Table 7.2   Epistemological tensions within economics and other social sciences

Traditional ideas	Complementary (or alternate premises)
Mechanistic	Evolutionary
Value neutrality	Value presence
Reductionist	Holistic
Objectivity	Subjectivity (interpretative)
Universal regularities	Contextualism, uniqueness
Logically closed	Logically open-ended
Mathematical models	Pattern models (images and so on)
One-directional causation	Multi-directional causation
Optimize (solve)	Illuminate and mitigate conflicting interests
Disseminate knowledge	Cooperative learning (interaction)

Source: Modified and extended version of table in Norgaard 1994, p. 62.

in mere 'either/or' terms but also as 'both/and'. In other words, the two opposing poles need not be mutually exclusive. One distinction can be made between 'mechanistic' and 'evolutionary' thinking where neoclassical economics tends to be mechanistic while institutional economics is rather evolutionary. Furthermore, the epistemological position of 'value neutrality' can be compared with the idea that 'value colouring' is unavoidable and that value premises are chosen deliberately, at least in part.

An approach may furthermore be 'reductionist' rather than 'holistic'. Here, there seem to be two different interpretations of the opposite poles, one referring to the broadness of a concept or study, for instance micro versus macro in economics, the other concerning one-dimensional versus multidimensional approaches or analyses. Taking an example from economics, an institutionalist like myself regards cost–benefit analysis as a case of 'monetary reductionism'. Models may furthermore be closed in logical terms or more open-ended. Related to this is the distinction between the two ambitions of presenting a complete or fragmented picture of the world or of a sub-set of phenomena.

Another deviation from traditional ideas of objectivity is that of phenomenology, where the subjective and interpretative elements are considered. Attention to various actors and their messages and standpoints is important in 'narrative analysis' (Kohler Riessman 1993) for example. Similarly, the popularity of case studies in the social sciences means that the search for universal regularities or explanatory laws is played down, while uniqueness and contextualism increase in importance.

The ideas of explanation and prediction on the basis of models of one-directional causation are similarly giving way to more complex models or multi-directed causation (compare systems thinking) and interactive processes. In economics, sensitivity to value issues and the imperatives of democracy suggest that ideas of scientifically correct 'solutions' for an issue on the societal level often should be replaced by a more modest and fruitful attempt to 'illuminate' an issue. The role of the analyst is no longer concerned with dictating 'correct' or 'optimal' solutions (with reference to a mathematical objective function), so much as interacting with various actors and interested parties in a process of co-learning (learning from each other) about values and possible options. Dialogue, negotiations, consensus building and conflict management are features of this differing approach to decisions in a democratic society.

POLITICAL ECONOMIC MAN (WOMAN)

As argued earlier, there is a political element in social science studies. I will now go one step further by arguing that the political element is an important aspect of all human roles and all behaviour and thus not limited to the professional role as scholar in economics or the social sciences. It is assumed that Man is a political being and it will therefore be suggested that Economic Man be replaced by Political Economic Man. Or, to couch it in the vocabulary of an actor-network model, Man is perceived as an actor who is enmeshed in a web of social relationships.

A symbolic representation of Political Economic Man (Woman) is given in Figure 7.1. It is assumed that for each individual, there is a set of relevant roles, R1 to Rk, a set of relevant activities, A1 to Am and a set of relevant motives or interests, M1 to Mn. The role R1 is assumed to be connected with the activity (or set of activities) A1 and with the motive(s) M1. For the individual, the total set of roles is integrated as part of an 'identity', whereas the total set of activities forms a pattern referred to as a 'life-style'. The total set of motives or

Roles		Activities		Motives	
R1		A1		M1	
R2		A2		M2	
R3	'Identity'	A3	'Life-style'	M3	'Ideological orientation'
.		.		.	
.		.		.	
.		.		.	
Rk		Am		Mn	

Source: Söderbaum 1993.

Figure 7.1   Symbolic representation of Political Economic Man, that is, a holistic and integrated view of an individual with his or her various roles, activities and interests

interests in turn combines to a valuational or 'ideological profile'. Even 'world view' (or '*Weltanschauung*') is a relevant description for such a holistic orientation, comprising cognitive as well as valuational elements. R1 may represent the role of market actor; A1, market-related activities of buying, selling, investing, and so on; and M1, motives and interests related to this role and these activities. So-called Green Consumerism implies that market-related roles, relationships and activities are important in social change, but Figure 7.1 also suggests that other roles may be just as relevant in relation to environmental issues. R2 may refer to the role of man/woman as a parent, R3 as a member of an environmental organization, R3 as a professional, R4 as a citizen, and so on. In order to understand the behaviour of an individual, all these roles, activities and motives are potentially relevant.

The individual is seen as a social being, that is a person 'embedded' in a web of social relationships. In spite of tensions and conflicts between various motives and interests, the individual is somehow held together by ideas of his or her role or identity in relation to each specific socio-cultural context. Dissonance theory, learning theories and other parts of social psychology are seen as relevant and useful in understanding behaviour. The individual strives for some congruence and balance between roles, activities and interests, and may experience such balance, but incongruence and tensions are equally characteristics of the human existence.

Egoistic versus 'other-related' (or community-oriented) motives are an example of such tensions. This points to a view of man as a moral being where responsibility in relation to others and society at large becomes a potential issue. Amitai Etzioni, for instance, has propounded an 'I & We Paradigm'

(Etzioni 1988), according to which the existence of a strong ego in each healthy individual is not sufficient reason to denigrate or exclude the social and ethical aspect of human life. Each individual plays a part in many groups, that is 'we-contexts', and such relationships involve a number of tensions and ethical issues. (Ethics is, of course, also relevant for 'we–they' relationships, for instance in situations of conflict.) Similarly, Amartya Sen, an open-minded, mainly neoclassical economist, has argued in favour of explicit consideration of ethics as opposed to the 'engineering tradition' in economics (Sen 1987).

While neoclassicists tend to see individuals as robot-like, optimizers who instantly react to price signals, institutionalists and many other social scientists point rather to the important role of habits in human behaviour. The individual is largely 'locked into' specific habits of thought and specific habitual activities that together form a pattern, referred to here as a life-style. At an early stage, Herbert Simon pointed to selective perception, limited cognitive capacity and search costs as relevant to an understanding of human behaviour (Simon 1945). As humans we tend to stick to familiar environments and use various rules of thumb to deal with complexity. However, this emphasis on habitual behaviour does not exclude the possibility of 'problemistic search' and conscious decision making. At times the individual perceives a problem and alternative courses of action. Habits are reconsidered and behaviour may change.

The theory of the consumer as part of neoclassical microeconomics is of some relevance when discussing environmental policy issues, for instance expected impacts of eco-taxes. Neoclassical public choice theory is similarly useful for understanding possible behaviour of individuals in professional roles. But a more holistic attempt to integrate various human roles seems to be warranted. The theory of the consumer is limited not only in the sense that one human role is emphasized at the expense of all others. Moreover, consumer tastes and preferences are taken as given. As part of an imagined value neutrality, the neoclassical scholar regards it as external to his or her role to problematize the values and life-styles of consumers. But if, as many suggest, environmental problems are connected with present consumer tastes and life-styles and more generally with dominant world views in industrialized countries, then the neoclassical approach implies that essential aspects of the problems faced are overlooked. Focusing instead on Political Economic Man and ideological orientation means that the different consumer preferences and life-styles of two individuals are no longer regarded as equally justified. Supported by a simultaneous, facilitating public policy or not, individuals may move in a step by step manner away from life-styles that are environmentally destructive toward those that are environmentally more beneficial. But again, whether such moves represent an advance is a matter of ethics and ideological orientation of the observer. In my judgement and in accordance with the Rio Declaration mentioned earlier, environmental sustainability *is* such an advance.

POLITICAL–ECONOMIC RELATIONSHIPS, NETWORKS AND ORGANIZATIONS

Individuals may act habitually or after consideration of competing alternatives. In either case, it is assumed that one's ideological orientation is of importance. If the individual feels that his or her practical behaviour deviates from the ideal or ideological orientation, then there is reason to reconsider either desired orientation or practical behaviour or both, to make them more compatible. Actually, decision making and rationality can more generally be seen as such a matching process (Söderbaum 1994). The individual looks for alternatives whose expected impacts suit the individual's ideological orientation.

Regarding individuals as political beings (compare Political Economic Man) who act in specific ways or engage in specific activities, is here equivalent to seeing individuals as actors. Actor A can engage in specific activities that only concern him/herself in the sense that no other actor is affected. Another possibility is that Actor A's activities influence the position of Actor B positively or negatively, in the sense that B's activities and life-style are affected. Such effects on B will be considered or not depending on A's ideological orientation. Rather than acting more independently of each other, A and B may also interact on more or less equal terms. They may cooperate for certain activities and consider impacts on each other. In this case, one may speak of a cooperative relationship – as opposed to a competitive or conflicting relationship.

Each actor is characterized not only by his or her roles, activities and interests (identity, life-style and ideological orientation) but also by his/her position with respect to power and resources. In some cases, two actors are mutually dependent on each other and neither is in a superior power position. In other cases, Actor A may regard himself as – and even in some objective sense actually may be – inferior to B in power terms.

A relationship between two actors A and B normally represents a link in a system or network of relationships with a number of other actors involved. The existence of organizations, each coordinating the activities of a set of individual actors, adds to the complexity. Just as individuals are seen as political beings, organizations can be interpreted as political entities, for instance in relation to environmental issues. As an example, rather than speaking of the business concept of a corporation, one may speak of its ideological or political orientation. When an increased number of companies argue that they have an 'environmental policy', this can be seen as one of many manifestations of the company's ideological orientation.

It should furthermore be emphasized that all kinds of relationships and networks are potentially relevant for an understanding of environmental policy issues and environmental performance. Public and private debate may be as relevant as market relationships or relationships within an organization. And of course not all organizations are business companies; some are universities, others can be described as environmental organizations. What goes on at universities, or among intellectuals more generally, may be as decisive for the sustainability issue as anything else.

It can be noted that in neoclassical theory, public and private debate is more or less neglected. To interpret relationships in terms of price signalling is not without interest, but rather petty in relation to many 'real world' problems and situations.

WHO IS RESPONSIBLE?

Let us now assume that a particular environmental problem has been identified. The issue of responsibility can then be raised by Actor A, from whose point of view four different cases or typical situations can be distinguished:

1. Nobody is responsible. The problem identified is seen as something that nobody can influence. Actor A may hold a deterministic view of societal development. 'If anything, the entire "system" should be blamed.' 'Nothing can be done to hinder globalization and the forces of the market.'
2. 'Others' are responsible. Actor A points out some other actor or actor category as being responsible. Actor A may point out his chief within an organization, the Ministry of the Environment on the national level or the bureaucracy on the European Union level, in an attempt to shift the burden of responsibility on to others, that is, in an effort to externalize responsibility.
3. Actor A sees him/herself as responsible, together with many others: 'I myself am responsible'. 'We are all responsible, but in varying ways and degrees.'
4. Actor A may see him/herself as exclusively responsible for the environmental problem observed.

How do various actors in society regard their own responsibility in relation to that of others? Some evidence is available from interviews carried out by Lönngren and Axelsson (1995). Bureaucrats in the environmental protection administration, politicians, industrialists, representatives of voluntary environmental organizations were approached in interviews and asked the following questions: 'As an actor facing environmental problems, you know very well how serious these problems are. What are you doing in your specific role to improve the situation?'. 'What are the potentials and limits of your role?' 'How do you see the roles and responsibilities of other actor categories?'

It is not possible here to elaborate on all details and shades in the replies of the various actors, but not unexpectedly, the authors found a tendency to blame others. A member of a specific actor category, say industrialists, tended to point to the power and responsibility of actors in another category, such as politicians, and sometimes to 'lock-in phenomena', that is deficiencies in how the 'system' or institutional framework (rules of the game and so on) functions more generally. Let us assume for the sake of simplicity that there are only two actors, A and B. Table 7.3 illustrates the possibility of what Lönngren and Axelsson called a 'responsibility trap'.

Table 7.3   Actors dealing with environmental protection issues may blame each other

Actor A	Actor B
'I am doing what I can' 'B is responsible'	'I am doing what I can' 'A is responsible'

In this situation, both of the actors apparently want to escape responsibility for developments in environmental terms. Various defence mechanisms are used to justify present behaviour. While not excluding the possibility that one of the actors alone can be held responsible, the way out of the 'trap' in most cases is probably a move away from 'either/or' reasoning to thinking in terms of 'both/and'. This would mean that each actor has a responsibility to act with the intention of improving the situation.

In addition to the above case of 'crosswise blaming', one can think of chains of responsibility externalization. A puts the blame on B, who in turn blames C, and so on. A may be employed by a business corporation. He may realize that his job has destructive implications for natural resources and the environment, but refers to his superior B, who is held responsible. B in turn argues that he is only doing his job in accordance with the expectations of C, for example the shareholders of the corporation.

Here again, each actor may reconsider his or her role and actions. An interesting issue is, for instance, whether A is well aware of B's preferences and whether B clearly knows what C wants. B has preconceived notions about the shareholders' preferences, but are these assumptions correct?

The usual assumption made is that the shareholders are homogeneous with respect to interests, that all of them see monetary profits and increased monetary value of assets as the exclusive consideration – in reality, however, there may be considerable differences among shareholders' preferences. Shareholders may actually constitute a rather heterogeneous category as regards the importance that is attributed to various monetary and non-monetary performance indicators of the company. In the present terminology, they may differ with respect to ideological orientation, some of them having internalized environmental concerns within their financial investment considerations. This example shows the importance of our models or theoretical constructs, a subject to which we now turn.

IDEAS AND IMAGES AS PART OF IDEOLOGICAL ORIENTATION

The ideological orientation of an actor is not seen as a mathematical objective function to be optimized. It is instead suggested that such orientation is a more or less fragmentary (or coherent) pattern of ideas and images. These vary with respect to kind and degree of simplification. Some ideas (images) allow of more complexity, others for less.

I will now argue that many of the ideas and images that are part of the ideological orientation of actors in our present societies are closely connected with the social sciences – and economics in particular. Business management literature also plays a significant role. In fact, the theories and models taught in economics and business administration legitimize application in practical affairs of these often very simplistic models or concepts.

If this is so, then it becomes important to discuss systematically all parts of the theoretical framework of neoclassical microeconomics. What are the ideas and images offered as part of these conceptual frameworks and what are the ethical implications of these concepts, models and theories? Are there alternatives to neoclassical microeconomics in its several parts and as a whole?

I have elsewhere (Söderbaum 1994) attempted to present an alternative microeconomics, or fragments thereof, in a way that I believe to be fruitful for analysis of environmental and other policy issues. Here, only a few examples are presented.

The reasons for my emphasis on Political Economic Man will now hopefully become more readily understood. Political Economic Man allows for the discussion and analysis of ethical and ideological attitudes, whereas theory based on Economic Man assumptions may be criticized as a subtle attempt to evade ethical issues. No questions are being asked about how Actor A maximizes utility, as compared with Actor B. It is merely assumed that each actor maximizes his/her own utility, whatever that will mean in terms of responsibility. Utility theory is a consequential ethic which does not raise issues of either responsibility or obligation (compare Westskog 1996).

Another example relates to ideas about economics and efficiency. The usual idea of money as a common denominator inherent in cost–benefit analysis at the societal level, CBA, means that only that counts which can be expressed in monetary units. Other Economic Man assumptions are: that all individuals are seen as consumers; that all phenomena that consumers value can be reduced to commodities, that all commodities can be traded in monetary terms, and that the specific market ideology (idea of correct societal valuation of specific impacts) of CBA are acceptable to all parties concerned. CBA furthermore involves a monetary reductionism, in three respects, all of which have their ethical or ideological implications. Impacts that are multidimensional are reduced to one-dimensional, monetary impacts; those that refer to different individuals or interested parties are reduced to a single aggregated sum of effects. Finally, impacts that refer to different periods of time are reduced to impacts at one point in time (in the form of a 'present value').

As an alternative, a holistic idea of economics more in line with institutional economics would mean that impacts of different kinds should be kept separate throughout the analysis, that impacts related to different interested parties and to different periods of time or points in time should also be segregated. An analysis in profile terms replaces the one-dimensional analysis of CBA.

Many actors in society have been indoctrinated at departments of economics and elsewhere into the reductionist concepts of neoclassical economics, which they may see as very practical and useful. Other actors regard this 'monetary reductionism' as being at the heart of the environmental problems we now face. Along these lines, it can be argued that environmental problems will never be taken seriously as long as environmental impacts are systematically being made more or less invisible in monetary calculations.

The list of concepts and views in neoclassical economics which have ethical and ideological implications can be extended and in each case alternatives with a different ethical and ideological content can be suggested. Examples of these neoclassical views which could be reconsidered or complemented are:

- the concept of an economy (where ecosystems and effects on ecosystems can be seen as fundamental to the functioning of the economy)
- the idea of development in GNP terms (where systematic measurement of a number of non-monetary indicators will complement the picture)
- ideas about the functioning of markets and about international trade in particular, or the national or global market economy as a whole (where an actor-network approach and attempts to elucidate the ethical issues involved, will change the picture)
- the concept of a firm (where stakeholder theory in business management literature and an actor-network model are two alternatives)
- ideas about social change (where actor-network theory changes the picture offered by public choice theory)
- ideas about relationships between Man and Nature.

SCIENCE: POWER WITHOUT RESPONSIBILITY, OR RESPONSIBLE BEHAVIOUR WITHIN A DEMOCRACY

Scientists themselves and actors in society also hold specific ideas about science and these views have different ethical implications. Traditional ideas about objectivity and value neutrality can – when faced with alternative epistemological views, as discussed earlier – be seen as an attempt to exercise power in society, while at the same time evading or belittling responsibility.

Gunnar Myrdal observed in his interaction with institutionalists in the USA in the 1920s that these scholars, while having similar ideas in other respects, were reluctant to admit that all theories and schools of thought in the social sciences are coloured by values (Myrdal 1975, pp. 6–7). Sometimes one feels that most representatives of the different schools in economics are afraid of relinquishing power by admitting the political element of their analysis.

This traditional idea of science furthermore implies that scientists are unusual people in the sense that they can exclude any influence of their ideological orientation on 'scientific analysis'. The scientists, and science as a phenomenon, would like to be regarded as innocent of and exonerated from responsibility for contemporary societal and environmental crises. While seeing themselves as readily serving society with solutions to specific problems, they tend to overlook or avert their eyes to the possibility that science with specific epistemological beliefs as its basis may equally well be part of the problem. While science has succeeded in certain respects, it has failed in other ways, more precisely in relation to a number of environmental problems. As scholars, we should therefore acknowledge and share responsibility for present problems and not merely propagate the view that science can do no other than foster progress.

Einstein once remarked that one cannot solve a set of problems by applying the same thinking that created the problems in the first place. This strengthens our argument that pluralism and paradigm co-existence is a good idea in present circumstances. It also suggests that various approaches that represent alternatives to the neoclassical paradigm, such as institutionalism, social economics, socioeconomics, and ecological economics, all have an important role to play.

TOWARDS A 'GREEN' POLICY

We all experience how societies undergo change. Andrew Dobson (1995) discusses various ways in which such changes can come about. He discusses, for instance, the possibility that some class in society that is suffering from current developments might attempt to attain power and even succeed, by parliamentary or other means. In Sweden we speak a lot about popular movements (*folkrsrelser*) as the main initiators of social change. The will of 'the people' is seen as being opposed to those currently in power, the 'establishment' or 'elite'. While the people apprehend new opportunities, representatives of the establishment are seen as those who benefit from the present situation. Inertia, with respect to thinking patterns and ideology, characterizes the establishment, according to this view.

Consider again the assumption about heterogeneity in each actor category. Some subset of 'the people' as well as some subset of the establishment may very well be described in terms of inertia or conservatism. But there is also a possibility that there are subsets in each of the two categories, of 'people' and 'establishment', who have sufficiently understood environmental problems to call for action. In addition to social movements of people outside the establishment, there may be 'establishment movements' which can play a significant role. Establishment actors within business, all forms of higher and adult education, environmental voluntary organizations, religious communities and within both local and national communities, all may push in roughly the same direction towards ecological sustainability.

If there is such a possibility of movements within the establishment, then the next question arises, whether such movements in a 'green' direction can be expedited. One such possibility that has already been touched upon is ideological debate, which brings in the conceptual framework of economics as an issue. A second is to form green 'establishment organizations' that can play a part in facilitating social change. 'The Natural Step' in Sweden is an example. Consensus building about environmental threats and about necessary steps to tackle and solve such problems in a business or in sectors of the economy, is an essential part of the strategy. Another thing is to create networks of actors on the basis of a common profession, for instance 'engineers for environment' 'economists for environment', 'consultants for environment'. The Natural Step is certainly not enough by itself, but in combination with the traditional environmental organizations, it has a role to play. Another course of action – in addition to scrutinizing the ethical and ideological content of economics as a discipline and the creation of Green establishment organizations – is to create new arenas for establishment actors where actors with a Green concern and orientation feel that they are welcome. Conferences in areas such as theory of science, sociology of science and responsibility of science may serve as an example. Conferences can also serve as arenas where national and international actors meet for a dialogue in the interface of science, politics and practice. Just as we scientists modify our arguments and roles when confronted by new and demanding situations, the same is hopefully true of actors from the World Bank, the United Nations Environmental Programme or the Global Environmental Facility, to mention but a few examples. In this way, more enlightened dialogue and policy initiatives will help us move toward environmental sustainability.

My conclusion, then, is as follows: to the extent that the conceptual framework of economics plays a role in public debate about environmental and other issues, it becomes important to abandon the present path of almost exclusive reliance on neoclassical economics in education and research. Neoclassical theory may in fact, in various ways, actively hinder an increased awareness about environmental problems and the consequent necessary ideological reorientation at all levels, from the individual, via organizations, to national and international forums. Scholars engaged in the ecological economics project are among those who can play a part in making economics more pluralistic. The institutional version of ecological economics that has been emphasized here will then represent an attractive option.

REFERENCES

Costanza, Robert (1989), 'What is ecological economics?', *Ecological Economics*, **1** (1), pp. 1–7.
Dobson, Andrew (1995), *Green Political Thought* (2nd edn), London: Routledge.
Eccleshall, Robert et al. (1994), *Political ideologies. An Introduction* (2nd edn), London: Routledge.
Etzioni, Amitai (1988), *The Moral Dimension. Toward a New Economics*, New York: The Free Press.
Kohler Riessman, Catherine (1993), *Narrative Analysis*, London: Sage.
Kuhn, Thomas S. (1970), *The Structure of Scientific Revolutions*, Chicago: University of Chicago Press.
Lönngren, Mats and Svante Axelsson (1995), 'Hinder och möjligheter för miljöarbete – en kartläggning av centrala aktörers problembilder' (Obstacles and possibilities for work on environmental issues, mapping the problem images of major actors), Swedish University of Agricultural Sciences, Department of Extended Education, Report 3, Uppsala.
Myrdal, Gunnar (1975), *Against the Stream. Critical Essays on Economics*, New York: Vintage Books, Random House.
_____ (1978), 'Institutional economics', *Journal of Economic Issues*, **12**, pp. 771–83.
Norgaard, Richard (1994), *Development Betrayed*, London: Routledge.
North, Douglass C. (1990), *Institutions, Institutional Change and Economic Performance*, Cambridge: Cambridge University Press.
Randall, Alan (1986), 'Institutional and neoclassical approaches to environmental policy' in Tim T. Phipps, Pierre R. Crosson and Kenneth A. Price (eds), *Agriculture and Environment*, Chapter 7, pp. 205–24, The National Centre for Food and Agricultural Policy, Annual Policy Review, 1986, Washington DC: Resources for the Future.
Sen, Amartya (1987), *On Ethics and Economics*, New York: Basil Blackwell.
Simon, Herbert (1945), *Administrative Behaviour*, New York: Free Press.
Söderbaum, Peter (1993), 'Values, markets and environmental policy: an actor-network approach', *Journal of Economic Issues*, **27** (2), (June), pp. 387–404.
_____ (1994), 'Towards a microeconomics for ecological sustainability', *Journal of*

Interdisciplinary Economics, **5**, pp. 197–220.

Von Wright, Georg Henrik (1986), *Vetenskapen och förnuftet. Ett försök till orientering* (*Science and Reason: Attempt at Introduction*), Stockholm: Bonniers.

Westskog, Hege (1996), 'The use of cost–benefit analysis to decide environmental policy – a dead end?', paper presented at the conference 'Ecology, society, economy: in pursuit of sustainable development' at the Université de Versailles-St.Quentin en Yvelines, 23–25 May, 1996.

8. How are we Doing?: An Analysis of Recent Attempts at Alternative Measures of Economic and Social Well-being

Charles M.A. Clark and Catherine Kavanagh

INTRODUCTION

Progress is one of those ideas that just about everyone supports and advocates. This is particularly true in the Western culture, where the ideal of progress has become a central aspiration. Yet, even though we would have a hard time finding opponents of progress, there are conflicting opinions about what 'progress' is. Progress for some could be retrogress for others. This is especially the case when one group's advancement comes at the expense of another group. Defining progress, and then measuring it, is an essential aspect of how a society will formulate and evaluate public policy and the state of the nation. The conception of progress, to a large extent, determines society's goals and propels the direction of its future development. Because of its role in public policy, defining progress and measuring it is an important element in the establishment and exercise of power. Commenting on what is and is not included in existing measures of progress, John Kenneth Galbraith (1958) has said, 'if it isn't counted, it doesn't count'. Thus, progress is politically, economically and socially one of the most significant elements in the running of a country.

Economists have settled on a notion of progress which they like to believe adequately and accurately reflects how a country is doing, whether it is experiencing progress or regression. This is national income accounting, and it is designed to reflect how much goods and services a society has produced in a particular year. Not only do most economists feel that this is an accurate measure of economic well-being, they also claim that it is value-neutral. National income accounting, they argue, merely sums all legal market expenditures on final goods and services. Yet, by including only 'legal' and 'market' expenditures and production, they are making very important value

144

judgements. In fact, they could not do otherwise, for all economic theory and analysis must base its efforts, at least to some extent, on values and value judgements.

Recently, there has been a growing critique of traditional measures of economic and social well-being. These critics argue that traditional measures exclude important social factors which reflect the quality of life in a country. They also object to the exclusion of important non-market production, such as child-rearing, which is necessary for a healthy society. Furthermore, environmentalists have noted that traditional measures do not adequately reflect resource depletion and environmental degradation. Economic growth based on natural resource depletion is not a sustainable path of development. The recent call by the European Union for all member nations to develop so-called 'green' accounting reflects the growing opinion that Gross Domestic Product (GDP) does not adequately consider environmental factors.

Our purpose here is to look at some issues raised by the critics of traditional measures of economic and social well-being and to explore some alternative measures. The second section examines the role of 'values' in how progress is defined and in the construction of measures of progress. This will be followed, in the third section, by a critique of the most widely used measure of economic and social well-being: GDP. The fourth section examines alternative approaches to measuring progress, such as the Genuine Progress Indicator, the Index of Social Health, the Human Development Index and the OECD List of Social Indicators. These measures are indicative of what has been accomplished in this field. Finally, the last section concludes with some comments on the need for alternative measures of economic and social well-being in transitional economies.

THE ROLE OF VALUES IN DEFINING PROGRESS

In *The Theory of Economic Progress*, Clarence Ayres notes that any conception of progress is based on a conception of a goal or end of progress.

> The traditional conception of progress is that of movement toward the attainment of an 'end'. Within the limits of day to day activity, finite and provisional ends are of course set up. Thus one may speak of progress toward the attainment of an academic degree. In a much more general but still limited sense one may even speak of the advancement of science as progress toward knowledge, or something of the sort. But the idea still persists that the attainment of such limited objectives constitute 'real' progress only insofar as these limited objectives contain some particularization of the universal 'end'. (Ayres 1944, p. 234)

The 'end' by which progress is defined and evaluated comes from the values of the individual, institution or community defining 'progress'. 'Ends' can never be neutral or value-free and they cannot be determined or evaluated solely by objective science.

For a little more than 100 years, professional economists have tried very hard to convince themselves and the public that economics is, or can be, a 'value free' science. This has not been a particularly successful effort. Only the most devoted and dogmatic disciples of neoclassical economic theory have accepted this proposition. All who have examined the proposition critically, especially philosophers and methodologists, have rejected this claim. As Gunnar Myrdal (1954) has noted, the attempt to develop a 'value free' economic science was in reality an attempt to dress up one set of values as scientific fact.

The problem of this research programme was that all theoreticians need an observation point before they can observe, and this observation point is the model or perspective with which the 'scientists' define and organize their observations. Values and value judgement are a necessary factor in the construction and adoption of theories and models. They are built into the hard core of the theory and therefore they necessarily influence the subsequent analysis. Furthermore, values play an essential role in the selection of what phenomena to observe and what to ignore. The selection of increases in the general level of prices (inflation) as the most important economic phenomenon (a common selection of most Central Banks) reflects a particular set of value judgements, whereas a different set of values might suggest that changes in the stocks of natural resources or other environmental factors are of paramount importance.

For the whole of the history of economic thought, the theory of value has been both a theory of the ordering properties of the economy and an expression of the legitimate goals and purposes (values) of the economy and society. The conception of value in neoclassical economic theory is at the root of the problem of why GDP is a poor indicator of economic and social progress. 'In the classical and much of the neoclassical tradition in economics, the maximal satisfaction of wants, notably consumer wants, has been and remains the basic criterion of judgement, the standard of value, the basis on which to distinguish between good and bad, proper and improper, and desirable and undesirable' (Tool 1986, p. 89). As Adam Smith argued, the goal or purpose of economics was to increase the production of goods and services so that the living standards of the masses could be improved. 'No society,' Smith writes, 'can surely be flourishing and happy, of which the far greater part of the members are poor and miserable' (Smith 1976b, p. 96), and 'consumption is the sole end and purpose of all production; and the interest of the producer ought to be attended to, only so far as it may be necessary for promoting that of the consumer' (ibid., p. 660). When generalized poverty and want are the economic problem, the solution is more production for consumption.

While the classicals placed their emphasis on production, the marginalists emphasized consumption. For them, value comes from, and is measured by, the utility derived in consumption. Yet, as Joan Robinson (1962, p. 47) has noted, the concept of utility is highly problematic: 'Utility is a metaphysical concept of impregnable circularity; utility is the quality in commodities that makes individuals want to buy them, and the fact that individuals want to buy commodities shows that they have utility'. The concept of utility, as used by economic theory, comes from Jeremy Bentham, and it is clearly intended to be both a measure of what is and what ought to be. In Bentham's famous words (quoted in Clark 1992, p. 98),

> [n]ature has placed mankind under the governance of two sovereign masters, pain and pleasure. It is for them alone to point out what we ought to do, as well as to determine what we shall do. On the one hand, the standard of right and wrong, on the other, the chain of causes and effects, are fastened to their throne. They govern us in all we do, in all we say, in all we think: every effort we can make to throw off our subjection, will serve but to demonstrate and confirm it. In words a man may pretend to abjure their empire: but in reality he will remain subject to it all the while. The principle of utility recognizes this subjection, and assumes it for the foundation of that system, the object of which is to rear the fabric of felicity by the hands of reason and of law. Systems which attempt to question it, deal in sounds instead of sense, in caprice instead of reason, in darkness instead of light.

The theory of marginal utility serves both of the functions of value theory: the ordering properties of society and the legitimation and evaluation of ends. For the neoclassical economist, something has value only in so far as it delivers utility to someone through the marketplace. The marketplace sums the total individual utilities of consumers and balances these against the disutilities of producers (cost of production) and reaches an equilibrium when these (demand and supply) are equal. The underlying order of the market is an expression of societies' values, yet only values that can be expressed in a market transaction are included. Economists often note that utility can be had outside of market transactions, but this is seen as a market failure and leads to inefficiencies. Thus they view the solution to all problems, economic or otherwise, as involving the establishment of property rights and a market for exchange.

Underlying this whole approach to economics is the utilitarian theory of human nature, in which humans are seen as, to use Thorstein Veblen's phrase, 'lightning calculators of pleasures and pains' (1919, p. 73). People are not seen as the causes or the effects, but as merely respondents to outside stimuli. This hedonistic conception of human nature states that all human activity is driven by the desire to maximize utility through consumption in the marketplace, thus the only thing which has worth in society (has value) is production for consumption. Given this conception of human nature, it is natural for economists to place all their emphasis on a measure of economic well-being that measures economic transactions, that is, the sale of goods and services to consumers. Whether these transactions actually contribute to social well-being or not is never asked, for the theory is based on the premise that individuals only engage in transactions if they receive utility from the transaction.

Furthermore, the question of the common good is excluded from the analysis. In neoclassical economics there is no common good, for there is no society. Neoclassical economic theory necessarily holds that society is a mental fiction, that only individuals have any real existence. Thus, for the common good to have any meaning in economics, it can only be the sum total of the utilities consumed by the individuals in a community. The net effect of this attempt to turn economics into a 'value free' or positive science has been to prevent economists from questioning the purpose of economic activity, and the role of the economy in improving the well-being of society. John Maynard Keynes was well aware of the limited usefulness of economists' exclusive attention to production and efficiency. He noted that increasing production was necessary at a certain stage of economic progress, and that at such a level of development, the institutions that promote production can be justified as necessary for solving the economic problem of generalized poverty. Nevertheless, he never lost sight of the overall goals of society. 'Our problem,' Keynes wrote, 'is to work out a social organisation which shall be as efficient as possible without offending our notions of a satisfactory way of life' (1963, p. 321). In his essay 'Economic Possibilities of our Grandchildren', Keynes argues that once the affluent stage of development is reached, society should and will rearrange its economic institutions to promote more laudable goals and aspiration than those that dominate in a society where poverty is the norm.

> When the accumulation of wealth is no longer of high social importance, there will be great changes in the code of morals. We shall be able to rid ourselves of many of the pseudo-moral principles which have hag-ridden us for two hundred years, by which we have exalted some of the most distasteful of human qualities into the position of the highest virtues. We shall be able to afford to dare to assess the money-motive at its true value. The love of money as a possession – as distinguished from the love of money as a means to the enjoyments and realities of life – will be recognized for what it is, a somewhat disgusting morbidity, one of those semi-criminal, semi-pathological propensities which one hands over with a shudder to the specialists in mental illness. All kinds of social customs and economic practices, affecting the distribution of wealth and of economic rewards and penalties, which we now maintain at all costs, however distasteful and unjust they may be in themselves, because they are tremendously useful in promoting the accumulation of capital, we shall then be free, at last, to discard. (ibid., pp. 369–70)

The pre-eminent position of production has led to the worst sort of commodity fetishism, the confusing of the GDP with the well-being of society.

In *The Affluent Society*, John Kenneth Galbraith (1958) has demonstrated how and why production has remained the primary goal of economics, even though the condition of generalized poverty has been replaced, in the developed nations, by generalized affluence. Where most of the population has attained a relatively high material standard of living and where poverty is the exception rather than the rule, the paramount importance of production should begin to fade. In a society where more people will die from eating too much than from not eating enough, and where the importance of production comes from the employment it creates rather than the goods and services it generates, the purpose of economic activity must be questioned and re-examined. Furthermore, when the progress of society, measured in human terms, does not seem to coincide with increases in economic output, the exclusive emphasis on production itself becomes a barrier to social progress.

Such a rethinking of economics has not taken place with the arrival of affluence. The mainstream of the economics profession has not altered its outlook. The reason most economists still view economic growth, and its primary measure, GDP, as the most important goal of economics stems from the values and assumptions which form the hard core of neoclassical economic theory. If one were to base an analysis of society and the economy on a different conception of value, then the measures used to analyse how society is doing would be different. If, instead of value equalling utility through market transactions, we adopted an alternative conception of value, then our conception of progress, and also our measurements of progress, would be very different. One alternative conception of value would be the promotion of human dignity and the common good, the value premises of the Catholic Social Thought tradition. A similar alternative is the 'instrumental value principle' developed in the American Institutionalist economics literature, most notably by Marc Tool. Under this approach, the criterion of social value is 'the continuity of human life and the noninvidious recreation of community through the instrumental use of knowledge' (Tool 1986, pp. 55–6). By using such a criterion, Thorstein Veblen, in *The Theory of the Leisure Class* (1899) was able to examine and evaluate the role of consumption in society. This approach allows the analyst to make the important, but often difficult, distinction between consumption which promotes human dignity and the common good and that which is based on creating invidious distinctions (conspicuous consumption). The ability to make such distinctions is essential if we are to understand, measure and promote 'real' progress. Our conception of progress cannot be limited to market transactions, but must include various social factors which fundamentally impact on human dignity and the common good. Ultimately, it is the acceptance of different values which has led to the creation of alternative measures of economic and social well-being.

WHAT IS WRONG WITH GDP?

The paramount position of GDP in modern capitalist societies can be seen in many aspects of daily life. News reports give us constant updates as to its past movements, in addition to its expected movements in the future. Its only rivals in coverage are the stock market, the weather and the sports betting line. Politicians continually debate its movements and the underlying factors behind these movements. GDP is the most widely used measure of social well-being, yet the narrow view of society which it portrays has resulted in it being severely criticized. Increasingly economists and other social scientists, as well as international agencies, are calling for, and developing, alternative indexes to measure social well-being.

National income accounting, of which GDP is one element, was developed as part of the effort to manage the wartime economy of the 1940s. Thus, it was not developed as a measure of social well-being. Essential to understanding the concept and use of GDP is its relation to power. 'GDP has mythic power because it is invoked as a measure of national power and prestige in international comparisons and as a political weapon in domestic politics' (Cobb 1995, p. 37). GDP is a measure of market transactions and its importance reflects the inherent power relations in a modern capitalist society. Market transactions involve economic activity in which goods and services are bought and sold, usually involving the earning of profits. The earning of profits, as all economists have noted, is an essential aspect of a capitalist economy: the driving force and raison d'etre of all 'legitimate' economic activity. The business community thus has a strong self-interest in promoting GDP as the most important economic statistic, for it measures the type of activity which benefits them. Economists since Adam Smith have assumed that the invisible hand of competition will ensure that profitable economic activity will be in the public interest. Yet their conception of the public interest is very narrow: the satisfaction of consumer demand. Much profitable economic activity is clearly contrary to the public interest, even as economists conceive it, such as the restriction of output to keep prices artificially high (monopoly pricing) or financial speculation.

As a measure of economic and social well-being GDP has many inherent problems. Most economists note that GDP often excludes transactions that are part of the economic life of a community, for example, the so-called underground economy. Economists have also noted the problem of externalities. An externality is an effect of a market exchange on individuals who are not part of the exchange. The fact that a nonparticipant is affected by a market transaction, according to neoclassical economic theory, means that utility or disutility is being experienced which is not being reflected in the determination of the transaction's price. The justification of free markets is essentially the theory that in a free market, prices reflect, in the long run, the sum of society's costs of producing goods or services (supply) and their desire for such goods and services (demand). If externalities exist, then there are costs and benefits that are not being fully expressed in the marketplace, therefore the market is not reaching the optimal equilibrium solution. If the problem of externalities can somehow be adequately addressed, most economists feel then that GDP will be an adequate measure of economic and social well-being.

Yet the limitations of GDP are more systemic than a mere information problem. GDP is a measure of economic transactions, and not all transactions can be considered a contribution to social well-being. Furthermore, much that contributes to social well-being might not be in the form of a market transaction. These two facts are at the heart of the current critique of GDP as an indicator of progress.

GDP measures transactions by their amount in monetary units. Any attached satisfaction is incidental to the transaction. Yet much of the growth in transactions stems not from increasing well-being (goods and services for consumers) but derives from the increased costs of living in contemporary society. Fear of crime motivates many to purchase various goods and services (engage in transactions) which are not designed to increase their level of happiness, but to protect their existing state. The purchase of cigarettes and the eventual expenditures on cancer treatment both add to GNP. When a couple gets a divorce, the level of transactions increases as two households now need to be provided for, and many non-market activities such as home child care, must now be purchased through the market. As A.C. Pigou noted , 'If a man marries his house-keeper or his cook, the national dividend is diminished' (Pigou 1936, p. 33). The reverse is equally true and is a more significant factor in modern economic life. In fact, the break up of the family is a major contributor to the growth in GDP. Other social ills, such as crime, drug abuse and juvenile delinquency, all lead to increases in market transactions and thus promote increases in GDP, but do not contribute to social well-being. Furthermore, the continual growth in waste and pollution, caused by the high level of economic activity, also generates significant increases in market transactions, either directly (the costs of cleaning up the environment) or indirectly (cost generated by illnesses related to pollution). In fact, pollution is a double bonus for it adds to GDP when it is generated, and it adds to GDP again when it is cleaned up (Cobb, Halstead and Rowe 1995). Thus, 'growth can be social decline by another name' (ibid., p. 65).

As a measure of market transactions, GDP necessarily leaves out non-market activity. The preparation of food at home contributes nothing to GDP, whereas having a restaurant prepare your food does. Paying for child care increases GDP, whereas raising one's own children reduces GDP in two ways. First, it removes a potential worker from the labour force and, second, it provides an economic service which does not pass through the marketplace, meaning the loss of an individual earning profits from the activity. Household labour and volunteer labour, both essential for society, do not contribute to GDP and crowd out possible profitable delivery of such services.

Economists have long noted the need to adjust national income accounts to take into account the consumption of capital goods. It is well known that a society which consumes not only its current income, but also consumes part of its capital stock, will be worse off in the future. Yet national income accounts are not similarly adjusted for the depletion of natural resources. This is particularly a problem in undeveloped countries where most of the economic growth comes from the cutting down of rainforests and depleting other natural resources. Such activities are clearly not sustainable.

In a similar way, the viability of a market economy necessitates a high level of what can be called 'social capital', the institutions and attitudes which allow for any economic activity to take place. In a market economy, respect for property rights is very important, as is a basic level of honesty and ethics. For a market economy to function, such attitudes must be second nature, the norm. The legal system operates around the fringes to support these attitudes, but it could not enforce them if even a small number of the population started to reject them. The socialization which creates civil society takes place, for the most part, outside of market transactions. As Adam Smith noted, it begins in the family, gradually extends to the local community and finally to society at large. Smith (1976a) knew full well that this socialization process was an essential precondition to the operation of what he called 'a society of perfect liberty' and what we call a market economy. The breakdown of this socialization process, which is at the heart of the rise in drug abuse, crime and the breakup of the family, contributes to the growth in GDP, but runs counter to the common good and the long-run sustainability of a social order.

When increases in GDP not only do not reflect improvements in the quality of life, but are created by social decline, then it is imperative to develop alternative measures of economic and social well-being. Furthermore, the values which underlie neoclassical economic theory and the use of GDP as the primary indicator of progress and social well-being are not those of any specific society, and certainly are not those of a civilized society. They reflect the values of a particular laissez-faire ideology and the small percentage of the population which benefits most from the exclusive promotion of private production over all other forms of economic activity.

SOME ALTERNATIVE MEASURES OF PROGRESS

In his recent overview of the topic of social indicators, Tony Fahey summarized the essential limitations of traditional measures of economic performance. 'National accounts aggregates such as Gross Domestic Product or National Income, no matter how well adjusted to take "green" issues into the reckoning, are designed as measures of economic activity, not as measures of welfare. Welfare is determined not only by economic activity but also by a wide range of additional dimensions of social life' (Scott, Nolan and Fahey 1996, p. 82). The problem with GDP is not just that it does not take into consideration such 'green' issues as sustainability, it is that it does not distinguish between economic activity that is positive and contributes to social well-being, and economic activity that is negative or contrary to social well-being.

An attempt to address both the sustainability issue and make the important distinctions between positive and negative economic activity is the Genuine Progress Indicator (GPI), developed for the United States economy by the group Redefining Progress. The purpose of the GPI is to replace GDP. It is an attempt at a comprehensive measure of the status of the economy. Cobb, Halstead and Rowe have described the GPI in a recent *Atlantic Monthly* article.

> We started with the same consumption data that the GDP is based on, but revised them in a number of ways. We adjusted for some factors (such as income distribution), added certain other factors (such as the value of household and community work), and subtracted yet others (such as pollution costs and the like). The result is a balance sheet for the nation that starts to distinguish between the costs and benefits of 'growth'. (Cobb, Halstead and Rowe 1995, p. 70)

Some of the factors which the GPI includes but which are excluded from GDP are: household and volunteer work; cost of crime; other defensive expenditures; distribution of income; resource depletion and degradation of the habitat; and loss of leisure. Estimates of the GPI are presented. Both the GPI and GDP grew at about the same rate throughout most of the 1950s and 1960s, but the indexes have diverged considerably since the early 1970s to the present. GDP has continued to increase steadily (with the exception of periodic recessions) while the GPI has either remained stagnant or declined.

Another alternative measure of social progress is the Index of Social Health (ISH), developed for the United States by Fordham University's Institute for Innovation in Social Policy. Unlike the GDP and GPI, the ISH is not meant to be a comprehensive measure of social well-being. Instead it is meant to be representative of how society as a whole is progressing. The index 'combines social indicators that measure some of the burdens and risks of life in this society with a set of socio-economic indicators that reflect the quality of our lives' (Miringoff, Miringoff and Opdycke 1996, p. 18). The indicators chosen are organized by the stages of life: childhood; youth; adulthood; old age; as well as some general indicators which affect all. Variables chosen are merely indicative of the health of society and the index does not attempt to be all inclusive. The ISH for the United States has only 16 variables. Furthermore, variables chosen are those which would have wide agreement as to their significance. Each variable is indexed to the best year the United States has experienced over the life of the index. Thus each variable is compared with the best performance it has achieved. However, the focus of the index is not primarily on each separate variable, but on the way in which they interact to create a social climate. Much like the GPI, the ISH also rose along with GDP up until the early 1970s and since then has stagnated or declined.

The Human Development Index (HDI) is another example of an alternative measure of social progress, developed by the United Nations Development Programme (UNDP). It was designed primarily to rank rich and poor countries. The index consists of three components: life expectancy, adult literacy and GDP per capita, which are combined in a single measure. Maximum and minimum values are set for each of the three components, and a country achieves a score of between 0 and 1 for each component. For example, minimum life expectancy is 25 years and the maximum set is 85 years. A country whose life expectancy is 70 years, for example, would then receive a score 0.75 for that component. The adult literacy component is constructed in a similar way. GDP per capita is constructed in Purchasing Power Parity terms with a minimum value of $200 and a maximum of $40,000. However, higher levels of income are discounted more heavily. Hence, a country which moves from an average of $1000 to $1500 per capita will have a bigger impact on the HDI than a country which moves from $30,000 to $30,500. The reasoning is that if a country already receives an above world average income per capita, further increases are likely to make a diminishing contribution to human development.

The HDI gives a very different picture of how countries are ranked when compared with just income per capita rankings. A limitation of the HDI is that it does not provide a sensitive measure of social progress within the developed countries. This is because many developed countries already have high scores on adult literacy and life expectancy, so that marginal changes are not reflected in the index. Thus the ability of the HDI index to provide a sensitive measure of progress, or lack of it, in society as a whole is open to question. The HDI is perhaps more suited to measuring progress in developing countries.

The OECD List of Social Indicators consists of 33 indicators which are broadly applicable across developed countries. The list includes indicators relating to education, health, employment, free time and leisure, quality of working life, the distribution of income and wealth, housing and physical environment, social environment and personal safety. The aim of the indicators is to supplement existing measures of activity and not to replace them. They provide information on the quality of life and hence provide a more complete picture of the social health of the nation. The indicators were designed under a set of criteria which included that they be relevant to policy, be applicable over a long period of time, be comparable across countries and be applicable to individual well-being. In this respect, the list can be regarded as a serious effort to produce measures of social progress that complement existing measures of economic activity.

Finally, according to the UNDP (1995), gender inequality represents a serious obstacle to human development. In the light of this, they produced two new measures of development which take account of gender issues. These are the Gender-related Development Index (GDI) and the Gender Empowerment

Measure (GEM). The GDI is closely related to the HDI, in so far as it adjusts the HDI for gender inequality. The GEM consists of three components combined in a single measure to capture gender inequality: female per capita unearned income; male and female percentage share of administrative, managerial, professional and technical positions; and percentage of parliamentary seats that are held by females and men. Again, both indexes produce different rankings of countries than does the HDI.

CONCLUSION

There is no 'scientific, value-free' definition of progress, thus we should not be surprised that there is not a simple 'value-free' measure. Much like the concept of value in economics, progress is a term we must continually define and redefine, as social and economic circumstances dictate. Just as Ricardo's search for an invariant measure of value was based on the incorrect view that the economy was controlled by natural laws, the notion that progress is not socially constructed and can be measured in a 'value-free' manner is similarly based on an attempt to understand the economy free of historical and social context. The value of emphasizing this fact is the value of political economy at its best. Ultimately, a society should, through an open and democratic process, decide what its goals are, what it will consider to be progress, and finally how it will measure progress. On that day economics will be demystified, and power will finally be in the hands of the people. And the discipline Adam Smith started over 200 years ago will finally serve its purpose, to have the economy organized for the benefit of the people, instead of having the people organized for the benefit of the economy.

REFERENCES

Ayres, C.E. (1944), *The Theory of Economic Progress*, Chapel Hill: University of North Carolina Press.

Clark, C.M.A. (1992), *Economic Theory and Natural Philosophy*, Aldershot: Edward Elgar.

_____(1995), 'From Natural Value to Social Value', in Charles M.A. Clark (ed.), *Institutional Economics and the Theory of Social Value*, Boston: Kluwer Academic Press.

Cobb, C. (1995), 'Imagery and Indicators', in Alex Macgillivray (ed.), *Accounting for Change*, London: The New Economic Foundation, pp. 37–40.

_____, T. Halstead and J. Rowe (1995), 'If the GDP is Up, Why is America Down?', *The Atlantic Monthly*, **276**, October, pp. 59–78.

Galbraith, J.K. (1958), *The Affluent Society*. Boston: Houghton Mifflin.

Keynes, J.M. [1932] (1963), *Essays in Persuasion*, New York: W.W. Norton & Company.

Miringoff, M., M. Miringoff and S. Opdycke (1996), 'The Growing Gap Between Standard Economic Indicators and the Nation's Social Health', *Challenge*, **39**, July–August, pp. 17–22.

Myrdal, G. (1954), *The Political Element in the Development of Economic Theory*, New York: Simon and Schuster.

Pigou, A. (1936), *The Economics of Welfare*, London: Macmillan.

Robinson, J. (1962), *Economic Philosophy*, Chicago: Aldine Publishing.

Scott, S., B. Nolan and T. Fahey (1996), *Formulating Environmental and Social Indicators for Sustainable Development*, Dublin: ESRI.

Smith, A. [1759] (1976a), *The Theory of Moral Sentiments*, Oxford: Oxford University Press.

_____ [1776] (1976b), *An Inquiry into the Nature and Causes of the Wealth of Nations*, Oxford: Oxford University Press.

Tool, M. (1986), *Essays in Social Value Theory*, Armonk, NY: M.E. Sharpe, Inc.

United Nations Development Programme (UNDP) (1995), *Human Development Report*, Oxford: Oxford University Press.

Veblen, T. (1899), *The Theory of the Leisure Class*, New York: Macmillan.

_____ (1919), *The Place of Science in Modern Civilization*, New York: Huebsch.

9. Institutional Economics in the Classroom: Increasing the Relevance of Economics Education

Janice Peterson

> The only serious grounds on which political economists for centuries have claimed significance for their work have been its alleged relevance to the resolution of real problems facing real people in real political economies.
>
> *Marc R. Tool (1979, p. 15)*

One of the defining characteristics of institutional economics is the belief that for economics to be relevant it must be concerned with solving the economic problems of the day. This concern is reflected in the professional activities and research agendas of many institutional economists. Research topics and methods are not, however, the only place where institutional economics makes a difference. Institutional economics provides the basis for introducing important and often controversial social and economic issues into our teaching, thus turning our classrooms into a 'site for social action' (Lewis 1995; Peterson 1995).

While other chapters in these volumes have chronicled and explored Professor Bush's many valuable contributions to the development of institutional theory and socially relevant scholarship, this chapter celebrates Professor Bush as a teacher. My belief that institutional economics provides an exciting framework for presenting economics in a meaningful way derives directly from my experiences as an undergraduate student in Professor Bush's Intermediate Micro- and Macroeconomics courses in the late 1970s at California State University–Fresno. Professor Bush brought his love for knowledge and his thoughtful, critical analysis into the economics classroom in a way that continues to serve as an inspiration to me in my own career as a professor of undergraduate economics.

This chapter begins with a brief discussion of the concerns that have been raised about economics education, and argues that institutional economists have a unique opportunity to address these concerns. Next, Professor Bush's approach to teaching microeconomic theory is presented as an illustration of how an institutional perspective can positively inform the way we present even the most orthodox material. This is followed by a discussion of how I have drawn on Professor Bush's approach to develop a meaningful framework for integrating distributional issues into my principles of microeconomics courses. The chapter concludes with a discussion of the pedagogical opportunities that are opened up by employing an institutional framework, and the benefits that derive from approaching economics education from an institutional perspective.

ECONOMICS EDUCATION: A NEED FOR RELEVANCE

The lessons that can be drawn from Professor Bush's teaching are perhaps now more topical and important than ever. The economics literature reflects an increasing concern with the way in which economists are being educated. The decade began with a surprisingly frank discussion of the state of graduate education in economics, summarized in the 'Report of the Commission on Graduate Education in Economics' (Krueger et al. 1991). Anne Krueger and the other commission members expressed concern over the relative emphasis on technique versus substance in the graduate economics curriculum. They also expressed the concern that creativity and communication skills are lacking in the training of economists (ibid., p. 1048). In addition, commission member W. Lee Hansen reported that a survey of graduate professors and students found a 'skills gap' in the training of graduate economists, where 'the mix of skills needed both for dissertation research and subsequent employment differed from the mix of skills currently emphasized in graduate programs' (Hansen 1991, p. 1072). He concluded that graduate education in economics was in need of reforms that would place more emphasis on creativity, critical judgement and communication skills.

This discussion, in combination with the negative trend in the number of economics majors nationwide and concerns about race and gender diversity in the profession, has drawn increased attention to the state of undergraduate education in economics (Ferber 1995; Bartlett 1995). Increasingly, members of the profession are expressing concerns about the relevance of what is taught in undergraduate economics programmes (Bartlett 1995). It is being argued that undergraduate programmes in economics need to reevaluate their missions and institute the reforms necessary to improve 'the preparation of economics students so that they can use the economics they learn in college in dealing with the problems they will face in the real world' (Colander 1995, p. 236).

Such changes require a 'rethinking of the method, content and pedagogy employed in economics courses' (Bartlett and Feiner 1992). Institutionalism is well suited to address this challenge, both by providing an alternative perspective to the orthodox views which dominate the traditional undergraduate economics curriculum, and by shaping the ways in which orthodox concepts are presented. The 'world view' brought to the classroom by institutionalists has important implications for method, content and pedagogy, even when institutional economics itself is not the primary topic under consideration.

Method

Training students to 'think like an economist' is viewed as the goal of undergraduate economic education by many in the field (Siegfried et al. 1991). Learning to 'think like an economist' is generally defined in terms of mastering the skills of abstract, deductive thought and acquiring the tools of mathematical modelling. Yet, exclusive emphasis on such abstract, deductive, mathematical methods acts to 'displace other methodological approaches to economic knowledge' (Bartlett and Feiner 1992, p. 559). As Robin Bartlett and Susan Feiner have argued, 'Economic science, especially in the distilled version taught in undergraduate classes, has been dominated by a single theoretical voice which has been authoritatively defined as THE valid approach to economic questions' (Bartlett and Feiner 1992, p. 560). The dominant theoretical voice in economics courses is neoclassical economics. The emphasis on this particular theoretical approach works to exclude the consideration of alternative approaches, thus creating 'a false sense of security about the "science" underlying the discipline' (Bartlett and Feiner 1992, p. 560).

Consequently, addressing the issue of method is one of the most important, and perhaps the most difficult, problems in reforming economics education. In many economics courses, and in most economics departments, it is the expectation that the neoclassical method be taught; teaching economics using a different method is often not an option. Institutional economics, however, can provide a framework for the discussion of neoclassical method in a way that allows for a meaningful exploration of a much broader set of issues. Professor Bush's intermediate microeconomics course provides an excellent example of teaching required, orthodox material in a historical, critical context.[1]

MICROECONOMIC THEORY: A HISTORICAL, CRITICAL APPROACH

Professor Bush began his intermediate microeconomics course by asking students to consider that there are two ways in which to view the study of microeconomic theory. First, the study of microeconomic theory provides us with skills – it allows us to master a set of analytical tools that may be helpful in examining certain situations or problems. Second, the study of microeconomic theory provides us with a 'world view', a particular picture of reality. Students were cautioned about accepting a particular set of theories as reality without careful consideration of the philosophical preconceptions and assumptions that define them. It was stressed that neoclassical economic theory – the traditional focus of a course in intermediate microeconomics – may provide useful skills that one needs to know to be an economist, but it does not provide the only set of useful skills, nor does it provide the only 'world view' for understanding the economy.

This theme was developed further by introducing students to the concept that any particular economic 'world view' had three components: the paradigm, its theories and its models (see Figure 9.1). Thus, the primary topics of the microeconomics course – the specific microeconomic models and their assumptions, logic and conclusions – were presented as part of a much bigger picture. This provided a framework that allowed students to examine the models of neoclassical microeconomics in a broader philosophical and theoretical context. This framework not only provided the opportunity for a historical and critical analysis of the models, but also made them more interesting to study. Instead of merely being abstract mathematical problems, microeconomic models became the key players in an intellectual contest over the meaning of reality.

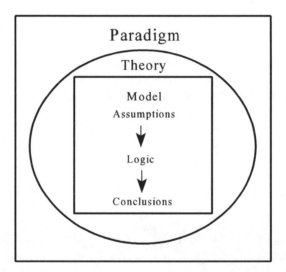

Figure 9.1   Paradigm–theory–model

THE FRAMEWORK: PARADIGM–THEORY–MODEL

The paradigm defines the intellectual domain under consideration, providing us with our conceptual map of reality. It is our primary frame of reference, providing the widest possible range of thought. It defines the intellectual sphere under consideration, and contains all of the relevant ideas to be examined.

Paradigms are defined by, and rest upon, a set of philosophical preconceptions – a philosophy of value, philosophy of knowledge, philosophy of human nature and philosophy of society. At the level of the paradigm, the philosophy of human nature is perhaps the most fundamental, providing the basic premise underlying all the other philosophical preconceptions.

To engage in meaningful economic analysis, we need to sharpen our focus on certain aspects of reality. This requires that we determine that certain things matter more than others. The things that matter the most in our analysis are the things that fall inside the boundaries of the specific theories within the paradigm. These boundaries are determined by the paradigm's philosophical preconceptions, which guide us in identifying and formulating intellectual problems and in developing explanations of and solutions for those problems (see Figure 9.2).

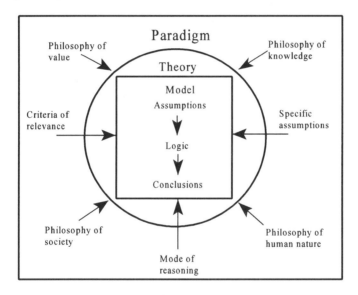

Figure 9.2   Philosophical foundations

Theories are systematic explanations that rely upon precisely formulated logical relationships. Theories contain models, which are constructed for the purpose of setting forth the logical structure upon which theoretical arguments rest. They are a type of language developed to increase the precision with which we communicate about economic problems. They are deduced from the basic axioms of the theory and reflect the underlying philosophy of knowledge. Developing models requires that we commit specifically to the study of certain relationships, defining some as relevant and others as not relevant. This requires that we make specific assumptions, establish criteria of relevance, and select a particular mode of reasoning.

After establishing this framework, Professor Bush used examples from the historical development of classical and neoclassical economics to illustrate the importance of the philosophical preconceptions of orthodox economics in defining the way in which the economy is defined and analysed. This provided the context for the presentation and discussion of the important microeconomic theories and models to be covered in the course.

The work of classical economist Adam Smith illustrates the importance of the philosophy of human nature in determining the way society is viewed in microeconomic theory. Smith began with a particular view of human nature, the proposition that humans have a natural propensity to engage in exchange. From this, he deduced the division of labour and his philosophy of society – the view that the propensity to exchange drives people to specialize, and thus become interdependent. This process provides for the efficient organization of economic activity, and is limited by the size of the market. Thus, the market becomes the controlling element in society.

Neoclassical microeconomics evolved to provide a precise analysis of the market mechanism. The evolution of neoclassical theories and microeconomic models illustrate the importance of the philosophies of knowledge and value in shaping economic analysis. The philosophy of knowledge underpinning neoclassical economics prescribes a certain mode of reasoning that determines the content of theories and structures of models. Neoclassical microeconomic models are based on a particular set of fundamental logical relations. The basic axiomatic structures are identical, reflecting the logic of constrained maximization. Models of constrained maximization, like all partial equilibrium models, require the setting of boundaries – determining what will be considered and what will not. This involves philosophical decisions about knowledge and reality.

Neoclassical economics argues that every society faces the fundamental and universal problem of scarce resources relative to unlimited wants. Thus, in this context, the problem of economics becomes one of choice. Economics becomes a system of thought to solve the problems of economic choice, and the core purpose of economic knowledge is to discover the universal logic applicable to the solution of this problem. In the neoclassical paradigm, it is argued that these problems can be solved, and an efficient allocation of resources uniquely determined, by the market system. Thus, the market equilibrium price becomes the measure of value. The values determined in the competitive marketplace take on a special significance, maximizing individual and social well-being and leading to a harmony of interests.

Consumer choice theory provides an excellent example of neoclassical theory and method. Discussions of neoclassical consumer choice theory typically focus on the use of models of constrained maximization to solve abstract problems of consumer decision-making, with little (if any) discussion of the importance of the philosophy of human nature in defining the boundaries of this theory. But the assumptions about human behaviour that derive from this philosophy – that individuals always prefer more to less, and that the individuals always know their preferences and can rank them in a consistent manner – are critical to specification of the models used in the analysis. The shape of the indifference curve, for example, is dependent on these assumptions. The importance of the convexity axiom illustrates the role of assumptions and logic (and the absence of empirical investigation) in neoclassical microeconomics.

In addition, the historical development of consumer choice theory provides an interesting illustration of how microeconomic analysis has evolved over time. An examination of the historical evolution of the definition of utility, and the important philosophical differences between cardinal and ordinal measures of utility, allows students to appreciate the concept as an intellectual construct that has been the subject of a great deal of controversy and debate. An examination of the changes in the scope and method of economic analysis that accompanied the shift from cardinal to ordinal utility measures illustrates how economic models always reflect current knowledge and assumptions and are subject to change.

The historical, critical framework employed by Professor Bush allows for the presentation of the neoclassical method as just that, a particular method for explaining economic phenomena. It allows students to see the role of values and assumptions in determining what will be examined by 'economic science' and what will not. It allows students to see the processes through which inquiry is guided into particular categories and modes of analysis. It allows students to see neoclassical economics as *one way* of viewing the economy, based on certain assumptions, and providing a particular set of skills and tools.

CONTENT

Economic method has important implications for the content of economics courses. The neoclassical emphasis on abstract modelling focuses more attention on the 'shape and form' of theories than on their content, thus abstracting from many issues of importance in the real world (Lewis 1995, p. 559). This is a particularly serious problem in principles-level courses, which provide many students with their initial, and in many cases only, exposure to economics.

Increasing the relevance of economics courses requires a shift in focus to real contemporary issues of importance. Using an institutional approach to define the scope and method of economics allows for contemporary issues to be brought to the foreground, emphasizing economics as a 'functional science', that enables society to 'more easily solve its various economic difficulties'

(Gruchy, quoted in Lewis 1995, p. 557).

The traditional lack of concern with current issues and problems is illustrated by the treatment of distributional issues in most principles of economics courses. In current 'real world' policy debates, distributional issues have taken centre stage. Articles on poverty, inequality and welfare reform appear in the newspaper almost daily. Yet, such issues are typically discussed in a very limited manner in principles of economics courses – often relegated to a general chapter on inequality at the end of the textbook. Policies concerned with the economic well-being of women and members of racial-ethnic minority groups – such as affirmative action – are becoming increasingly controversial, yet discussions of the economics of race and gender have been virtually absent from the majority of economics texts (Feiner and Morgan 1987).

The neglect of distributional issues in the traditional principles of economics course provides students with a distorted view of the US economy and leaves them unprepared to analyse and respond to current policy debates. This omission reflects the fact that traditional notions of what 'thinking like an economist' entails – the core concepts presented in principles courses – may exclude analyses of distributional issues, most particularly those that focus on race, class and gender (Shackelford 1992; Bartlett and Feiner 1992).

Four core concepts are particularly important in shaping the discussion of distributional issues: the definition of economics, the performance criteria chosen to evaluate economic outcomes, the role of values in economic analysis and the economic functions of government (see Table 9.1). Addressing the limitations of these neoclassical core concepts is a necessary first step in reforming the content of economics courses and setting the stage for a meaningful discussion of contemporary issues in the economics classroom.[2]

Definition of Economics

The definition of economics is critical in determining the conceptual framework and goals of the principles of economics course – determining what questions will be asked and how they will be addressed. The traditional definition of economics focuses on rational individual choice under conditions of scarcity. Economics is presented as the 'science of choice' – the study of how individuals/societies allocate their scarce resources to satisfy alternative and competing human wants. Constrained maximization, fundamental trade-offs and opportunity costs become the focus of most introductions to the discipline.

The necessity of choice, imposed by scarcity, constitutes 'the economic problem'. This forces all societies to answer the 'three economic questions': What goods and services should be produced? How should they be produced? For whom should they be produced? The focus of most principles of economics courses is on how these questions are answered through the maximizing behaviour of individual decision-makers in a market economy. The priority

Table 9.1   Core concepts and distributional issues

Neoclassical	Institutional
Definition of economics: The study of the allocation of scarce resources under conditions of scarcity. Inequality and poverty are issues of productivity and choice; reflect the failure of individuals in the economy.	*Definition of economics*: The study of the process of social provisioning. Inequality and poverty are issues of status and power; reflect the failure of social and economic institutions.
Performance indicators: Efficiency vs equity trade-off. Emphasis on market efficiency.	*Performance indicators*: Efficiency and equity are interrelated goals. Emphasis on provisioning and economic security.
Role of values: Positive vs normative economics. Economics should be a 'positive science'.	*Role of values*: All economics is shaped by values and ideology. Economics should focus on problem-solving.
Role of the government: The government functions as a 'policeman'; the optimal policy is one of laissez-faire. Income support programmes have negative incentive effects.	*Role of the government*: The government and the economy define each other; laissez-faire is a myth. The government plays a critical role in the provisioning process.

assigned to each of the questions is important in determining what will be discussed and what will be excluded from consideration.

In the neoclassical framework, distributional issues – those associated with the question 'for whom?' – are not given a high priority. To the extent that they are discussed, it is in the context of individual behaviour and market outcomes. Poverty and inequality are viewed as issues of individual productivity and choice, reflecting the failure of individuals in the economy.

Institutional economics is grounded in a very different definition of economics, a definition that views economics as more than the study of individual choices made in order to cope with some abstract concept of scarcity. Economics is defined as the study of social provisioning – the processes by which societies secure the material goods and services necessary to maintain and reproduce themselves. Social norms, customs and institutions play an important role in defining and guiding the economic process and determining how individual choices are made.

Under an institutional definition of economics, resource allocation and income distribution decisions are viewed as interrelated parts of the ongoing process of social provisioning. Social practices and institutions play an important role in defining and guiding the economic process and determining how the 'three economic questions' are answered. For example, consumption decisions are viewed in the context of economic class, social norms and corporate power; production decisions are viewed in the context of the legal/institutional environment, social rules and market power; the distribution of income is analysed in terms of social custom, bargaining power, and race and gender discrimination (Brown 1988). In this framework, consumption, production and distributional questions define each other and are linked in ways that go beyond individuals interacting in markets. In this context, inequality and poverty are not outcomes that can be explained away in terms of inappropriate individual choices and scarcity. They are the result of institutional processes based in invidious distinction and sustained by enabling myths; they are approached as issues of status and power. Inequality and poverty distort the process of social provisioning and limit social and economic participation, and thus are central issues in the study of economics.

Performance Criteria

The neoclassical definition of economics is associated with a very narrow set of performance criteria for evaluating economic outcomes. Efficiency is emphasized over other criteria and is defined in ways that set it in opposition to other goals, such as equity. Economic efficiency is defined in terms of rational individual choice and market equilibria. Both allocative and technical efficiency are achieved through the maximizing decisions of consumers and firms in competitive markets. Equity concerns, on the other hand, are associated with the distribution of income and are said to be based in society's notion of fairness. Such notions are generally placed outside the realm of economic analysis.

Economic efficiency is often discussed in terms of 'Pareto optimality' – a situation where no one can be made better off without making someone else worse off. This limits the discussion of distributional issues, since any income redistribution can be seen as making one group worse off and, therefore, a violation of this principle. Thus, societies are confronted with one of the 'fundamental trade-offs' – the trade-off between efficiency and equity. This trade-off suggests that pursuing distributional goals necessarily takes away from the pursuit of efficiency, thus imposing economic costs on society.

Institutional economics rejects the neoclassical 'efficiency vs equity' trade-off and the privileging of market efficiency over other goals. Institutionalists argue that efficiency and equity are, in fact, interrelated concerns. Economically efficient outcomes are always defined in terms of a particular distribution of income – decisions about what constitutes an acceptable distribution of income are implicit in discussions of efficiency. Focusing on market-based indicators of efficiency obscures important (and often negative) distributional outcomes and distorts our picture of economic success.

An institutional treatment of the three economic questions illustrates the interrelationships between efficiency and equity issues. The question of what should be produced, for example, will be answered differently for different distributions of income. Thus, allocative efficiency is only meaningful in terms of a particular distribution of income. How goods and services are produced is determined as much by social norms and the institutional structure as by the market for factors and individual technology. The treatment of costs – what is included in their measurement and who bears them – reflects the underlying distribution of economic power. Thus, technical efficiency is also socially determined in many ways and reflects distributional concerns.

Institutionalists argue that the provision of economic security is necessary for the pursuit of other social and economic goals – it is necessary for the full participation of all individuals in a meaningful way. Consequently, performance indicators related to the provision of economic security (poverty rates, unemployment rates, and so on) play a central role in institutional analyses of the economy. Economic policies are judged in terms of their contribution to the success of a society in sustaining and reproducing itself, not narrowly defined benefit–cost analyses.

Role of Values

The neoclassical discussion of the role of values in economics takes place within the framework imposed by the 'positive vs normative dichotomy'. 'Positive analysis' is defined as an 'analysis of what is' based on scientific fact, while 'normative analysis' is defined as an 'analysis of what ought to be' based on value-judgements. Neoclassical economics argues that economic analysis must be 'positive' analysis because 'conclusions based on value judgements do not advance one's understanding of events' (Boyes and Melvin 1994, p. 10).

This severely limits the topics seen to be acceptable for economic analysis and the role of the economist in policy discussions. Distributional issues, in particular, are viewed as 'values-issues' and unacceptably normative. In this context, the division of the analysis implied by the three economic questions takes on particular importance. The resource allocation questions ('what?' and 'how?') are associated with efficiency concerns that can be evaluated with 'positive scientific analysis', while income distribution questions ('for whom?') are associated with equity concerns and involve 'normative value-judgements'. Thus, the first two questions fall much more clearly into the realm of 'legitimate' economic analysis and receive far more attention in the traditional economics curriculum.

Institutional economics rejects the neoclassical 'positive vs normative' dichotomy, arguing that value-free economic inquiry is simply not possible. Knowledge is always socially constructed, reflecting the values and biases of the individual researchers, social system and culture that produced it. The presentation of a particular theory as 'value-free' acts to obscure the particular values and priorities embedded in that theory.

Institutionalists replace the quest for value-free analysis with the belief that for economic inquiry to be worthwhile it must be activist and explicitly address 'values-issues' (Petr 1984, p. 4). The explicit purpose of economic inquiry is to provide the tools to actively guide the processes of social provisioning to outcomes that promote the full participation of all individuals and the noninvidious recreation of community. Thus, the analysis of inequality and poverty, and the development of policies to address these problems, take a top priority in an institutional approach.

Role of the Government

In neoclassical economics, the economy and the government are defined as separate entities, known as the private and the public sectors. It is argued that the questions 'what?' 'how?' and 'for whom?' are most legitimately answered in the private sector through the maximizing decisions of individuals in markets. In this framework, the government exists outside this process, 'intervening' or 'interfering' in the market economy through its policy actions. The self-regulating market system is seen to work best without such interference, and the optimal policy stance is one of laissez-faire.

Thus, the primary role of the government is that of a 'policeman', enforcing the 'economic rules of the game' that facilitate the operation of the market economy. Additional economic functions of the government are presented in terms of increasing degrees of interference in the market. Government policies concerned with promoting competition and correcting market failure are discussed in terms of efficiency goals and are seen as less intrusive than policies concerned with distributional issues which are associated with equity goals. Distributional policies are analysed in terms of their impact on individual behaviour and are generally seen to have negative 'incentive effects'.

Institutionalists reject the neoclassical 'policeman' view of the role of government, arguing that the government and the economy are inseparable and define each other. The government, through its definition and enforcement of the working rules, defines the economy and legitimizes the power relationships, institutions and beliefs that shape economic outcomes. Thus, laissez-faire has never meant an absence of government involvement in the economy. By not 'interfering' in the economy, the government tacitly supports the status quo distribution of income and power (Samuels 1989, pp. 427–33; Brown 1988, p. 60).

Institutional economists argue that the conceptual separation of the economy from the government found in neoclassical economics provides an incomplete and distorted picture of both the operation of the market economy and the broader provisioning process. The neoclassical emphasis on 'private' market activity devalues the necessary economic activities of the government. Institutionalists argue that the state is intimately involved in the process of social provisioning and has a necessary role to play in the provision of economic security. The 'policeman' view of the state is replaced with a broader view of the political economy. Distributional policies are not analysed in terms of their intrusiveness into an otherwise free market, but are evaluated in terms of their contribution to the social provisioning process.

CONCLUSION

Traditionally, teaching students 'to think like an economist' has focused on the mechanics of neoclassical models, which constitute a very small part of a much bigger picture. Professor Bush placed this discussion in a much broader perspective, beginning with the premise that any particular model may or may not have lasting relevance. Since models become obsolete, it is necessary to understand more than the mechanism; it is necessary to develop a deeper understanding of their significance. This requires placing them in the context of the broader paradigm that defines them, exploring their history, and comparing them with models based in other paradigms.

This type of historical, critical approach to teaching economic method provides a framework for expanding the content of economics courses. Examining neoclassical economics in this way illustrates how the traditional definition and presentation of core concepts has shaped the discussion of current issues. In particular, it shows how the scarcity definition of economics, the efficiency vs equity trade-off, the positive vs normative dichotomy and the 'policeman' view of the government have limited meaningful discussion of distributional issues in many economics courses, particularly at the principles level. Introducing an institutional perspective at the level of these core concepts broadens the scope and goals of the principles of economics course, thus allowing for a more complete and thoughtful discussion of current issues and problems.

The changes in method and content introduced by an institutionalist perspective have important implications for pedagogy. Pedagogy is critically important since, as Jean Shackelford has argued, 'knowledge goes hand in hand with process . . . how one teaches is as important as what one teaches' (Shackelford 1992, p. 571). The method and content of economics courses influences pedagogy because 'the content and context of economics derive from the questions asked and the conclusions made by economists concerning teaching traditions. What is and what is not important revolves around the goal of teaching students to "think like an economist"' (Shackelford 1992, p. 572). The traditional view of what it means to 'think like an economist' has had important implications for the ways in which economics has been taught. April Aerni has described traditional pedagogy in economics as the 'banking style of teaching where the teacher deposits information in students, the students feed it back on tests, and the teacher hopes to earn "interest"' (Aerni 1993, p. 7). The banking style of teaching fosters an inherently passive approach to learning. Despite the fact that many economists view themselves as scientists, most economics courses offer few 'hands on' or laboratory-type experiences that allow students to actually 'do economics' (Bartlett and Feiner 1992, p. 562).

One consequence of the traditional approach to teaching economics is that 'economic pedagogy is unnecessarily constrained', which contributes to the exclusion of many students from economics, particularly women and people of colour (Bartlett and Feiner 1992, p. 562). Research in the field of education indicates that there are many learning styles, and that diversifying teaching techniques increases learning in general and helps the material reach a wider range of students (Bartlett and Feiner 1992, p. 562; McGoldrick and Sanborn 1995, p. 1). Introducing more cooperative and 'hands on' exercises allows students the opportunity to connect the materials from the course to their own experiences and to current issues, making the study of these materials a more worthwhile and interesting venture (Bartlett 1995, p. 364).

Encouraging a more active and participatory classroom, and creating opportunities for students to relate the course material to their own lives, is an essential part of the process of increasing the relevance of economics courses. Institutionalism provides a framework that encourages creative innovation in the ways in which economics is taught. Institutionalism is fundamentally activist in nature (Petr 1984, p. 6), and thus is conducive to pedagogical practices that encourage active learning and critical thinking. As Margaret Lewis has argued, institutionalism is rooted in the same pragmatic philosophical tradition as feminist and active learning pedagogics. An institutional approach opens up opportunities for the adoption of these pedagogical practices that emphasize 'active and critical engagement' and encourage 'doing' (Lewis 1995, p. 556).

Two examples of active/experiential learning pedagogies that are very compatible with institutionalism are 'field work' and 'service learning'. 'Field work' can be defined as 'sending students into the field to observe and interview participants in economic activities and to collect data and information that they bring back into the classroom to analyse and integrate into their understanding of issues' (Lewis 1995, p. 556). Introducing field work into the economics classroom is consistent with the 'fact-based' nature of institutionalism (Petr 1984, p. 8).

'Service learning' is also consistent with an institutionalist approach, reflecting the activist, instrumentalist, process-oriented nature of the paradigm (Petr 1984). The main concept behind service learning is to 'integrate experiences in the community with those occurring in the classroom' (McGoldrick and Sanborn 1995, pp. 3–4). Service learning provides students with 'direct experience working with communities in need and/or organizations that promote the public good', thus explicitly addressing values and social change (McGoldrick and Sanborn 1995, pp. 3–4).

Thus, the institutional approach to economic inquiry calls for an active, comparative approach to teaching economics, where explicit attention is given to the role of values and ideology in shaping the way economists engage the world. A comparative, institutional approach gives students insight into the controversies within the discipline and into current public policy debates. This provides students with a more honest and accurate picture of the discipline and makes learning economics more interesting and relevant (Moseley and Wolff 1995).

This active, comparative approach to teaching economics also has the benefit of fostering critical and creative thinking. Critical thinking requires a recognition of the evolutionary nature of knowledge (Thoma 1993, p. 128) and the importance of underlying values and beliefs (Cohen 1993, p. 243), both of which are essential elements of institutional economics (Petr 1984). Active learning pedagogies, that encourage 'doing economics' through hands-on assignments, field work and service learning, also foster critical and creative thinking. The holistic method of institutional economics encourages such practices by combining 'empirical evidence, appropriate analytical frameworks that emphasize the interaction of institutions and values underlying the issues at hand' (Lewis 1995, p. 559). This allows students' own experiences to 'be incorporated so they understand the relevance of the issue to their own lives' (Lewis 1995, p. 559).

Thus, the institutional approach employed by Professor Bush in his teaching lays the foundation for a variety of creative approaches to teaching economics. These creative approaches address many of the concerns that have been raised about economics education, particularly the lack of creative and critical thinking skills, and the need to make economics more relevant to a more diverse group of students. The institutional approach shifts the focus of economics education away from abstract technique to the development of the skills and knowledge necessary to take on the tasks that give economics its real significance – 'the resolution of real problems facing real people in real political economies' (Tool 1979, p. 15).

NOTES

1. The discussion that follows is based on my class notes from Professor Bush's Intermediate Microeconomic Theory course, taught at California State University, Fresno.
2. The arguments in this section were originally presented at the annual meeting of the Association for Evolutionary Economics (Washington, DC, January 1995) and were published in the *Journal of Economic Issues* (see Peterson 1995).

REFERENCES

Aerni, April (1993), 'Using Feminist Pedagogy in the Economics Classroom', a paper presented at the Eastern Economic Association Annual Meeting (Washington DC, March).

Bartlett, Robin (1995), 'Attracting "Otherwise Bright Students" to Economics 101', *American Economic Review*, **85**, May, pp. 362–6.

Bartlett, Robin and Susan Feiner (1992), 'Balancing the Economics Curriculum: Content, Method and Pedagogy', *American Economic Review*, **82**, May, pp. 559–64.

Boyes, William and Michael Melvin (1994), *Microeconomics*, 2nd edition, Boston: Houghton-Mifflin.

Brown, Clair (1988), 'Income Distribution in an Institutional World', in Garth Mangum and Peter Philips (eds), *Three Worlds of Labour Economics*, Armonk: M.E. Sharpe, pp. 51–63.

Cohen, Mel (1993), 'Making Critical Thinking a Classroom Reality', *Political Science and Politics*, **26**, June, pp. 241–4.

Colander, David (1995), 'Reform of Undergraduate Economics Education', in David Colander and Rueven Brenner (eds), *Educating Economists*, Ann Arbor: The University of Michigan Press, pp. 231–41.

Feiner, Susan and Barbara Morgan (1987), 'Women and Minorities in Introductory Economics Textbooks: 1974–1984', *Journal of Economic Education*, **18**, Fall, pp. 376–92.

Ferber, Marianne (1995), 'The Study of Economics: A Feminist Critique', *American Economic Review*, **85**, May, pp. 357–61.

Hansen, W. Lee (1991), 'The Education and Training of Economic Doctorates', *Journal of Economic Literature*, **29**, September, pp. 1054–87.

Krueger, Anne et al. (1991), 'Report of the Commission on Graduate Education in Economics', *Journal of Economic Literature*, **29**, September, pp. 1035–53.

Lewis, Margaret (1995), 'Breaking Down the Walls, Opening up the Field: Situating the Economics Classroom as Site of Social Action', *Journal of Economic Issues*, **29**, June, pp. 555–65.

McGoldrick, KimMarie and Robert Sanborn (1995), 'Experiential Learning: An Application for Economics Students', a paper presented at the Eastern Economic Association Annual Meeting (New York, March).

Moseley, Fred and Richard Wolff (1995), 'Alternative Theories in the Teaching of Economics', in David Colander and Rueven Brenner (eds), *Educating Economists*, Ann Arbor: The University of Michigan Press, pp. 243–8.

Peterson, Janice (1995), 'For Whom? Institutional Economics and Distributional Issues in the Economics Classroom', *Journal of Economics Issues*, **29**, June, pp. 567–74.

Petr, Jerry (1984), 'Fundamentals of an Institutionalist Perspective on Economic Policy', *Journal of Economic Issues*, **18**, March, pp. 1–17.

Samuels, Warren (1989), 'Some Fundamentals on the Economic Role of the Government', *Journal of Economic Issues*, **23**, June, pp. 427–33.

Shackelford, Jean (1992), 'Feminist Pedagogy: A Means for Bringing Critical Thinking and Creativity into the Classroom', *American Economic Review*, **82**, May, pp. 570–76.

Siegfried, John, R. Bartlett, W. Lee Hansen, A. Kelley, D. McCloskey and T. Tietenberg (1991), 'The Status and Prospects of the Economics Major', *Journal of Economic Education*, **22**, Summer, pp. 97–223.

Thoma, George (1993), 'The Perry Framework and the Tactics of Teaching Critical Thinking in Economics', *Journal of Economic Education*, **24**, Spring, pp. 128–36.

Tool, Marc (1979), *The Discretionary Economy*, Santa Monica, CA: Goodyear Publishing.

Index

175